THE IMAGE: A PROPHETIC BIRTH

By

Deeva Denez

This book is a work of non-fiction. Names and places have been changed to protect the privacy of all individuals. The events and situations are true.

ISBN: 1-4033-8522-X (e-book)
ISBN: 1-4033-8523-8 (Paperback)

Library of Congress Control Number: 2002095154

This book is printed on acid free paper.

Printed in the United States of America
Bloomington, IN

1stBooks - rev. 03/19/03

ACKNOWLEDGEMENTS

I would like to make a special acknowledgement to Tawanna Caston and Tosh Fomby for helping me to get this book together.

Dedication

This book is dedicated to my daughter, who is the image and prophetic birth, Mariah Kellie Marie Mitchell.

INTRODUCTION

Our lives are so enveloped in the physical realm because God made us from physical matter. Therefore, when we experience a spiritual phenomenon, it can either be from God or Satan since they are spirit beings. The two images I saw in '95 were, however, from God. He showed me what was to come in my life.

This story, *The Image: A Prophetic Birth* is the fruition of the two images. The first image was a baby wrapped in a blanket. The second image was a very pregnant image of me with a BIG book suddenly coming in front of the pregnant image. Although God showed me two images, this book reveals a third image or work that God is doing with mankind. As the story unfolds, the third prophetic image takes form.

Chapter One

Raymond slowly paced back and forth as I descended the stairs with the poem in my hand. I was anxious to give it to him, but the expression on his face told me to wait. I sensed he was ready to leave minutes ago. This was not the time to delay him any longer. The poem would have to wait until a more opportune time. I hoped before the day was over.

"What took you so long?" Raymond asked with a sour disposition.

"I was getting your keys," I said, handing them to him as I put the poem in my pants pocket. "You are the rightful recipient since you are my husband. Don't you agree?"

"Thanks," he said as he took them from my hand. "I'm really hungry. Let's go get the kids, so we can eat," he said, putting the keys on his keyring.

"Don't I get a kiss or a hug before we leave? This is our wedding day."

"Vanessa, I love you more than anything else on this earth. I am a very happy man at this moment. I'm also very hungry. Can we save the kisses for later?" he asked, walking to the door.

"Just one kiss before we leave, please. I am a new bride," I said, standing in front of the door.

"Mrs. Miller, didn't Reverend McCauley say our wedding kiss was the longest he had ever seen?"

"Yes."

"Well, that kiss should stay with you for a while. I'm all kissed out," Raymond said, moving me from the door.

"Raymond Miller, I demand that you kiss your new wife right now!" I said, holding my ground.

"Okay, okay Mrs. Miller, if a kiss is what you want, then a kiss is what you will get," he said, pulling me into his arms giving me a long passionate kiss.

"That's more like it," I said when the kiss was over, "Now, I feel like a married woman."

"Mrs. Miller, can we leave now to pick up Francine and Raymond?" he asked, still holding me, looking into my eyes.

"Only if you promise to give me another kiss like that one when we come back home."

"I promise."

"Good. Now we can leave," I said, opening the door. We left embraced in each other's arms. Raymond was my man, and I was his woman. His disposition had changed to the warm, loving man I loved and married. This marriage was destined to last until death do us part, I thought as we reached the car.

The ride over to the school was rather hurried. I wasn't sure if Raymond was anxious to get to the kids or was really very hungry. I didn't bother to ask. I figured it didn't matter one way or the other. All that mattered, at this point, was that we were together. I did wonder, however, how the kids would take the news of our marriage. I would find out soon because we were ten minutes away from the school.

The ride to the school was quiet. Raymond seemed absorbed in thoughts. We barely spoke a word as he drove. Once he mentioned how happy he was that I was his wife. He also asked me where I wanted to eat. I told him it didn't matter. Whatever he decided would be fine.

He released his hand from mine as he pulled into the school parking lot. I hoped he didn't sense my nervousness when he pulled his hand away.

"Do you want to go inside?" he asked, turning, looking in my eyes.

I wanted to say, yes, but I said, "No. I'll wait in the car. How do you think they will take the news?" I asked still nervous.

"I don't know. You'll find out soon."

"When do you plan to tell them?"

"As soon as possible."

"Tell them inside. I want to see their reactions when they come to the car."

"Okay, sweetie," he replied opening the door. "You're sure you don't want to be with me when I tell them?"

"I'm sure. I think this way is better," I said, reclining in my seat.

Raymond walked on the pavement that led to the side door of the after school program. He knocked on the door, and moments later someone let him inside. I waited ten minutes before the door opened again. To my surprise and delight, Raymond Jr. and Francine ran to the car happy and excited. I got out of the car to meet them with opened arms.

"Mommy! Mommy!" they shouted in unison as they ran toward me.

The three of us embraced with a firm hold. Raymond stood behind the kids. Francine was the first to break free.

"I knew you were going to be my mommy," Francine said, grinning.

"How did you know?" I asked perplexed.

"Do you remember when we went to the mall, and I threw a penny in the fountain?"

"Yes, I remember," I replied still holding on to Raymond Jr..

"Well, I made a wish."

"What did you wish?" I asked curious to know.

"I wished my daddy would marry you, and I would have two sisters," she said, proudly.

"I don't want no more sisters," Raymond Jr. added. "I already have three sisters. I want a brother."

"I'm sorry to disappoint you, Raymond, but you will have two more sisters. You have two brothers, Little Carl and Carlos."

"Ahh, they don't count. Carlos hates my guts, and Little Carl is too old," Raymond Jr. responded.

"Come on, everybody in the car," Raymond demanded. "I've heard enough. I'm ready to eat."

We all got in the car as Raymond commanded. I was still stunned by Francine's reply. I thought it was odd that she wished for two sisters, the exact number of daughters I was prophesied to have. I then thought about the two miscarriages last year and the image I saw in '95. I could see it clearly. First, the image of the baby, wrapped in a blanket, looking at me through the windshield as I drove. I could still hear my words, "I'm coming, I'm coming, baby girl. Mama's coming soon," I said, before the image disappeared. Then, I remembered the second image of me being very pregnant. A big book came in front of the pregnant image. A voice said, "Your book will be published first, then you will deliver." The book, *Uncaged* was published December 22, 1997. Today was January 15, 1998. I knew from the second image, my baby could be conceived at anytime. Now, with the marriage with Raymond, my baby was coming soon.

The school was only minutes from the apartment. By the time I finished reminiscing, Raymond was turning into his complex. The kids were excited in the back and couldn't wait to tell their grandmother the good news. The kids gathered their belongings as Raymond parked the car. He opened the door for Francine and me while Raymond Jr. ran to the apartment. Francine slid her hand inside mine as I walked with Raymond holding his hand.

"I'm glad you're my mommy. I can't wait to tell Grandma Carrie," she said, tightening her grip.

"I'm glad you're glad," I said, smiling into her big brown eyes,

"I'm going to pick up a few things to take back to the house. We'll leave the kids here tonight because they have school tomorrow," Raymond commented as we approached Raymond Jr..

Mrs. Simmons stood in the door after letting Raymond Jr. inside. He had already told her the news. She smiled when she saw us at the steps.

"So you got married?" she asked as we crossed the threshold.

"Yes," Raymond and I responded together.

"That's nice," she replied, walking from the door with her crutch. "Welcome to the family. I hope this marriage lasts."

"It will," I said, sitting on the sofa by the door. "This marriage will take us to the grave. We're in it until death do us part."

"Mama, don't worry. This marriage will last," Raymond added as he went to his room. "It won't end like the other two."

"Grandma, I'm going to have two more sisters," Francine said, putting her school bag and coat on the living room table.

"Are you pregnant, gal?" Mrs. Simmons asked, concerned.

"No," I answered, laughing, "not yet. But I will be soon."

"What's for dinner, Grandma?" Raymond Jr. asked, coming from his room. "I'm hungry."

"Go wash your hands. I'll fix your plate," Mrs. Simmons answered, walking toward the kitchen.

"Mine, too," Francine responded. "I'm starving!"

"Wash your hands, too. Your plate will be ready in a minute," Mrs. Simmons added. "Vanessa, you want something to eat, too?"

"No, thank you. Raymond and I are going out to eat."

"Ooohh, can I go?" Raymond Jr. asked.

"Me, too?" asked Francine.

"No," Raymond answered, coming from his room with a small suitcase. "I'm taking my wife out to eat, then we're going to her house to spend the night."

"Our house," I corrected.

"Right, our house," he continued. You have school tomorrow. We'll be back to get you after school. Mom, is that okay with you?"

"It's alright as long you bring me some snuff back tomorrow. I'm getting kinda low," Mrs. Simmons, replied, fixing plates.

"Let's go, Mrs. Miller," Raymond said, reaching for my hand. "Kiss me goodbye kids. We're leaving," Raymond added.

"Okay, Dad," Raymond Jr., said walking towards Raymond.

"Do you have to go?" Francine asked with tears in her eyes.

"Yes. I'll be back tomorrow. Be good for your grandmother. Give me a kiss," he said, leaning down to kiss her.

"I get kisses, too," I said, reaching to kiss Raymond Jr..

We all kissed goodbye then Raymond and I left. When I asked him where we were going to eat, he answered, "Steak and Ale."

We reached the Steak and Ale by Cumberland Mall within thirty minutes. The hostess seated us at a cozy table in a room with four other patrons. Raymond ordered steak, and I ordered Hawaiian Chicken. We headed for the salad bar as soon as our waiter left. After filling our salad plates, we went back to our seats and Raymond said grace.

"Dear Gracious and Merciful God, thank you for blessing this day and allowing me to marry my wife. Bless our marriage, the union that You have put together. Prevent the hand of Satan from ever destroying this marriage. Show me how to please my wife and instruct her how to please me. Let our love be perfected by Your Holy Spirit and Son, Jesus Christ. Thank You for this food. There is someone, somewhere, who needs You. I pray that You will visit them and provide food for those who are hungry at this time. I ask this in Your Son, Jesus Christ. Amen."

"Thank you for a beautiful grace," I said picking up my fork. "How does it feel being married again?"

"You can't imagine the joy I'm feeling, sitting in front of you as your husband. I thought I had lost you forever," Raymond said, smiling, holding his glass of tea.

"Life is unpredictable. You never know what will happen. Most times you just have to live it one second at a time," I said putting my fork down and picking up my tea. "Make a toast to your new wife."

He laughed. So, Mrs. Miller, you want me to make a toast?"

"Yes, I do. Hurry up! I'm ready to drink my tea."

"Okay," he said, lifting up his glass. "To my lovely wife, Mrs. Raymond Miller, may our marriage be filled with all the fruit of God's Holy Spirit. May we both be happy all the days of our lives together," he said, hitting my glass. "Now, it's your turn, Mrs. Miller."

I lifted my glass after I finished drinking from his toast. "To my dear husband, Raymond Eugene Miller, the bearer of the sign. Let today be the beginning of a very special relationship. May our marriage exemplify Jesus Christ and The Church. Let me be the wife of your expectations and more. And you be the husband I desire," I said, touching his glass with mine.

"Very good, Mrs. Miller. If we live up to our toasts, we should have a very happy marriage," he said putting the glass to his lips.

The waiter came to the table with our food as we finished drinking our tea. He placed the steak dinner in front of Raymond and the chicken dinner in front of me.

"More tea?" he asked as he placed my plate down.

"Yes," we both responded.

"Is there anything else you need?" he asked.

"No," we both said.

"Very well. I will be right back with more tea," he said, as he left the room.

"This looks good," I said, picking up my fork and knife to cut my chicken. "How is your steak?"

"It's good, especially to a hungry man. I haven't eaten all day," he said, putting another big piece in his mouth.

The waiter returned with a pitcher of tea and refilled our glasses then left.

"Mrs. Miller," Raymond said, as the waiter departed.

"Yes, Mr. Miller," I replied biting my pineapple.

"Today, you have made me the happiest man on earth!"

"I hope you can say that everyday of our marriage," I said, as we devoured our food.

While we ate, we reminisced of the past and talked about our future plans. Raymond promised me he would never take me for granted. Since we were both tired and full, we decided to call it a day. The forty-minute drive home seemed liked fifteen because we talked all the way. Our happiness radiated like a light.

I gave Raymond the poem after we showered and were ready for bed. I slipped it in his hand before he turned off the light. He read it and smiled.

"I like it," he commented, as he finished reading it. "So, you're confident you married the right man?" he asked, repeating the last phrase of the poem.

"Yes!" I shouted with confidence.

"Because I am the bearer of the sign?"

"Yes!" I shouted again.

"Well, Mrs. Miller, I have something very important to tell you before we go to bed," he said turning off the light.

"What is it?" I asked, puzzled.

"We can't consummate this marriage tonight."

"Why not? We're married," I asked walking to the bed.

"Those are the doctor's orders because of my medication and treatment. I still have a problem getting an erection," he announced, pulling back the covers.

"You do?" I asked disappointed, resting my head on my pillow.

"Yes, I do. Good night, Mrs. Raymond Miller," he said, pecking my lips, wrapping his arms around me. "Sweet dreams."

"Good night, Raymond," I said cuddled in his arms thinking of Douglas, and my Jamaican treat.

CHAPTER TWO

All night long, I thought of Douglas although I was Raymond's wife. If I had married Douglas, we would have made love all night. He would have lit my fire and kept the flame going. I would not be in my bed thinking of another man on the day of my marriage. I would be too happy with the one I had.

As my eyes opened, I saw the back of Raymond's white T-shirt and head. Seeing him in my bed instead of Douglas snapped me back into reality. What if, I had married Douglas? I asked myself as I stared at Raymond. Then I told myself, I must not think of Douglas anymore. I must concentrate on my marriage and commitment to Raymond, my husband. He deserves nothing but the best from me. He deserves all that I have to give.

Being perfectly still, I continued to stare at Raymond. He turned around as if he felt my eyes fixating on him.

"Good morning, Mrs. Miller," he said, reaching for me. "How is my lovely wife today?"

"I'm fine. How are you?" I asked, sliding into his arms. "I'm finding it hard to believe that I am your husband. It's good to wake up and have you in the bed with me," he said, softly stroking my hair.

"It's hard for me to believe, too, that we're married. I have to pinch myself every now and then just to make sure."

"I'm still the luckiest man on earth," he said, pulling me even closer to him.

"And, I'm the luckiest woman," I said, snuggling up to his chest.

"I didn't tell you this yesterday, but I'm off until the 27th."

"I'm just off until tomorrow night because it's my weekend to work," I said, putting the sheet over me. "Why did you take off?"

"I couldn't function at work. You saw what shape I was in when you came to the apartment yesterday. I couldn't do anything but cry. I asked for time off to get myself together. I couldn't take seeing you, knowing you were with someone else and looking at me as if I was a stranger. I love you too much to know that you didn't love me anymore," Raymond said with tears in his eyes.

"You don't ever have to worry about losing me again. We'll be together until death do us part."

"I can use my days off to get settled. I just remembered today ends the semester for the kids. We couldn't have chosen a better day to get married if we had planned it."

"Looks like God planned everything to a T."

"Yes, He did. Everything except one thing."

"What?" I asked, anxiously.

"With both of us working nights, who's going to stay home with Raymond and Francine? As my wife, you don't have to work full-time. I will pay all the household bills. I want you home with the children."

"I'll ask Becky next week about working part-time. Since you work Tuesday through Saturday, I'll ask to work Sunday and Monday nights. That way, someone will be home with the kids every night, and I can still get a paycheck to pay my bills."

"That sounds good. I'm sure everything will work out," he said, nibbling on my ear.

"Stop, Raymond. Don't get nothing started you can't finish," I said, squirming from him. "How long do we have to wait, anyway?"

"A month. I go back to the doctor next month."

"What will happen if we cheat?"

"I don't know. I didn't ask the doctor that question because we weren't together the last time I saw him."

"Since we can't have sex, let's eat breakfast. What do you want?"

"You."

"Me? What do you mean?" I asked, turning to look at him.

"I want to hold you and feel your body next to mine. I love you, Vanessa. I don't have to have sex."

"You're different from any man I've ever known, and I love the difference," I said, as I snuggled up close to Raymond and dozed off, wrapped in his arms.

When we finally got out of bed, Raymond unpacked his few things, making himself at home. I promised to empty Carl's old dresser, so he could make room for the rest of his belongings. During my single years, I used Carl's dresser for my writings and extra clothes. I didn't know where I was going to put all of my stuff, but I had to find a place soon.

I thoroughly enjoyed our first day of marriage together. I cooked a light dinner before we went to get the kids from school. I knew, once we picked up the kids, our honeymoon was over. It would be time for us to roll up our sleeves and work the marriage.

Starting a marriage with Raymond felt different from the marriage with Carl. Back then, I was young, eighteen years old, and didn't have a clue what getting married really meant. I had lived at home with Mom and Dad and hadn't experienced a lot of things in life. I also realized during my marriage with Carl that I had not developed into my full person. Some of the things I did and liked as a teenager at home was different from the things I liked being grown, on my own. Then the boys came at the age of twenty-five and thirty, my likes and dislikes changed again. I had matured into the woman I was today, the woman that Raymond married.

Raymond was the man I needed for the changed woman I had become. Our character traits were very similar, whereas, Carl and I were opposites. Being opposites, worked for a while, but at this time in my life, I needed someone more like me. Raymond was good for me. He was a hard worker, a family man, and a man with morals. He was not a man to run around or hang out with the guys. I loved those qualities about him the most. The fact that he didn't drink, smoke, curse, or gamble were icing on the cake.

Raymond taking time off made the transition easier. He packed all the clothes and brought them to the house. He planned to move the furniture by the end of February because he had to pay February's rent since he did not give thirty days notice. His mother stayed at the apartment to guard the furniture.

Raymond Jr. and Francine chipped in and helped move. They were glad to leave the apartment and live in a house. I was glad, too, because the children in the apartment were too rough for them. After we found a place for everything, we gathered in a circle and held hands. Raymond led us in prayer, then I followed. We asked the kids if they wanted to say a prayer, too. They both were thankful to have a family. Listening to them made me realize even more how important it is for children to have a family with a mother and a father. I prayed to God to let me be a loving mother to them. I wanted to love them as my own because when I said, "I do," they became my children.

We stayed up for another hour then called it a day. Raymond beamed with happiness. We all did. God had put us together the day before through His infinite wisdom. We had the rest of our lives to be together as a family. All of us seemed ready for the challenge.

Saturday night at work, everybody congratulated me for getting married. That night I worked with Tia, my soul sister coworker. We hadn't talked since I got married. She was in the office drinking water when I clocked in.

"Who did you marry?" Tia asked as I laid the phone down.

"Raymond, I told Abeba to tell everyone I married Raymond Miller Thursday after I got married," I said, looking for a pen and marker.

"What happened to Douglas? When you left out of here Thursday morning, you were in love with Douglas and had broken up with Raymond. Jenny and I spent all Thursday night discussing who you married. She said Raymond, and I said Douglas."

"You were right. When I left work Thursday morning, getting married was not on my mind. Sit down, this will take a few minutes to explain," I said, sitting in the black supervisor's chair.

"Girl, this must be good. Let me get another cup of water first," she said as she poured another cup.

"Do you remember telling me my son called while I was out of the lab Thursday morning?"

"Yeah, but what does that have to do with you marrying Raymond?" Tia asked, bewildered.

"Everything."

"I can't wait to hear this. It must be some story. Let me sit down," she said, sitting in the blue chair, next to the door.

"It is. Okay, Tia, here goes. After I clocked out Thursday morning, I called my son to see what he wanted, but the phones at the house were disconnected. He had told me earlier he was having trouble with his car. Since Carl moved, Little Carl had to drive to school because he and Carlos were not on the bus line for the schools they attended."

"Vanessa, what does this have to do with you getting married? I don't get the connection," Tia said, agitated.

"Be patient, Tia. This whole incident with my sons explains how I got married. Because if it wasn't for that phone call, I would still be single."

"This must be deep. Go on," Tia commanded.

"I drove to Carl's house in Clayton County when I left here Thursday morning. I wanted to make sure the boys had a way to school. When I drove up, Little Carl's Toyota was gone. I rang the doorbell to be sure they weren't inside. To my delight, nobody was home. So I drove to my house in Decatur. The first thing I did when I got home was turn the ringer off on my phone downstairs, like I always do. As I reached for the phone upstairs to turn its ringer off, the phone rang. I picked it up, thinking it was Douglas. It wasn't. It was Raymond on the other end crying like a baby."

"You're kidding?"

"No, I'm not. He was crying so hard, I didn't know who he was. Anyway, I offered to go over to his place to console him. He said he had to call me sometimes to get through his crying episodes."

"Girl, I wished I could have seen him, all broken up. Serves him right for breaking up with you anyway," Tia added crossing her legs.

"Tia, you would not have wanted to see Raymond in the condition he was in. I wasn't prepared for what I saw. Raymond was crying with snot coming from his nose. He said he had been like that for a while."

"Didn't he work Thursday morning? I remember you saying he didn't want to speak when you saw him in the hallway."

"That's right. The incident in the hallway is the very thing that tore him up. He said, he couldn't stand for me to look at him like he was a stranger when he loved me so much."

"Wow, I bet you never knew how much he loved you," Tia commented, drinking the last of her water.

"He showed me then that he loved me with his whole being. I realized, I had been wrong about him. He loved me more than anything else in the world. At that point, I knew I had my man, so we set out to marry the same day and did."

"Weren't you engaged to Douglas?"

"Not officially. We had planned to get counseling and get married in May."

"Have you told him you're married?"

"Yes, I told him as soon as we got to the house," I said, frowning.

"I know he was shocked."

"I broke his heart. That's the only thing I regret. Douglas was good to me. He didn't deserve to be hurt like that."

"Excuse me," Elaine from the evening shift said as I finished my last sentence, "all the controls are done in the back. I left two urines spinning."

"Well, I guess we better get to work," Tia said, getting up. That's some story. I refuted Jenny all night Thursday that you had married Douglas. I'm glad you told me what happened," Tia said, walking out the office.

"Oh, congratulation," Elaine added as she picked up the phone to clock out.

"Thank you," I said, getting up walking to Tia.

"How is the honeymoon?" Tia asked, walking to the window to accession a blood gas.

"It's fine although we haven't consummated the marriage."

"Why not?" she asked, picking up the specimen in a bag of ice.

"It's another long story."

"I have eight more hours. Let me run this blood gas first," Tia said, walking to the back of the room.

CHAPTER THREE

While Tia ran the blood gas specimen, I couldn't decide if I wanted to explain Raymond's problem or not. Looking at the chemistry analyzer, I realized I had patients to verify. Taking the last results of the Hitachi specimens off the analyzer, I walked to the computer terminal. As I studied the paper, I noticed one patient had a critical glucose that had to be repeated. Another patient had an elevated dilantin level that needed diluting. And a third patient had a low sodium result that had to be repeated also.

As we worked, more specimens came in. Tia went to the window to accession, and I made my dilution. We worked like dogs for three straight hours. I had forgotten about our former conversation until Tia reminded me when the work stopped.

"So, why haven't you and Raymond consummated the marriage?" Tia asked, as we went to the office to take a break.

I hesitated speaking. I still couldn't decide if I should tell her or not.

"Vanessa, what's wrong?" Tia asked, sensing my apprehension. "Is it something you don't want to discuss?"

I thought about it for a minute before answering. Let me get a cup of water first," I said, reaching for a cup by the cooler. "I'm glad the work slowed down. I need to get off my feet for a while," I said, filling my cup with water.

"Me, too," Tia added. "It's been crazy in here! I think I'll eat my banana," she said as she grabbed it from the desk.

We each sat down and relaxed before I spoke. "Tia, do you remember me telling you that Raymond had not been in a relationship for five years when we met?" I asked, then drank my water.

"Yeah, I think so," she answered as she peeled her banana.

"Well, he was celibate during that time."

"The whole time?" she asked, biting her banana.

"As far as I know, he was for the whole time. Anyway, because of his celibacy, he has problems maintaining an erection."

"Doesn't that get on your nerves? How do you have sex?" Tia asked, devouring the last of her banana.

"It can be difficult sometimes, but we managed in the past. You know when you're horny, can't nothing stop you. You'll work something out."

"I don't understand. If you had sex in the past, why you aren't having sex now?"

"Raymond went to the doctor to find out what his problem was and what could be done to make him right."

"What was the problem? Maybe, he needs to go to another doctor."

"His problem was poor penile circulation due to lack of use. He's taking medication to correct the problem. The doctor told Raymond on his last visit to abstain until his next appointment in three weeks," I said, leaning back in the chair.

"You have to wait three weeks before you can consummate the marriage? Girl, if I were you, I would get me some. From what you just told me, having sex will solve his problem," Tia said, getting up. "I guess my break is over. I hear more work being clocked in."

"You could be right, but I'll wait," I said getting up walking to the water cooler. Tia's words penetrated me like lotion. I wondered if indeed she had the solution to our problem.

By Sunday evening, built up passion had gotten the best of Raymond and me. When we were in bed, Raymond passionately kissed me, and I snuggled up to him. His kiss ignited a desire for intimacy. I tried to fight the urge, but the more I resisted, the more my body demanded to be satisfied. My hand accidentally touched Raymond's penis, which was as hard as a brick. His hand slid between my legs. We began to massage each other's genitals.

"Raymond, we'd better stop before we do something we're not supposed to," I said low, trying to ignore my body that was screaming for more.

"I can't take this any longer. I don't care what the doctor said. You are my wife, and I am your husband. Now, is the time we make it official," he said, mounting me.

Our bodies moved synchronously like a fine watch. We were in so much heat it didn't matter if Raymond was healed or not. We didn't stop until we were both satisfied.

I loved my husband. It didn't matter to me if he could perform or not. I married him as he was. I was thankful Viva was gone from my life. Otherwise, we would have problems. God knew she had to leave. He knew what I would be up against.

Tuesday morning, I told Becky, the assistant supervisor, who was in charge of scheduling, I needed to go part-time, immediately. She pulled out the schedule book and told me she could schedule me off on the nights Jenny, Tia and I worked together. However, I couldn't officially go part-time until Tia came back from vacation, February 10. Since I wanted to work Sunday and Monday nights, I could start February 8.

Thursday, February 5, was Raymond's urologist appointment. Raymond said he still wasn't one hundred percent. He was closer to seventy-five percent. Each lovemaking session made him more frustrated although he had found a way to satisfy me, which made me very happy.

Raymond went in to see Dr. Travis Fuller when the receptionist, a short, stout black woman with brown eyes and a beautiful smile, called his name. I remained in the waiting area reading a magazine. Twenty minutes later, the same receptionist called me to join Raymond. When I entered Dr. Fuller's office, Raymond was sitting in an olive green chair facing the doctor. Dr. Fuller, an elderly, pecan brown skinned man with graying hair and small, square glasses, motioned me to come inside. I sat next to Raymond in an identical chair.

"How are you Mrs. Miller?" Dr. Fuller greeted me cheerfully, "I am Dr. Travis Fuller," he said extending his hand.

"Nice to meet you Dr. Fuller," I said, shaking his hand.

"Is there anything else you need me to do before I leave?" the receptionist asked as she stood in the doorway.

"No, Dorothy. That will be all. Thank you," Dr. Fuller said, smiling, showing his white teeth.

Dorothy nodded then left the room.

"Mrs. Miller, I sent for you to join your husband. I have examined him and prescribed medication that should remedy some of his problem. I need your help to alleviate the rest."

"How can I help?" I asked, bewildered. "You're the doctor."

"Mrs. Miller, sometimes doctors can't do everything to help the patient. Sure, I have my part, which I have done, but in your husband's case, I need you, too. It's called teamwork. You're an important member of this team. Don't you agree, Raymond?"

16

"Most definitely, Dr. Fuller," Raymond answered, reaching for my hand.

"Okay, doctor. What do you want me to do?" I asked, calmly.

"Mrs. Miller…"

"Please, call me Vanessa," I interrupted.

"Very well, Vanessa," he said, pausing to exhale, "there is an exercise I need you and your husband to perform during intercourse that will allow him to maintain a full erection. I've already explained it to your husband."

"What is it?" I blurted out, looking at Raymond.

"Don't worry Mrs. Miller, I mean Vanessa, it's very simple. At the height of intercourse, before an ejaculation, Raymond must pull out. When he does, you have to grab the base of his penis and squeeze it as hard as you can for a few seconds then continue with intercourse as before."

"Won't I hurt him?" I asked, feeling apprehensive.

"No. It will feel like a pinch to your husband."

"How can he maintain an erection? Won't it hurt?" I asked again.

"Vanessa, it's not as bad as it sounds. Let me explain what you're doing. By cutting off the circulation of the penis during intercourse, you are forcing the blood vessels to supply more blood to the penis to compensate for being cutoff. Thus, making the penis harder than before. You're helping to build up a larger blood supply to the penis. The more blood, the bigger and harder the penis becomes. Which means, more sexual pleasure for you and your husband."

"How long do we have to do this exercise?" I asked still uneasy about the whole thing.

"Well, that depends on how often you have intercourse and how well you do your part. Say, you have intercourse four to five times a week, and you cutoff the circulation correctly. I'd say anywhere from six to ten weeks, Raymond will be able to have normal erections."

"Are you sure this will work?" I asked, clasping Raymond's hand.

"It should work, but if it doesn't, I have something else you can do," he said, peeping over his glasses. We talked a few minutes longer before leaving Dr. Fuller's office. He reassured us we should see an improvement within three weeks. We hoped he was right because we were ready for Raymond to be healed.

Since it was 12:30 in the afternoon when we arrived home, we decided to practice before the kids came home from school. During intercourse, Raymond pulled out, and I squeezed the base of his penis as hard as I could for a few seconds. I was surprised my actions didn't seem to bother Raymond. I released my grip, and we continued. He came within seconds. Judging by the intensity of his orgasm, the exercise heightened the sexual experience rather than diminishing it.

I prayed as our bodies separated that one day Raymond would be healed, and our daughters would come. Raymond held me close and told me how blessed he was to have me for his wife. He also said, he wished he could perform like his old self. I told him I was happy to be his wife, and his performance in bed did not change how I felt about him. I love him unconditionally, like Christ loves The Church.

As I lay in Raymond's arms, I thought about our relationship, how it paralleled with Jesus and The Church. I remembered before we got married, after we had broken up, Raymond said he loved me so much; he would have given his life for me. That's the same way Jesus feels about His Church or people, who are the called out ones. In I Peter 2: 9-10 *"Christians are a chosen generation, a royal priesthood, a holy nation. Christ's own special people, that we may proclaim the praises of Him who call us out of darkness into His marvelous light; who once were not a people but are now the people of God, who had not obtained mercy but now obtained mercy."* Jesus gave His life for us that we might live righteous and holy.

The more I thought about the similarities of Raymond and Jesus, the more love I felt for both. Raymond was my physical husband now. Jesus will be my spiritual husband to come. At His second coming, Jesus, the bridegroom, will gather His people from the four corners of the earth to partake in the marriage of His Church. Revelations 19: 7-9 tells of this marriage. *"Let us be glad and rejoice and give Him glory, for the marriage of the Lamb has come, and His wife (The Church) has made herself ready. And to her it was granted to be arrayed in fine linen, clean and bright, for the fine linen is the righteous acts of the saints. Then he (a voice) said to me, 'Write: Blessed are those who are called to the marriage supper of the Lamb!'..."*

I must have dozed off thinking of Raymond and Jesus because the next thing I knew, Raymond was waking me up to get ready before the kids came home from school. He also asked me if I was interested in visiting a church Sunday that one of his officer's attended. I told him that would be fine. Then I asked him, "Which church?"

He answered, "Word of Faith with Pastor Dale C. Bronner."

Sunday, we all went to The Word of Faith Church by Greenbrier Mall. We arrived while the choir was singing. A cordial male usher seated us on the second row from the front. Raymond and I were surprised to get such good seats since we were late, and the church was full. As the choir took their seats, a young, light-skinned man wearing a brown suit stood up to preach. Since I had never seen Pastor Bronner, I assumed the young man was he.

"I had prepared one message for you today, but the Lord wants me to bring you a different message, one that is close to my heart," the preacher said as he wiped his forehead, walking from the podium. "Last week, Pastor Bronner spoke about babies being birthed. He mentioned both physical babies and businesses. The Lord told me that a birthing will take place," he said, squatting in a birthing position. "God will bring forth children to worship and obey Him. He is a jealous God and will no longer tolerate His people to put other gods before Him. Therefore, He will give birth to a new generation of offspring, who will obey Him and love Him with their whole being. His offspring are presently in the womb of The Church, waiting to be delivered," he said, walking to the left side of the pulpit, squatting again. "Literal births will take place as well as spiritual births of God's people. I don't know why the Lord wants me to speak on this today, especially since Pastor Bronner talked about it last week. But there must be somebody here today who needs to hear this message. I think back on my three-week-old daughter. My wife and I lost our son before she conceived our second daughter. She didn't experience any complications with our first daughter, who is four years old. After we lost the second child, the doctors wanted to do genetic testing before we tried again. They had us thinking something was wrong with us. I told them we didn't need any testing. There was nothing wrong with my wife or me because we had a healthy little girl of our own. Jesus had told me not to worry because everything was going to be all right. We would bring forth a normal, healthy child because we feared Him and walked in His ways. He reminded me of His promises in Psalm 128. Let's turn there and read," he said as he walked to the podium. He flipped pages in the opened Bible then read, *'Blessed is every one who fears the Lord, who walks in His ways. When you eat the labor of your hands, you shall be happy, and it shall be well with you. Your wife shall be like a fruitful vine in the very heart of your house, your children like olive plants all around the table. Behold, thus shall the man be blessed who fears the Lord...'*

Today, when I look at my daughters, I thank God for His Son Jesus Christ and His Word, which can not fail," he said, leaving the podium again. He got back down into a birthing position and said, "God will bring forth children. A supernatural birthing is taking place in our very lives. Will you be born? Or will you abort? God desires that all of His children make it to the birthing when Jesus Christ returns. Right now, we're being nourished and protected by The Church that Jesus started before His death. Literal babies and businesses will be born as well as spiritual children of God. I feel the Spirit of God moving in me to confirm what I'm saying to you is true," he said, standing upright. "Choir can we please have a selection? I feel like shouting and praising The Almighty God!" he asked before stomping his feet.

I listened to the choir, knowing my daughters will be born!

CHAPTER FOUR

The Word of Faith minister completed his sermon after the choir ended their selection. He picked up where he left off. His message was so timely for me that I knew God had sent us there. After leaving the church, I was so full of hope, I rejoiced all the way home. No longer was I concerned about my two miscarriages last year. I knew beyond a shadow of a doubt, my two daughters were going to be born!

Since my daughters were sure to come in my mind, my next order of business was to promote *Uncaged*, which was published December 22, 1997. Lisa, my publisher had my first book signing scheduled for Friday, February 20, from 6 to 8 p.m.. She also had arranged for me to appear on the Connie Flint Gospel Morning Show with Brother Edmond Patterson on radio WAOK, 1380 AM at 8:30 a.m.. Friday was a big day for me. It was the beginning of a long awaited opportunity.

When it was time for my radio debut, Raymond went with me. The station was located at Colony Square. We walked around several minutes and asked several people how to get to the station. Finally, a hostess at a nearby restaurant gave us the right information. We arrived at the station by 8:20 a.m.. I looked for Lisa, who was supposed to be on the air with me, but she wasn't there yet. A young black woman showed us where to go. We saw Mike Roberts and Carol Blackman performing on the FM, twin station, V-103.

I had on a blue dress with heels. Raymond had on a gray suit. Brother Patterson was dressed to kill in a brown and beige suit with matching brim. Connie, however, was dressed for radio with a navy jogging suit and sneakers. Her hair was in braids that extended to her shoulders. She greeted us by waving her hands as we came inside the studio. She had on a headset, talking into a microphone, while looking for a tape. I smiled and took my seat in front of another headset. Brother Patterson was sitting on a stool to my left, and Raymond sat in a chair to my right, close to the door.

At 8:30 a.m., Connie acknowledged over the air that I was in the station. I was nervous and didn't know what to expect. I was determined, however, not to let my nervousness get the best of me or ruin my radio debut. Fifteen minutes later, after more music, the news and traffic updates, it was time for me to speak.

"We have in our studio a new author, Deeva Denez. Her book is titled, *Uncaged*," Connie said, over the air. "Miss Denez, I haven't read your book, but can you tell my audience about your book?"

"Sure. *Uncaged* is my life story."

"You need to get closer to the mike. I can hardly hear you. Don't be bashful," Connie scolded, laughing.

I took a deep breath and continued. "The story begins shortly after my conception when my parents wanted to abort me, then it covers the next thirty-eight years of my life."

"What's so special about your life that you had to write about it?" Connie asked, coldly.

"I was commissioned by God in '94 to write my story in '95. He told me to write it the end of April '95 or the beginning of May '95. He said, it will be written and published. I was just following orders."

"You still haven't told us much about your life or what's in the book. I'll give you a few minutes to think about it while we pause for the news and traffic update," Connie said, cutting me off.

During the break, I thought about what to say. I couldn't wait to get back on the air.

"For those of you, who are just tuning in, we have in our studio today, Deeva Denez, author of *Uncaged*. It's her life story. Deeva, how did you come up with the title *Uncaged*?" Connie asked when it was my time to be on the air again.

Uncaged described me during a period of my life toward the end of the book. It was a time in my life when I was set free from the mental and emotional bondage of my past because of past hurts."

"How did you become uncaged?" Connie asked as if she was really interested.

"Through forgiveness. I had to forgive those who had mistreated me in the past. By doing so, I became healed of my mental and emotional wounds that I had been harboring for years."

"Forgiveness is powerful," Connie commented, smiling.

"Yes, it is. Forgiving others can set you free. It's like being born-again. God forgives us of our sins toward Him and He expects us to forgive others of their trespasses against us. When we forgive others, a healing takes place inside of us. At least, that's what I experienced and want others to experience, too," I replied as Lisa entered the room and sat in front of a headset.

We're almost out of time. Do you want to tell the audience where they can purchase your book?"

"Yes. *Uncaged* can be found at B. Dalton Bookstore at South Dekalb Mall. I'm having a book signing there, tonight from 6-8 p.m.. It can also be found at Brother's Three at Shannon and Southlake Malls; Two Friend's Bookstore at West End Mall; The Heritage Bookstore on Wesley Chapel; and Medu Bookstore in Greenbrier Mall."

"You have one minute. Is there anything else you want to say?" Connie asked, congenially.

"I'll let my publisher, Lisa Brown, have the last minute."

"Tomorrow, Deeva will be at Shoney's on Memorial Drive from 10 a.m. to 1 p.m.. And I will have her coming out party at Fine Arts By Todd at the Galleria across from Cumberland Mall at 8 p.m.." Lisa said.

"My, my, my, you have a lot going on. Well, it's been my pleasure to have you on my show. I wish you much success with your book, *Uncaged*."

"Thank you Connie for having me," I said.

"Now, we will hear from your friend and mine, Brother Edmond Patterson," Connie said, continuing her program.

Raymond and I gathered our things and left. Lisa came with us. I asked Raymond how I did as soon as we entered the elevators? He said, fine. I was glad he was with me. I was glad I didn't have to be at my radio debut alone. To celebrate, we decided to go to IHOP for breakfast. We parted ways with Lisa in the lobby. We would see her again, tonight, at B. Dalton for the book signing.

Once again, Raymond went with me to the book signing. We made it a family event by taking the kids. They strolled through the mall while I signed books. Periodically, they checked on me to see my progress. At the end of the two hours, I had sold twenty-one books, which was a good count according to the bookstore manager.

The next day at Shoney's, I didn't sell as many books, but I gave a book to Regina Slaughter, a radio personality on WYZE, 1480 AM. Several friends showed up to support me. Lisa and Tracey Lawrence, my publicist, were also present.

That night at the coming out party, Lisa made me feel like royalty. She had finger foods spread out on a table. Other authors saluted me with either kind words or recited pieces of their work. It was the most wonderful experience I had ever received in my life! I felt very special and loved by everyone present. I thought about all the long hours I had put into writing *Uncaged*. It wasn't until the party that I realized every second I put into my work was worth it. My moments of glory were worth the year and a half of labor to complete *Uncaged*.

The excitement from my coming out party weaned when my cycle started the next day. I was hoping to get pregnant this month, especially after hearing the sermon from The Word of Faith minister. I didn't tell Raymond how I felt. I didn't think he would understand. Fortunately, I didn't have time to sulk because I was too busy promoting *Uncaged* and writing its sequel, *The Bearer of the Sign*. Tuesday, March 3, I spoke at the Gresham Library about *Uncaged*. The president of a writer's group read *Uncaged* and loved it. He wanted me to share my story with his people. I was elated to speak to his group. My mother, brother, and niece also came. They made the event more special.

My message of forgiveness was well received. I emphasized how forgiveness releases the other person from causing you anymore hurt. Wounds are healed. The past becomes the past and not the present. I told them how my body was in the present, but my mind was in the past. I relived, over and over again, the negative things that were done to me in the past until I forgave the offenders and released them from causing me pain. By releasing them, I became free, mentally and emotionally. Thus allowing me to be uncaged from my own mental bondage.

The next morning, I was on Regina Slaughter's radio program from 8:30-9:00 a.m.. She contacted Lisa after she read *Uncaged*. She loved it, and said it was the first book she had read in many years with the exception of the Bible, which she read daily. Regina was so excited about *Uncaged* all I had to do was show up. Her enthusiasm dominated the half hour.

"Ladies and gentlemen, I have a special guest with me this morning, Ms. Deeva Denez, author of *Uncaged*. I must confess, it's the best book I've read in a long time. It's her life story, and it has a lot of interesting incidents in it. I must say, I especially liked it when you started talking about the blue carpet," Regina said, laughing.

"Listeners, you're in for a treat. Don't go away. We will have Deeva Denez tell her story after this next selection, "No Charge" by Shirley Ceaser."

Regina played the next selection then took two calls from the audience before getting to me. I was sitting in front of the microphone in a room outside the radio studio. A large glass window and a door separated us. Regina's room was soundproof, mine wasn't.

"Now, it's time to hear from our guest, Deeva Denez, author of *Uncaged*, a fascinating book! Deeva, in *Uncaged*, you tell us about your childhood growing up with an abusive father. How is your relationship with your father now?"

"Let me clarify abusive," I stated, not wanting the listeners to get the wrong impression. "Growing up, my father slapped and punched me all the time. That happened until we got in an altercation when I was eighteen years old. I left home the next day. My relationship with my father has improved every since I left. You must also realize that when I became uncaged, I was able to forgive him of how he treated me. Thus, getting rid of all the hurt I had experienced for years."

"You mentioned being, "uncaged". Can you explain what you mean?" Regina asked, enthusiastically.

"Uncaged, describes me. It means being freed from mental and emotional bondage. At one point in my life, before I became "uncaged", I wasn't living. I was only marking time, waiting to die. I was very unhappy and felt trapped in a marriage I no longer wanted to be in. Through forgiveness, I was set free."

"That's a powerful testimony, Deeva," Regina commented, smiling.

"Forgiveness is powerful! Christ wants us to forgive others, first, so He can forgive us of our trespasses against Him. And when you think about it, our trespasses are always greater than what anyone else can do to us."

"You're absolutely right, sister! It's time for another selection. Then we will be back with our local author, Deeva Denez," Regina said, as she played, "Oh Happy Day" by the Staple Singers.

Regina played two more hits and Stephanie gave a news update before I got back on the air. My time was almost up. Five minutes were left.

"It's time again to hear from Deeva Denez, author of *Uncaged*. Deeva, you have to explain the blue carpet before we leave," Regina coaxed.

"When I left home, at eighteen, I got married eight days later to Carl Lewis. The marriage had three distinct phases: a six year honeymoon; seven golden years; and six years of depression followed by a year of release, which occurred when I became uncaged. During the golden years, our house had gold carpet in it, which was replaced with blue carpet that symbolized and ushered in six years of depression."

"We only have a few minutes left. Is there anything else you want to say to my listeners?"

"Writing *Uncaged* allowed me to get rid of a lot of mental and emotional baggage. I feel like a brand new person. Life is worth living again. And most of all, my past is now my past and not my present. I know others have suffered things in the past that they need to be healed of. Forgive your offenders, so that you, too, can be freed or "uncaged". *Uncaged* was written for that very purpose. To allow people to live a happy abundant life that Jesus died for us to have!"

"Very well put, Deeva. Listen, we are all out of time. I want to thank you for coming."

"Thank you for having me," I said, feeling good about the program.

"You have to come back. The next time, I'll let my listeners call in. It's time to wrap it up, once again. I hope everyone has enjoyed the program. I have enjoyed being your host. I love you. I really do. Goodbye, Pooh," Regina said, going off of the air.

Quickly, I gathered my things because the person who was on next was sitting beside me waiting. As I left the room, his program began. Regina met me outside the studio by the door. She couldn't say enough good things about *Uncaged*. I liked her interview better than Connie Flint's. I think the main difference was she had read the book and Connie had not. If today was any indication of how well *Uncaged* would do, I knew I was on the road to success.

CHAPTER FIVE

Regina really made me feel good. Her enthusiasm intensified my courage to go forward. I didn't know what was ahead. I had to trust in The Almighty God.

Raymond taped Regina's program while I was at the station. I felt as if he was my husband, fan club, and manager all rolled into one. He was everything I needed in a mate. Things were going well with us. We had even gotten our lovemaking down to a science. We had discontinued the pull out and squeeze exercise. It had become too bothersome. Besides, Raymond was performing well without it. I felt both blessed and happy being Raymond's wife.

The kids seemed to be adjusting well with the exception of Raymond Jr.'s seizures. Raymond had not told me how to respond to Raymond's seizures until he had one in the hall bathroom one morning before school. Raymond came in our bedroom when Little Raymond's seizure was over and gave me instructions on what to do. He told me to lay Little Raymond on the floor and tilt his head back to clear his air passage and prevent him from biting his tongue. Then hold him down until he stopped any jerking movements.

I never saw Little Raymond have a seizure, but after that incident, I noticed he'd stare into space as if he was someplace else. Raymond said those were small seizures. Consequently, Raymond took our son to his neurologist because the seizures were occurring frequently. His neurologist started him on 250 mg of Depakote E.C..

Little Raymond's seizures weren't as big of a problem to him as was my lack of free time. It bothered him that I couldn't spend much time with Francine and him. I was too busy writing my next book and promoting my first. I tried to explain to them I had to work twice as hard now to get more free time later.

Most of the time when Raymond and I were dating, I wasn't writing nor was I a published author. The kids enjoyed all the fun things we did like going to the park, the movies, skating, and watching TV together. Both Raymond and I were working on building up our businesses. His was a financial empire; mine was an established author. Our goal was to have a better life later. Therefore, today, we had to sacrifice the fun times with the kids.

Saturday, March 7, I had a book signing at Shoney's from 6-8 p.m. on Main Street in East Point. Lisa and I showed up, but no one came inside the room we were in to buy a book. I was naturally disappointed. We couldn't figure out what we did wrong.

The following Friday I had a book signing at Medu Bookstore in Greenbrier Mall from 4-6 p.m. I sold twelve books. The turnout and atmosphere were good. The only bad thing was an obvious friction between Lisa and Tracey. They argued when it was over.

The next day, Tracey had scheduled another book signing with Brother's Three at Southlake Mall from 4-6 p.m.. As my publicist, Tracey made contacts for my book signings and radio interviews. She really kept me busy.

Tuesday, March 17, I went to an interview with Twanda Black, a radio personality for 104.1 FM, WJZF, Jazz Flavors at 11 a.m.. Her show aired on Sunday mornings from 8-9 a.m.. Twanda had read *Uncaged.*

I arrived at 10:45 a.m.. The receptionist said Twanda was with someone and should be with me shortly. I sat down on a beige sofa, across from the receptionist desk and in front of a brick fireplace.

Ten minutes later, a short, dark-skinned woman with short black hair and a tall medium-brown skinned man came in the room talking. The man called her Twanda. After they finished their conversation, the receptionist told Twanda I was waiting for her. She and the man walked over to me and introduced themselves. He gave me a business flier and asked for a copy of my book when I told him I was an author. Since I had two copies with me, I sold him a copy. He talked a few more minutes before Twanda walked him to the door. I stood up as she turned around.

"I will be with you in a minute," Twanda said, going to the desk, shuffling papers.

I continued to stand hoping she meant what she said. Glancing at my watch, the time was 10:56 a.m.. I thought about Lisa and wondered where she was. She'd better hurry if she wanted to be a part of this interview.

"I'm ready, Ms. Denez," Twanda said, facing me. "Sorry to keep you waiting."

I walked toward her. "That's okay. I understand," I said, standing beside her.

"Let's go to my office. I have everything ready for the interview. Follow me," she said, leading the way.

We walked past several rooms before we reached her office.

"Have a seat next to the microphone," Twanda instructed, sitting behind her desk. "It won't take me but a minute to put the tape in. Make sure you're comfortable."

I placed my purse on the floor and took a deep breath as I positioned myself close to the mike.

"I'm ready," Twanda announced. Are you ready?"

"Yes."

"Good morning. I'm Twanda Black. Your host today. You're listening to 104.1 FM, WJZF, Jazz Flavors. My first guest is a local author, who has written an amazing book called *Uncaged*. Welcome to the show Deeva Denez."

"Thank you."

"How long did it take you to write *Uncaged*?"

"I started writing April 21, 1995 and completed it on November 13, 1996."

"I understand it's your life story. Why did you write it?"

"I was told by God in April of '94 to write a book. He told me it would be written and published. He also told me when to write it. He said write it at the end of April or the beginning of May of '95."

"You have several prophesies in *Uncaged*. Please, explain a prophesy in the book."

"In 1980, I went to see a seer, who told me of several events in my life. *Uncaged* is the fulfillment of some of her prophesies. The seer, Madame Lee, told me I was going to have four children, two boys and two girls. At the time she told me, I had just found out my husband was sterile. She also told me I was going to leave my husband, which I did in '95. I had two sons by him. I knew I had to get out of the marriage in order for my daughters to come."

"What about the six initials?" Twanda asked.

"Madame Lee gave me six initials of men, who would be important to me. I met all six and recently married one of the men. He was the bearer of the sign I prayed for to identify the next man in my life."

"At the end of *Uncaged* you were involved with three men. Did you marry one of them?"

"I'm not saying. You have to wait and read my next book, *The Bearer of the Sign*."

"How much have you written of your next book?"

"I'm on chapter sixteen. It's coming along, nicely."

"You talk a lot about your sons. How are they doing?"

"My sons are fine. They live with their father. In *Uncaged*, I wrote of how much they loved their father. And because I made a promise to my oldest son that I would never separate him from his father, I struggled with getting a divorce. I have legal custody of my sons. They lived with me at first but preferred living with their father."

"What is the message of *Uncaged*?"

"It is to show how I was freed from mental and emotional bondage and to help other people be delivered also."

"Explain how you were freed?"

"Through forgiveness. I had to forgive those who hurt me in the past. By doing so, I released them and freed myself."

"Where can your book be purchased?"

"Medu Bookstore at Greenbrier Mall, B. Dalton Bookstore at South Dekalb Mall, Heritage Bookstore on Wesley Chapel Road, Two Friends at The West End Mall, and Brothers Three at Shannon and Southlake Mall."

"I wish you much success with your book."

"Thank you."

"Thank you for being on my program," Twanda said, turning off the tape.

I took a deep breath when it was over. I felt good about the interview. Twanda looked at me with her soft black eyes as she put her hands in front of her on her desk.

"Now, tell me. Who did you marry, the Muslim or the security guard?"

"I'm not telling. You have to read *The Bearer of the Sign* to find out," I replied, laughing. She really wanted to know and thought I would give her the answer without being taped. We talked ten minutes more about personal matters because she saw herself in Vanessa Lewis. They had a lot of the same struggles. *Uncaged* shed some light in her life. I was glad my book helped her and hoped it would help others.

Twanda escorted me to the front after our talk. As we stood talking, I felt queasy like I was pregnant. It only lasted a second, long enough to get my attention.

When I got home, I told Raymond about the interview and the queasy feeling. I told him, I thought I was pregnant. He had a wide grin that covered his face. The glee in his eyes said it all. I told him my cycle was due in five days.

Three days later, on Friday the twentieth, I re-appeared on Regina Slaughter's radio program. That evening I had a book signing at Two Friends Bookstore at The West End Mall from 6-8 p.m.. Regina's program was another success. Her enthusiasm made the difference again. I received a call from Stephanie's mom, who said she loved *Uncaged* and couldn't wait for the sequel.

Lisa was with me at the book signing that evening. I sold ten books. Lisa told me Tracey was no longer working for her because her fees were too expensive. During the book signing, the queasy feeling returned. I knew if my cycle didn't start Sunday, I would take a pregnancy test Sunday night at work.

Sunday, I met with a book club called The Meeting of the Minds. I arrived at two o'clock, but was told it didn't start until three. Since the host, Charlotte Alexander, was not ready, I waited in my car, outside, until she waved for me to come inside. Charlotte had prepared refreshments and told me to help myself. I drank the punch, ate fruit and wings while we waited for the other members to show up. Two hours later, no one came. Charlotte explained that two of her faithful members had just had babies, and she didn't know what happened to the other seven. She didn't want to wait any longer because she wanted to see Angela Davis at the Shrine of the Black Madonna. Two of her friends showed up to go with her to the Shrine and bought a copy of *Uncaged*. While I was at Charlotte's, the queasy feeling returned. I knew when I left, I was definitely pregnant!

I told Raymond about the queasy feeling returning. And I knew I was pregnant. He grinned again, holding me close to him. However, he wouldn't be convinced until I took the pregnancy test that night. I told him, I didn't need to take the test because I knew I was pregnant. But I would take it anyway for the record.

That night at work, I collected a urine specimen to take a urine pregnancy test. The plus sign for a positive result appeared before the

five minutes were up. The joy I felt was overwhelming. My baby girl –
the image, a prophetic birth – was on the way.

CHAPTER SIX

The excitement I felt, knowing I was pregnant, was more than I could bear. Knowing another human being was developing inside of me – taking form – gave me an unspeakable joy. It also gave me a sense of added responsibility. God had granted me another opportunity to help mold a young mind to conform to His ways. It was an honor to be given a chance to bring forth one of God's children into existence.

Jesus showed me an image of a baby wrapped in a blanket in March of '95. Now in March of '98, the image was being made a reality. I'm reminded of the time in Genesis 1:26 & 27 when God made man. *"Then God said, 'Let Us make man in Our image, according to our likeness; let them have dominion over the fish of the sea, over the birds of the air, and over the cattle, over all the earth and over every creeping thing that creeps on the earth.' So God created man in His own image; in the image of God He created him; male and female He created them."* Man is made in the image of His Creator. We have the same form and likeness as God. But we are flesh, and God is spirit. However, the good news of the gospel, that Jesus proclaimed and shed His blood for, was to change our bodies of flesh to spiritual bodies like God and Jesus, our Father and Brother. I Corinthians 15:21-24, and 42-49 explains. *"For since by man came death, by Man also came the resurrection of the dead. For as in Adam all die, even so in Christ all shall be made alive. But each one in his own order; Christ the firstfruits, afterward those who are Christ's at His coming. Then comes the end, when He delivers the kingdom to God the Father, when He puts an end to all rule and all authority and power....So also is the resurrection of the dead. The body is sown in corruption, it is raised in incorruption. It is sown in dishonor, it is raised in glory. It is sown in weakness, it is raised in power. It is sown a natural body, it is raised a spiritual body. There is a natural body and there is a spiritual body. And so it is written, 'The first man Adam became a living being.' The last Adam became a life-giving spirit. However, the spiritual is not first, but the natural, and afterward the spiritual. The first man was of the earth, made of dust; the second Man is the Lord from heaven. As was the man of dust, so also are those who are made of dust; and as is the heavenly Man, so also are those who are heavenly. And as we have borne the image of the man of dust, we shall also bear the image of the heavenly Man."*

In the case of my daughter to come, I saw the spiritual image first, followed by the physical. God has an awesome plan for mankind after our spiritual birth in His image. Blessed will be those who are part of the second, spiritual birth.

Raymond took the news well of our soon to come arrival. He began writing down a list of things to do before the baby came. His desire was for me to be a full-time mom. Actually, it was both our aspirations. He wanted his business to first replace my income then replace his. I wanted my book sales to be my source of income instead of Grady Hospital.

Tuesday, March 24, I had a book signing at The Heritage Bookstore on Wesley Chapel Road from 6-9 p.m.. It was a dismal failure. I sold three books. There was very little traffic in the bookstore. In addition, my table in the back, made it hard for me to prospect the few customers who did come inside the store. The bright side of the evening was it gave Lisa and I another opportunity to talk. I always enjoyed our time together. I told her I was pregnant and had gone to the doctor earlier that day. My due date was November 29. She congratulated me.

The next afternoon, I went to Grady's Birthday Bash at Hirsch Hall from 2:30-3:30 p.m. as a guest speaker for the Grady employees who had birthdays in March. It was the first time Grady advertised for entertainers for the Birthday Bash. I responded to the announcement in a weekly Friday Update, Grady's newsletter, and was selected. I talked about *Uncaged* and read from it, in the fifteen minutes I was allotted. I received good responses from the thirty or so people who were present. Regardless of how anyone else felt, I was excited because being there gave me another chance to talk about *Uncaged*.

Friday, March 27, I had a book signing at Shoney's on Wesley Chapel Road, from 9 a.m. -1 p.m.. This was my last book signing scheduled because Tracey was no longer working for me, and Lisa was not going to promote me without a publicist. I felt betrayed. But, I was determined not to let Tracey or Lisa dictate the fate of *Uncaged*. It was the work of The Almighty God. Jesus would allow it to prevail, regardless of what obstacles I came against.

The book signing was a success. I sold seventeen books. The manager placed my table up front by the cash register. He persuaded a few customers to purchase books. His enthusiasm and selling skills paid off for me. He also gave me some pointers for future book signings. I really appreciated his input. At the conclusion of my book signing, the manager invited me to his Rotary Club meeting, Thursday, April 2, at his Shoney's from 7:30-8:30 a.m.. I accepted his invitation. He said prominent business people from the community would be present.

I left the book signing both happy and tired. The pregnancy was causing me to feel drowsy. All I wanted to do was go home, kick off my shoes, and crawl into bed to take a nice long nap. Maybe, Raymond was still in bed, too, I thought as I drove home. Cuddling up next to him would be the perfect ending to my afternoon.

To my disappointment, however, Raymond was up when I got home. He was at the kitchen table reading. He barely looked up as I entered the house.

"I was hoping you would still be asleep," I said, putting my purse and books on the coffee table.

"I couldn't sleep," he said, turning a page.

"Would you like to sleep with me?" I asked, walking toward him.

"No. I'd rather read," he answered, coldly, with his head still bent, facing his book.

"The kids won't be home for another hour and a half. Let's go upstairs and cuddle."

He placed his finger where he was reading and looked me straight in the eyes. "I said, I'd rather read."

"What's wrong with you? You act like you're mad at me or something."

"You don't have time for me, lately. When you're not here, which is most of the time, I read. Would you please finish this conversation, so I can read."

"Oh, so that's it. You're upset because I've been busy having book signings. That I haven't spent much time with you," I said, getting pissed.

"I have said all that I'm going to say," he said as he drifted back to his book.

I went back to the coffee table, picked up my books and took them downstairs with the other *Uncaged* books. Raymond was still reading when I came back up. He never looked up as I went upstairs to take a nap. I took off my shoes and laid face down across the bed, pulling the covers around me. Back flashes of Douglas kept entering my mind. The fun times we had. The dinners. The kisses. The conversations about getting married. The warm embraces that I longed for with Raymond. The more I tried to erase the memories, the more vivid they became. I also thought about Raymond's baby I was carrying and Righteous, the baby girl Douglas saw in a vision that I handed to him. Was his vision correct? Was I going to have both Raymond and Douglas's babies? I asked myself before I dozed off to sleep.

I answered my own question when I woke up. My subconscious mind had figured it out while I slept. It reminded me, Raymond was the bearer of the sign. He was the man I was to spend my last days with. There will be no other man in my life after him. Therefore, I need to get over Douglas and move on with my life with Raymond, my husband.

I turned to look at the radio clock on my nightstand. It read, 2:49. The kids will be home soon, I thought as I rolled out of bed. Feeling the fullness of my bladder, I immediately went to the bathroom. Raymond came to the door as I flushed. He smiled at me while I washed my hands. I looked at him, not saying anything, wondering what changed his disposition.

"How do you feel?" he asked still smiling.

"Fine. Why do you ask?"

"While you were sleeping, I was thinking about us."

"So was I. What were you thinking?" I asked drying my hands on the towel hanging on the shower curtain.

"So much has been happening since we got married, we need to slow down and spend more quality time together. You're busy with *Uncaged*, and I'm busy trying to get my business started. Let's do something special next week while the kids are in school."

"I wish you had thought of that earlier. We could have done something special today, when I came home, like make love," I said, walking to him laying my head on his shoulders and embracing him. He wrapped his arms around me. His touch felt wonderful. After some time passed, he lifted my chin to kiss me.

"I knew that's what you had on your mind when you came home," he said after the kiss.

"If you knew that's what I had on my mind, then why didn't you follow through?" I asked, looking into his eyes.

"I wanted you to experience how I feel when I come home, and your mind is not on me, but on other things.

"So, you're saying that I've been so busy doing other things, that I have neglected you, the one person, who is supposed to be first in my life, next to God?"

"Yes. That's what I'm saying."

"What would you like to do next week?"

"That depends on your behavior the rest of this week," he responded, lowering his hands to my waist.

"I promise you, I'll be on my best behavior," I said, rubbing his butt. "I can't wait to see what you have in store," I said as the doorbell rang.

"I guess, we'll have to continue this later," he said, releasing his hold to answer the door for the kids.

"I hope we can pick up where we left off," I said as he walked off.

"We can do better than that. We can pick up where you wanted to start when you came home," he said, walking out the door.

I smiled and followed him downstairs. He was opening the door as I reached the bottom step. Little Raymond entered first, running past both of us to use the bathroom. Francine dropped everything she had in her hands at the door. Her two plaits were disarrayed on her head. Loose hairs were everywhere. She didn't care anything about her hair when she played. She was only concerned with having a good time. I had grown accustomed to seeing her come home looking a mess.

"What's for dinner?" she asked, walking to the kitchen.

"Aren't you going to say hello first?" Raymond asked, locking the door.

"Hello, Daddy. Hello, Mama."

"Hello, Francine," Raymond and I replied in unison.

"What's for dinner, Mom?" Little Raymond asked, jumping down the steps as he opened the bathroom door.

"You have to say hello first, Raymond, before you can ask what's for dinner," Francine responded. "That's what Daddy told me. Isn't that right Daddy?"

"Yes, that's right."

"Hello, Mom. Hello, Dad," Little Raymond said, kissing my cheek. "What's for dinner?"

Little Raymond and Francine always asked, "What's for dinner?" when they came home. I anticipated the question before they came through the door although sometimes, I found it irritating. "Today is Friday, the day we eat out," I answered, walking to Big Raymond. "Where would you like to eat, today?"

"It's my time to decide, Francine," Little Raymond snapped, "You chose McDonald's last time."

"Let's go back to McDonald's," Francine retorted, "I want a Happy Meal."

"I want to go to Taco Bell," Little Raymond replied. "I want tacos!"

"I don't want tacos," Francine said, "I want a Happy Meal."

"Francine, we're going to Taco Bell," Raymond said, holding my hand. "It's Raymond's time to decide. We went to your choice last week."

For some reason, I felt like this was a good time to tell the kids I was pregnant. "Raymond and Francine, I have some good news to tell you," I said, hoping to ease the friction. "We'll be having a new addition to our family soon."

"What do you mean?" Francine asked.

"I'm pregnant with your sister."

"Oh, no. Not another sister!" Little Raymond shouted. "I don't want another sister. I already have three!" He was referring to Francine, Brandy, his oldest sister by his father, and Robin, his younger sister by his mother.

"Sorry, Raymond. That's the way it is. Your fourth sister is in the oven cooking," I said, squeezing Raymond's hand.

"What do you mean?" Francine asked.

"Speaking of cooking, let's go eat," Big Raymond said. "We'll explain it to you while we eat our tacos."

We left for Taco Bell. I rubbed my abdomen as I walked out the door and said a silent prayer.

Dear Lord, protect this unborn child from all harm and danger. Let her be healthy and normal. Let her blend in with the rest of the kids. And help them to love her unconditionally, the way You love us.

Help me to love each child equally, showing no favoritism. Give me the wisdom, strength, patience, and love to be a mother to all of my children, regardless of the circumstances. Amen.

I went to the car reassured that Jesus was in charge of the situation. He wouldn't put anything on me that was more than I could handle. I knew, He would bring this new child into existence. It was guaranteed.

CHAPTER SEVEN

The drive to Taco Bell was noisy. Francine and Little Raymond stayed into it with each other over one thing after another. First, Francine's leg touched Little Raymond's. Then, Little Raymond couldn't find a piece to go to his action figure, and he accused Francine of taking it. I bit my lower lip to keep myself from exploding or saying something I might regret later. I was hoping Raymond would jump in and correct the situation like he usually did. Since he didn't say anything, I didn't either.

Once we settled at a table with our food and said grace, I explained to Francine what "cooking in the oven" meant. Her eyes grew large when she understood I was having a baby. Little Raymond was upset, but not enough to not eat his food. As a matter of fact, he ended up eating one of Francine's tacos because she was too excited to eat it.

Raymond's face filled with joy as I spoke about the baby to come. His arms slid across my shoulders allowing my head to rest on his arm as we watched the kids eat. A feeling of happiness enveloped me. I laid my hand on my abdomen again to reassure the fetus it was already loved and wanted. We would patiently wait until her time arrived when we could see her face-to-face.

I wondered if her face would look exactly like the face of the image I saw through the windshield? A face I could never forget. The image had large, piercing eyes that stared serenely at me, as if she was waiting on me to make my move. That's why I said, "I'm coming, I'm coming, baby girl. Mama's coming, soon." Now, I'm waiting on her, I thought as I sat with my family.

"Mama, when will my sister come?" Francine asked, wiping her mouth after she finished eating.

"She's due at the end of November," I replied still resting my head on Raymond.

"What do you mean by due?" she asked, picking up her soda.

"Due means when the baby will come," Little Raymond answered before I could speak. "Duhhh. Don't you know anything?"

"I'm just seven, Raymond. I don't know everything yet."

"You mean, you don't know nothing, yet," Little Raymond teased.

"Leave me alone!" Francine snapped, getting upset. "Why do I have to have you for a brother, anyway?"

"Cause, I was born first. Duhh, dumb-dumb."

"That's enough!" Raymond interjected. "Finish eating your food, Raymond, so we can go. If I hear another word from either of you, you will get it when we get home."

An awkward silence followed Raymond's words until Francine broke it with the sucking sound coming from her empty cup.

"Francine, stop it!" Raymond instructed. "You've drunk all of your soda. Stop sucking on your straw!" Raymond said exactly what I wanted to say.

I sat up because my tranquility had been broken. At that point, I was ready to leave, and Little Raymond had just finished eating. "Since everybody's through eating, clean off the table," I commanded. "Raymond, wipe your mouth. You have sauce on your face," I said, clearing off my space. "It's time to leave."

Little Raymond picked up all the paper off the table and discarded it. Francine placed the dirty tray over the trashcan. Raymond straightened the chairs, and I wiped the table with a napkin. Our table looked better when we left than when we arrived. Raymond held my hand as we walked to the car.

The ride home was quiet. I guess, the kids still had Raymond's words imbedded in their minds. They knew their dad meant business when it came to discipline. He followed through with his warnings. I loved that about my husband. He believed in being the man of his house. He didn't rollover and play dead like Carl.

Thinking of Carl also reminded me of the time shortly before our divorce, three years ago. He thought we were going to get back together, and he was going to be the father of my daughters. I told him, I was going to have two daughters, but I didn't tell him they wouldn't be by him. He thought, I needed time and space to sow some wild oats. He thought, I would come running back into his arms after I realized he was the best thing that ever happened to me. He also thought he would then father my two daughters, and we would live together happily ever after. Boy, was he shocked when I didn't give him a chance to come back.

Then I thought about all the opposition Raymond had before we were married. They were Viva, my wretched flesh, who hated his guts. Bryson, my married lover, who Viva loved. Herman, my male church friend, who was very interested in me, but I couldn't get into him because I was a friend to his ex-wife. My mother, who didn't like Raymond because he had two children, and she felt like he didn't have a damn thing. Last, but not least, Douglas Jefferson, D.J., the man who I was pre-engaged to before I married Raymond. We were waiting on premarital counseling to set our May wedding date. Through all of this, Raymond, my Little David, the conqueror, prevailed. He successfully overcame all his oppositions. He won me as his prize and the privilege to father my daughters.

Raymond snapped me from my reminiscing when he gently held my hand while he was driving. A smile spread across my face as I thought about his conquests. I reminded myself again that I married the right man despite all we went through in the past.

"Thank you for being a wonderful wife," Raymond said, squeezing my hand.

"You're welcome," I responded, turning my head, smiling at him. "Thank you for being a great husband."

He smiled, but kept his eyes on the road. "You have a way of making me very happy."

"I'm glad. I hope you will always be able to say that. I hope each day together gets better and better," I said, squeezing his hand back.

"I'm sure they will," he said as we pulled into our driveway.

We all got out and went inside. I was glad the kids were calmer than when we left. I planned to write when we returned unless Raymond had other plans. Their calmer disposition would make writing easier with fewer interruptions from settling their disputes. Since Raymond had to work, I knew he would be retiring soon to get some sleep, and I would be up with the kids.

I had a good writing session that evening. *The Bearer of the Sign* was really beginning to take form. My goal was to complete it before the baby was born. Since I didn't have anymore book signings scheduled, I could spend more time writing.

I wrote for three and a half months without another book signing. Saturday, July 11, and Friday, July 17, at Medu Books in Greenbrier Mall ended this no book signing period. Tuesday, July 14, I had book signings at B. Dalton, South DeKalb Mall because of the Black Arts and Heritage Festival from 2-4 p.m. and 5-8 p.m., respectively. I had called myself to schedule the book signings for B. Dalton's. I had, had enough of being idle. I knew the potential of *Uncaged* had not been reached. I felt the festivals would be the perfect opportunity to get started again.

During my down time, I kept telling Jesus that I knew He was with me. That He would never forsake me like He said in His Word, even when everyone else had. And, even when the way was dark and uncertain.

I recited Hebrews 13:5&6 daily. *"Let your conduct be without covetousness; be content with such things as you have. For He Himself has said, 'I will never leave you nor forsake you.' So we may boldly say: 'The Lord is my helper; I will not fear. What can man do to me?'"*

Saturday at Medu, the crowds were thick, but the sales were slow. I had anticipated selling lots of books. I was very disappointed, however, when I only sold five. Two of them were to my ex-sister-in-law, Nette. I prayed while I drove home that Tuesday at South DeKalb Mall would be better.

On Tuesday, July 14, as I entered South Dekalb Mall to go to my book signing, a young boy handed me a pamphlet with various authors and the times and dates of their book signings. I looked for my name but didn't find it. I thought it was strange since I had two signings scheduled. On my way to B. Dalton's, I noticed an unfamiliar book cart filled with books and several authors signing. As I paused to look, a smiling face came over to me.

"Go over and meet the authors," a tall, slim, dark-skinned man said, wearing a beige cap with AIRPLAY on it. "Get an autographed copy of their books."

"I don't have time. I'm on my way to B. Dalton's for a book signing."

"Check this out. You can stop here first, then go to B. Dalton's. We have great authors here," he said, leading me to the authors' tables.

"You don't understand," I said resisting his persuasion. I am an author, going to my own book signing. But, I didn't see my name in this pamphlet," I said, showing it to him.

"Oh, that's for my authors. Would you like to join us this week? I have some vacant slots."

"I don't have time, now, but I will be back when my book signing is over at eight. Will you still be here?"

"I'm not going anywhere as long as the mall is open, and people have money in their pockets," he said, smiling, showing most of his teeth.

"What is your name?" I asked, turning to leave.

"Mike, but my friends call me AIRPLAY."

"I'm Deeva Denez, Mike. I'll be back," I said, walking away. "I don't want to be late for my book signing." We both walked in opposite directions.

I arrived at B. Dalton's at 4:58 p.m.. William, the manager, had a table set up for me at the entrance with a Kinte cloth. I used the employee restroom before setting up for the signing.

It felt wonderful sitting behind the table, talking to people about *Uncaged*. Anytime I book signed, I also ministered to people. For some reason, people had a tendency to open up to me and tell me private things. I used the opportunities to teach about Jesus Christ. He is the answer to all of our problems.

At the end of the three hours, I had sold seventeen books. Not bad, I thought, for a new beginning. Several people said they didn't have any money then but would come back later to purchase a book. I also met several people who had read *Uncaged* and loved it. It always made my day to meet those people.

I saw Mike on the way out and signed up for three days, Thursday at twelve-noon, Friday after B. Dalton, and Sunday at 2 p.m.. I could have stayed that evening but was tired and decided to call it a day.

I rejoiced all the way home, thanking Jesus for the doors He opened to me. I knew when He opened a door, no man could close it. I thanked Him for allowing me to meet Mike. I knew that it was He that brought us together.

Before my twelve-noon book signing with Mike, I had a 10:30 a.m. ultrasound appointment. Since I was twenty weeks along, it would be able to determine the sex of my fetus. I already knew I was having a girl. The ultrasound would prove it to everyone else. The ultrasound technician kept gliding the instrument across my gelled abdominal area, typing information on a keypad. Finally, at the end of the session, after she told me the status of the fetus, I asked the technician what was the sex of my child? She moved the instrument several more times, turning the screen for me to view.

"Can you see this area?" she asked pointing to the screen.

"Yes," I answered, looking at the fetus moving.

"That's a hamburger. You're having a girl."

"A hamburger," I repeated. "Does that mean boys have hot dogs?"

She laughed. "No. Boys have penises. Dairy Queen has hot dogs."

"I knew I was going to have a girl before I got pregnant," I said, smiling, still looking at the screen. "You've just confirmed what I've been waiting on for three years."

"Actually, all babies start out as girls until twenty weeks of gestation when the Y chromosome kicks in. It's dormant up until that time. You can sit up now. I'm finished. I know you have to go to the restroom. Your bladder is really full," she said, wiping the gel off of me, then helping me to sit up.

"Thank you," I said, sitting erect. She was right. I did have to urinate, but I was so excited I didn't care if I peed on myself. All I could think of was my baby girl was cooking in the oven.

Full of joy, I left the ultrasound facility headed for South Dekalb Mall. I had already told Mike, I might be a few minutes late due to my appointment. I arrived at 12:08 p.m.. He and I were the only ones working. To put the icing on the cake of a wonderful day, The Dekalb Neighbor Newspaper took my picture signing my book to a couple, who had their daughter in a stroller. The photographer said my picture should be in the July 22, issue.

The fact that I only sold six books did not diminish my joy. My picture was going to be in the paper next week, which should generate more sales. Dollar signs started registering in my head as the photographer left. I kept paraphrasing an old saying, "One picture should be worth a thousand or more sales."

I was back at it again, the next day. First, B. Dalton's then Mike. I sold fifteen books at B. Dalton's and four with Mike. The mall drew a nice size crowd who came to browse instead of spend. Vendors were lined up, selling their wares. My only regret was not having enough money myself to buy some of the fine art I saw. Such was life. One day, I'll be able to buy whatever I wanted when I wanted it, I told myself as I left the mall thirty dollars richer.

I took Saturday off to rest and go to church. The Lord knew we needed a day of rest, otherwise we would work ourselves to death. Saturday or the Sabbath was my spiritual renewal day — a day I looked forward to each week.

Sunday, as I approached the mall entrance, I noticed a bus parked to my right. People were boarding the bus. I felt disappointed that I had arrived too late to sell to the passengers. Then, my eyes focused on a dark-skinned man talking to a light-skinned woman. She was slim and attractive with shoulder length, brown hair. She faced me while I saw a side profile of the man. They looked as if they had just come from church. Everyone boarding the bus did, too. As she turned to board the bus, he turned his body slightly, while still holding a conversation she was obviously trying to end. I kept walking as I watched. It suddenly dawned on me that I knew the man. I almost didn't recognize him in the black slacks, gray dress shirt, black dress shoes and black suspenders.

"Douglas!" I said, as our eyes met.

CHAPTER EIGHT

Douglas turned completely around, facing me. I couldn't believe his outfit. When we were together, he only wore his work uniform everywhere, including church. His gray shirt was brand new because the folded creases were very visible. Douglas still was not a dresser, even with his new look.

"Vanessa!" he shouted, walking towards me. "I thought, I'd never see you again." His eyes traveled to my bulging midriff as our distance decreased.

My eyes searched his to determine his reaction. I kept thinking of Righteous, the girl he said would be ours. I hoped he wasn't thinking the same thing. "What are you doing here?" I asked, standing a foot away.

"Are you pregnant?" he asked not answering my question.

"Yes. I'm having my daughter. I found out last week."

"When are you due?" he asked, looking me over from head to toe.

"November 29. Look Douglas, I'm here for a book signing," I said, walking toward the entrance. I can't stand out here and talk."

"I'll walk with you, if that's all right?"

"Sure. I think, we both have a lot of catching up to do," I said as we walked side by side to the mall.

Douglas opened the entrance door, allowing me to get in front of him. I picked up my pace once we were inside, realizing I was late. Douglas, a slow walker and slow talker, however, kept up with my pace. He was not going to let me get away from him again. In my haste, neither one of us bothered to talk.

Finally, we reached my destination. Mike greeted me as I took my place behind the table he had waiting for me with my books neatly arranged. Mike was a stickler for displaying books in a professional manner.

"Deeva, I have you ready to go," Mike said, as I walked to my table.

"Thanks, Mike," I said, putting my purse next to my chair. "The table looks great! How have sales been?"

"Slow. But since you're here, I'm sure things will pick up. Hey man, get your autographed copy of Deeva's book," he said to Douglas.

"I've read it, man," Douglas replied with an annoyed expression that Mike understood.

"Alright, man. I feel you. Deeva, let me know if you need anything," he said as he disappeared.

I put the finishing touches to my table while Douglas talked.

"Vanessa, I bought you a card and started to mail it, but decided not to. I didn't know how you felt about me no more," he said, sadly, looking into my eyes for the answer.

Douglas was good at reading my eyes. That was one reason I fell in love with him so quickly. But today, I wanted to conceal my true feelings. I was married now. What we had was over although neither one of us wanted it to be that way. I wanted to tell him, I still cared for him, but fought the feelings daily. I had convinced myself, I had married the right man, Raymond. Now, carrying his child, nothing else or no one else mattered – not even Douglas.

"I picked up the phone to call you on numerous occasions but changed my mind," he continued. "I read your book. You have a bloodline curse. I now know that we were never meant to be together. We would have made a big mistake," he said as his eyes continued to search my face.

My eyes dodged his. He wasn't the same man I fell in love with, I told myself. He was different. A difference, I didn't like. He continued to talk as if I didn't need to say anything. He wanted to clear his head.

"I went to Jamaica by myself. I couldn't change the tickets no more."

My heart did a flip-flop. We were supposed to go to Jamaica for our honeymoon, the week of May 10th. He was originally planning on going to Trinidad but changed to Jamaica for me. "Douglas, I'm sorry for hurting you," I finally said. "You were good to me. I never wanted to hurt you. Once I got married, I knew it was over between us. I had started a new life without you. I had moved on. The only thing I hated about getting married was hurting you."

"I was so upset, I didn't go to work the next day. I cried the rest of the day," he said, solemnly.

"I'm sorry for hurting you, Douglas. You are a good man and deserve a good woman," I said, looking into his small round eyes.

"I met a yellow woman in Africa. She has big eyes like you. I'm going back in a couple of weeks. She reminds me of you," he said, forming a semblance of a smile and looking at me as if he had not gotten over me.

Douglas, who was black as night, had this thing for yellow women with big eyes. I was glad he had found someone else. "How is Keith?" I asked, wanting to change the subject.

"I don't work with Keith no more. I received my certification in May and changed jobs. I now make over $100,000 working with computers."

I thought about Raymond's job as a Grady security supervisor. His salary was nowhere near $100,000 and never would be. "That's great, Douglas. It seems as if you're doing very well."

"God is good," he said, smiling.

A slender, forty-something woman wearing a white shorts set walked up to my table and picked up a copy of *Uncaged*. "That's a true life story," I said, turning toward the woman. She read the front then flipped it over and read the back.

"This seems like it's good!" she exclaimed. "How much is it?" she asked, still reading the back.

"Fifteen dollars," I replied, moving closer to her. "Douglas, I have to go. It was good seeing you again," I said as he walked off.

"I think, I'll get one," the woman said, handing me the book.

I signed her book then directed her to Mike to pay for it. I told her more about *Uncaged* as I signed. She had been married twice and could easily relate to everything I said. She also had a friend who was in a bad marriage. I told her *Uncaged* would be a good book for her friend to read, too.

After Cheryl left, a cocoa brown man came to my table. He looked at *Uncaged*. He said, "The cover looked interesting." I told him my book was about coming out of mental and emotional bondage. He said, he had a radio program in Columbus, Georgia. I gave him a book, and he gave me a card. He wanted me to give him a few days to read it then give him a call. If he liked my book, I could be on his program. His name was Dr. Hud of Foxie 105 FM, WFXE and WOKS 1340 AM.

When Dr. Hud walked away, I thanked Jesus for allowing Dr. Hud to come to my table, and prayed that He would make it possible for me to be on his program. I was so excited from seeing Douglas and meeting Dr. Hud that it didn't bother me the Heritage Festival was coming to an end. God had really blessed this week. It was one that I would never forget.

I called Dr. Hud, Thursday, July 23. He had read *Uncaged*, liked it, and wanted me to be on his show the up coming Monday from 6-7 p.m.. He would conduct a telephone interview. I was instructed to call him at 5:55 p.m..

When I hung up from Dr. Hud, I called Mike. I needed connections to do a book signing in Columbus next week. Since I was going to be on the radio, I wanted to capitalize on it as much as possible. I had never been to Columbus. I didn't even know where it was. Wherever it was, I would be there next week signing *Uncaged*.

Mike told me about Brother's Three Bookstore at the army base. He knew the owner and would call to schedule a book signing at the base. He also told me about Books-a-Million and Walden Books at the mall. While I was in Columbus, I could make connections for future books signings.

Mike called back twenty minutes later. He had arranged for me to go to the base Thursday, July 30, after the radio interview with Dr. Hud. He gave me directions to the mall and the bookstores before he hung up.

Monday evening, I was slightly nervous. I said a quick prayer before I dialed the radio station for the interview. Friday, Mike faxed Dr. Hud ten questions I had written for the interview at Dr. Hud's request. Since I knew the questions, giving the answers would be easy. I told myself as the phone rang, this should be a piece of cake.

"WOKS, 1340 AM, this is Dr. Hud," the voice said on the other end.

"Dr. Hud, this is Deeva Denez."

"Deeva, I will put you on hold until our interview starts. You'll be able to hear me while you're on hold. I have your questions."

"Okay," I said, as he left the phone. I heard him over the phone while I waited for him to return.

"We have a special guest with us this evening, Deeva Denez, author of *Uncaged*. Deeva, welcome to the show," Dr. Hud said, returning to the phone.

"Hi, Dr. Hud. Thanks for having me," I replied glad to start the interview.

"Deeva, I read your book. It was enlightening. You had a lot about dogs in it. Can you explain about the dogs?" he asked, not reading from the submitted questions.

I laughed. "You're talking about the barking at my birth, and the letter that I wrote referring to how I felt about myself?"

"Don't forget about Big Mama's Butch, the dog that got run over by your dad before your delivery, and the barking at the end," Dr. Hud added. "Deeva Denez is not your real name either."

"Wow, I'm impressed. You really did get into *Uncaged*," I said still laughing. "I'm sure a lot of people feel like I felt during that time in my life - - like a dog. My book does have a lot about dogs, now that you mention it. But let me add, my dog days are over now."

"That's good. What made you write *Uncaged*, and how did you get it published?"

"I explain in chapter twenty-three how God told me to write a book in April of '94. He told me to start writing it the end of April '95 or the beginning of May '95. He also said, 'This book will be written and it will be published.' All I had to do was be obedient to God, and I did."

"*Uncaged* is your life story. How long did it take you to write it?"

"I get asked that question all the time. I started writing *Uncaged* April 21, 1995, and I completed it November 13, 1996."

"Deeva, give my listeners an overview of *Uncaged*. In my opinion, it was a source of healing for you," Dr. Hud commented.

Uncaged begins shortly after my conception. It tells of the untimeliness and adverse circumstances my parents faced during that time, namely they were living with my great-grandmother, who was a hell raiser from Summerhill. She wanted my parents to abort me. My father thought it was a good idea although my mother objected. I then tell about my childhood, which included finding love at an early age, as well as being slapped and punched by my father. Most of the book though describes my twenty-year marriage of mental abuse. The title *Uncaged* exemplifies me when I reached a turning point in my life. It was then, that I loved myself and no longer thought of myself as nothing or a dog because that was how I had been treated. I also had to forgive my father and husband for the way they treated me in the past. Through forgiveness, I was set free to live a happy life based on my God given potential."

"I think you summed it up very well," Dr. Hud added. "Your story is worth reading. I've told several people about it."

"Thank you. *Uncaged* was written to free others as well. Too many people are bound up in their minds and are hurting because of something that happened to them in the past. They need to release their offenders and be set free, too. You're only half living when you live with anger, hatred, bitterness, and strife."

"You're absolutely correct. Look, Deeva, we're almost out of time. Do you have one last thing you want to say?" Dr. Hud asked, candidly.

"Sure. God has work for each of us, but He can't use us wounded. This is a time of healing, so that we can become whole again to do His work according to His Will."

"I agree with you. Deeva, it was a pleasure having you on my program. I'm sure my listeners found you intriguing.

"Thanks again for having me, Dr. Hud."

"I wish you much success with your book. It has been my pleasure having you on my show. You're listening to WOKS, 1340 AM. We have just been hearing from Deeva Denez, author of *Uncaged*," Dr. Hud said before he hung up the phone.

I slowly laid the receiver down in the phone cradle, smiling as I thought of the interview. I felt it was a success. I hoped the listeners did, too.

Raymond came inside the bedroom while I was still thinking of the interview and looking at the ten questions Dr. Hud didn't ask. I wished he had asked question #9. Where can your book be purchased? I thought as Raymond opened the door.

Our eyes met as he crossed the threshold. I could tell he had something on his mind. What, I didn't know.

No longer could I concentrate on the questions. My mind was now on my husband of six months. A husband, I now realized, I had neglected.

CHAPTER NINE

I continued to look at Raymond. For some reason, he had my undivided attention. The expression on his face told me to leave him alone, to let him enjoy being withdrawn in his cave. But there was something inside of me telling me differently. It said to penetrate his barrier and find out what was on his mind.

"How did your interview go?" he asked walking to his dresser a few feet from the door.

"It went well. I was very pleased with Dr. Hud's interrogation although he didn't ask the ten questions I submitted earlier," I answered, talking to his back while he rearranged the top of his dresser. I slowly stood on my feet and walked toward him. I had an urge to embrace him from behind and hold him in an arm lock. My plans were interrupted, however, when he suddenly walked to the bathroom. I followed behind him determined to hold him close to me.

"I'm going to take a sit," he announced, noticing I was at his heels.

I wanted to wrap my arms around him before he went into the bathroom, but decided not to because he might be in a tight. I patiently waited for Raymond to do his business before I held him lovingly around his waist. He felt like putty in my arms. I felt as if I held his very soul at that moment. A softening of his spirit as we caressed reassured me of his love. A love that had been smoldered lately with neglect.

As our bodies touched, I promised myself that I had to give him all the love and attention he deserved. Putting all my energy into my work had to end. The Lord had given me a good man to spend my last days with. I had better count my blessings and honor my wedding vows, to love and cherish him all the days of my life.

"I love you," I said softly, placing my head on his shoulders.

"I love you, too, sweetie, but I have work to do downstairs," he said, releasing his arms from me. "I just came up to take a sit."

"Can't you give me five more minutes?" I asked, wanting more.

"No!" he said sharply. "I have to get back to my work, and you need to get some sleep before you go to work. Don't try to be superwoman tonight. I care about you, sweetie. You need to get some rest, and I need to get back to work," he said walking towards the door.

"Five minutes wouldn't make a difference one way or the other, Raymond. You can give me five minutes of your time. When we were dating, time was no object."

"Marriage changes things, doesn't it, Mrs. Miller?" Raymond asked as he walked out the door, smiling.

I felt my blood pressure rise as Raymond walked out the door. His words cut through me like a knife. He was right, as usual. He had a way of ending an argument before it started. He also had a way of leaving me speechless when I had something to say.

Looking at the clock radio on my nightstand, I saw the time was 7:17. I had less than three hours for a nap. I couldn't decide if I'd rather sleep or write. I decided, I'd make up my mind after I iron my clothes for work and take a long hot bath. If I was sleepy, I'd take a nap. If I wasn't, I'd write.

The hot water and bubbles were like therapy. They caused me to relax, thinking back on the good times I had. My mind drifted back to the time when Raymond and I dated. I thought about the many days he came over on Thursday evening, his first night off, and stayed until four or five in the morning. He'd go home to shower and take a quick nap then come back by nine or ten that morning. He stayed until it was time to pick the kids up at six or when Carlos came home from school at three. A lot of times, I'd go home with him, leaving Carlos at home alone because he didn't want to go with us. I laughed aloud, thinking about how Carlos couldn't stand Francine and Little Raymond. His feelings hadn't changed either since I married Raymond six months ago. Raymond would get his kids settled in then come back to my house until four or five in the morning.

Those were the good times when we spent as much time together as we could. Now, that we were married, it seemed as though we had no time for each other. Everything else took up both of our time. Why does the romance end when the marriage begins? I asked myself as I continued to reminisce.

Suddenly, I remembered the fireball kisses Raymond gave me all the time. His kisses use to light my fire within a second, and I stayed lit for the evening. Now, I get pecks on the lips three times a day. An, I'm home from work, good morning, peck. An, I'm up from my sleep peck. And, I'm off to work peck. Peck, peck pecks, that's all I get!

I'm tired of pecks. I want real kisses like I use to get. Each time I told Raymond how I felt, he'd give me another peck and send me on my way. Men truly are from Mars, I thought as I let my bath water out and dried off.

The bath and reminiscing made me desire a nap more than writing. After ironing my clothes for work, I took a two-hour nap. I knew sleeping would allow me to think about the past more. I was thankful, I had good memories to think about. At one point in my life, my past was negative. God truly is good. Life is fair.

Feeling refreshed from the nap, I quickly got dressed as soon as the alarm went off. For some reason, I looked forward to going to work. I told myself, I was still excited because of the interview. Whatever the case, I felt good and was happy with everything in my life, including my relationship with Raymond.

Raymond was at the table working when I came downstairs to leave. He got up from the table and walked me to the door as usual. Giving me my goodbye peck at the door, I left for work.

Jenny was clocking in as I entered the lab. I rushed past her to clock in too on the office telephone. Tia walked in as I put the receiver down.

"Do you know what station I'm on?" Tia asked me while filling a cup with water.

Jenny and Tia never could keep up with the weekly rotation. They always asked me at the beginning of the week. "You're accessioning, "I replied, looking for an ink pen and marker on the supervisor's desk.

"What am I doing, tonight?" Jenny asked, laying her purse down on the desk.

"You're the back," I answered, picking up a pen and marker from the box.

"I'm glad somebody can keep up with what I'm doing," Jenny said, looking as if she hadn't gotten any sleep.

"Jenny, did you get any rest?" Tia asked. "You look like you can barely keep your eyes opened."

"I'm okay. I stay tired these days, no matter how much sleep I get," Jenny responded, still looking very tired. "I'll live," she said, walking out the office.

"Tia, as tired as Jenny is, she can still out work both of us and everybody else half her age. I don't know how she works like she does at 59, but she does. If I felt like she looks, I'd be at home in my bed," I said, walking past Tia.

"Me, too. No way, I'd come to Grady half dead," Tia added. "They work us like machines as it is."

"They have us working worse than machines. We work like dogs when it's really busy."

"You got that right," Tia said as I walked out the office.

I retrieved my lab coat from the rack, near the Hitachi, my station. Jenny had just gotten her lab coat and walked away when I reached the rack. Elaine, the evening shift tech, filled me in on what was going on with the Hitachi. She and the other evening shift techs soon clocked out as the midnight shift took their places.

The Hitachi had six specimens running. Two labs had just printed out and needed to be verified. I pulled the paper from the printer, walked to the Hitachi terminal, and answered the results. Tia brought me ten more specimens as I verified the last patient. Her long dark-brown hair was pulled back in a ponytail that covered three-fourths of her back. She grabbed the end of her hair and twirled it with her fingers.

"Vanessa, I want to have a baby, but my husband is not ready. He thinks we should start trying next year, but I'm ready now. I'm not getting any younger. I turned twenty-eight this year. What do you think I should do?" Tia asked still twirling her hair.

"Relax Tia, you have plenty of time. Look at me, I'll be forty-two when I have my baby."

"I don't want to have my children after I'm thirty-five. I want to have two children, a boy and a girl, but at the rate I'm going, I will only have Peaches, my dog."

"I think your husband is enjoying you too much. He's not ready to share you with a child. He wants your undivided attention. When you add a child to a marriage, the husband's time with his wife is practically cut out."

"I'll give Derrick his time. He's being selfish. Don't you think?"

"I think the two of you need to sit down and talk about it. Having a baby is not as easy as you think it is. A baby adds to a marriage as well as take away time from the couple. Derrick is wise to put off having a child if he is not ready to be a father with the added responsibilities," I said, downloading the new samples. "Raymond and I both wanted more children. That was a big issue with us that we both agreed on."

"Derrick acted like he wanted children before we got married four years ago."

"People change. Maybe, he did want children then. He may want children now. Whatever the case, the two of you need to agree on when to start a family. There will be sacrifices made from both of you, especially you as the mother. Whatever you do, don't rush Derrick. You might end up raising your child by yourself," I said, standing up to put the new specimens on my instrument.

"You don't want to be like me," Jenny added from the other side of the room. "I raised my three sons by myself since the oldest was five years old. Although my husband wanted our sons, he didn't stay around to help me raise them. Having kids is not easy. If your husband is not ready, wait until he is. Mind you, that's no guarantee he will stay with you until the kids are grown, but your chances are better that he will," Jenny said, tearing her urinalysis results from the analyzer.

"I'm still ready to have a child. I'm not getting any younger," Tia screeched.

"You have more time than you realize," I said walking to the Hitachi. Pray about it. Let God change Derrick's mind. Later on, you may be glad for the delay."

"I wished, I had waited," Jenny replied sitting at the microscope to do her urine microscopic. "I had my first child at twenty-three, a year after I got married. Everything happened so fast; I wished I had more time with my husband alone and more time to mature. I realized later, I really wasn't ready."

"I feel like I'm ready," Tia chimed. "I only wished Derrick was. I'll never have a baby if I wait on him!"

"Tia, you don't have a choice," I scolded. "You have to wait on Derrick and The Lord. Sometimes waiting is the hardest thing to do, but sometimes it is the right and Godly thing to do. Pray about it. Leave it in God's Hands and enjoy your life. At the right time, you will get pregnant and have your baby."

"You're right. I'll pray about it and let Jesus work it out. I won't nag Derrick anymore about having a baby."

"Good. Just remember me. I knew eighteen years ago I was going to have my daughter. I never dreamed I would be this old having this baby. But I tell you what, I'm glad everything worked out the way it did. If I had had my daughter earlier, I don't think I would have been as excited as I am now. You don't know what lies ahead. God does. Trust Him to bring forth your child at the right time, according to His plan and will in your life."

"I need blood!" an Emergency Clinic female employee shouted through the window holding blood release papers.

Tia rushed to the window to sign out two units of O Negative blood. I placed my new specimens on the Hitachi and took the results of the old samples off to verify them. My daughter moved inside of me as I walked to the computer. Feeling her movements gave me a joy that could not be put into words. I prayed silently for Tia that one day she too could experience the joy of having a child.

Tia and I talked more concerning her situation. It weighed heavily on her mind. I completely understood how she felt because I was in her shoes eighteen years ago. God answered my prayer to have a child. I prayed that He would answer hers, too.

All night and on the way home, I thought of Tia. As I pulled into the driveway, I said another prayer. Walking up the steps, I felt excited about being home. For some reason, I couldn't wait to see Raymond. I had thought about him most of the night, too. All the lights were out as I entered the house. Our bedroom door was closed. Quietly turning the bedroom doorknob, I opened the door. Raymond's back was facing me as he lay in bed. I quickly slipped my clothes off and snuggled up close to him. I wanted him to turn around, put his arms around me, and make love to me.

"Good morning," I whispered in Raymond's ear, laying my head on his pillow.

He slowly turned over facing me, putting his arms around me and pecked my lips. "Good morning, sweetie," he said opening his eyes.

"I want more than a peck," I said cooing in his face.

He tightened his arms around me and smiled, giving me another peck on my forehead. "I'll give you two pecks," he said, smiling more.

"Baby, don't you want to make love?"

"No," he answered, quickly.

"Well, I do," I said, gliding my hands over his behind. I felt his manhood respond to my touch. He kissed my lips, passionately moving his hands to my breasts. His touch felt wonderful and my body wanted more.

"I'll take a shower in the hall bathroom and you take a bath in ours," Raymond instructed, ending what had gotten started.

"I can't wait that long," I moaned. "Let's start now!"

"On second thought, I think I'd rather go back to sleep," he said, pecking me on my lips and turning over.

Fuming, I laid next to him. I felt our baby move again. In my mind, I told her to kick his ass, something I wanted to do. She'd be here soon I consoled myself. I would teach her the correct way to live with a man, something I was having a hard time doing.

CHAPTER TEN

Since Raymond had killed my desire for both sleep and sex, I decided to work on *The Bearer of the Sign*. My goal was to finish it before my daughter arrived. Writing was my escape from reality. I could make love on paper although I couldn't in real life. Writing to me was wonderful! It allowed me to be everything I wanted to be.

Towards the end of my writing session, my mind drifted to my next book signing at the base in Columbus, Georgia. I felt somewhat anxious because I'd never been to an army base before. I kept wondering what it would be like. In the back of my mind, I hoped the soldiers would have an open mind about *Uncaged*.

When Friday finally arrived, I rushed through my morning rituals so I wouldn't be late. Each book signing gave me a high that surpassed any alcohol consumption. My head was spinning like a top. I convinced myself to calm down before something tragic happened. I would hate to be late or miss a book signing over an anxiety attack.

The drive to Columbus was very pleasant. Clear, blue and white clouds covered the sky. It was the kind of day you'd like to spend outside, on a blanket, eating fried chicken, potato salad, baked beans, and bread. I promised myself, I would have a picnic the first chance I could. With more book signings coming up, I'd better hurry before the weather changed.

Listening to my gospel favorites such as Shirley Ceasar, The Brooklyn Tabernacle Choir, John P. Kee, The Mississippi Mass Choir, and James Bignon, the two and a half hour drive seemed like thirty minutes. I beamed as I saw the Columbus sign to my right. "Mike gave me excellent directions", I blurted aloud to myself. Normally, I'd get lost if the directions weren't perfectly clear.

Looking intently at the signs, I followed them to the base. Finding a good parking spot close to the commissary, I smiled and pulled right in. I was told the bookstore was located near it. As I walked toward the commissary with a box of *Uncaged*, my eyes scanned the crowd. Watching the soldiers, dressed in fatigues, going to and fro made me think of Douglas, no matter how hard I tried to block him out of my mind. Movements from my unborn daughter, however, made me think of Raymond. I entered the building leaving all my cares and thoughts of Douglas behind.

Once inside the threshold of the building, I saw the commissary straight ahead. My eyes darted back and forth, looking for the bookstore. Finally, not being able to locate it, I stopped the first person that crossed my path.

"Excuse me," I said to a short, older, black woman wearing white shorts and a red and white T-shirt, "do you know where the bookstore is?"

"There's only one place that sells books in here, and it's not in a store," she replied, smiling, chewing gum, and pointing at the opposite end of the building. "It's down there, at the food court. You'll see the cart. You won't miss it, if you tried," she said, walking away.

"Thank you," I said as she walked off. Smiling, I walked in the direction of her finger. Sure enough, nestled between a burger and a chicken fast food restaurant, I spotted the cart of books. It was only a few steps away.

About two-dozen businesses filled the gap from the commissary to the other end of the building. A long corridor separated the businesses allowing half to be on each side. The businesses ranged from shoe repair, dry cleaning, a barbershop, a novelty shop, custom made T-shirts and other art works, the bookstore cart and a few other businesses. I saw some shops I wanted to patronize while I was there. Since I didn't have much money, I needed to sell some books if I made any purchases.

Suddenly, my eyes focused on a young, dark-skinned woman sitting on a high stool in front of the cash register. Although she was facing me, she was not looking in my direction. Her head was down as if she was either reading, sleeping, or praying. I couldn't decide which.

By now, the box of books in my arms was getting heavy. Then I became more concerned with finding a resting place for my books than deciding what she was doing. Reaching a long empty table that appeared to be where I would do my book signing, I put my books on it and walked over to the young woman. Her head jerked up as I approached her, as if I had startled her.

"Hi, I'm Deeva Denez, the author of *Uncaged*. I am in the right place for my book signing, aren't I?"

"You're in the right place, all right," she said, getting off the stool revealing the long slit in her ankle length blue jean skirt. "It's so slow around here, I was about to go to sleep, but I started reading, then started praying for customers. I guess, you're the answer to my prayers. Here's where you will have your book signing," she said, standing at the table. "I had a few of your books on the table earlier, but sold out. I hope you brought more with you?" she asked, not noticing the box on the other end.

"Sure, I have a box full," I said, walking to the box. "I'll spread some out, then we will be in business. Is it always so slow?"

"You have to realize everything around here revolves around the first and the fifteenth, the two paydays. Today is the end of the month, and the end of the money, if you know what I mean."

"Yeah, I know exactly what you mean. I get paid every other Thursday and quarterly for my book sales. If anything comes up after I've written my checks on payday, it'll have to wait until the next check," I said, sitting in the tan chair in front of the table with copies of *Uncaged* strategically displayed just how Mike Austin taught me.

"So, you feel me?" she asked with a mystic look on her face. "I have a plan, Deeva, to help sell your books. We both need the business, don't you agree?"

"Of course! What's your plan? By the way what is your name?"

"Angel, but I'm really devilish. You just don't know how bad I want to smoke a cigarette right now."

"Go ahead. I'll be all right. You can tell me your plan when you return."

"Hey, Joel, this is Deeva Denez!" Angel shouted at him as he approached the table while we were talking. "Deeva, tell Joel about your book while I step outside a minute."

"You wrote this book?" Joel asked, picking up a copy flipping it over. "What's it about?"

"It's about my life."

"Why should I read about your life, Deeva? What makes your life so special? Right here it says, 'Vanessa Lewis got married for all the wrong reasons. He's handsome, supportive, seems understanding and is a great lover. But, he's the wrong man. Her Mr. Right, the man she thought wanted her, too, is having an affair with her best friend....' Hell, your life is just as fucked up as everybody else around here! We all can write a book. Hell, I know I can!" Joel exclaimed with his brown almond shaped eyes inflamed. "Shit, I don't need to read this. I might want to fuck somebody up!" he said as he slammed the book on the table with his large, yellow hand. "See ya, Deeva," he said, walking away. His long, black T-shirt danced in the wind.

Angel returned to the table before Joel was out of sight. "Deeva, what on earth did you say to make him leave like that? I heard him from outside. That's why I came back."

"All I said was, '*Uncaged* is about my life.' He read the back then lit a fuse."

"I have a plan, Deeva." Angel said, pulling a chair next to me. "Let's hope it works before we lose another customer." Her back was to the corridor as she faced me. I was all ears, eager to hear her plan.

"What is it?" I exclaimed softly.

"I told several of my associates that you would be here today. They all said they would come by to see you and buy a book. I've read *Uncaged* and thought it was great. I told them bits and pieces, and they agreed. I said all that to say this. Now, here's the plan: I will go to the different booths and tell people you are here. I will tell them *Uncaged* is about love, sex, and money. It tells you how to find the right mate, so that you can be sexually satisfied in order to work at your maximum potential and find your God given talent, so that you can be happy and prosperous. Thus, becoming uncaged from the bondage of poverty, loneliness, and low self-esteem."

"Angel, don't you think you are stretching the truth?"

"You mean, lying?"

"That's exactly what I mean."

"Not at all. Isn't *Uncaged* about your relationships with John, Carl, Zakee, and Bryson?"

"Yes."

"Didn't you love them?" she asked with a conniving grin.

"Yes."

"Didn't you have sex with Carl and Bryson?"

"Yes," I answered shaking my head in agreement, smiling and understanding what she was doing.

"By marrying Carl, didn't you stay broke as hell and frustrated?"

"Yes."

"Don't you think you would have been more prosperous either being by yourself or marrying someone else?"

"Yes."

Deeva Denez

"So Deeva, since you were both frustrated and unhappy in your marriage to Carl, you were in bondage and were not able to live up to your full potential. Am I correct?"

"Yes, Angel, you're correct."

"So Deeva, am I still lying?"

"No, you're not. I guess I never thought of *Uncaged* like you worded it, but you're right. You little devil."

We both laughed. Afterwards, she carried out her plan. Despite Angel's plan, the customers slowly came to my table. Some were interested in buying *Uncaged* but didn't have any money. I understood. At the end of two hours, I sold six books.

Angel asked me if I didn't mind coming back the next day. Since it was "payday," I should be able to sell more books. She was right. On "payday" I sold twelve books. Before my departure, I left ten books for her inventory.

During my drive home, I thought about Angel. I had grown fond of her, the two days we worked together. Once she told me business was very slow. There had been talk of closing her branch of the bookstore. She already had another job lined up because she saw the handwriting on the wall. I prayed for her and others in her position at the base. I also prayed that *Uncaged* could heal some of the broken relationships on the base. While I was there, I heard several accounts of adultery, this person with that person's mate, and other such ungodly accusations. I wondered if that was another reason things were bad at the base. At any rate, prayer can change things. Prayer can heal that which is broken, bind that which is loose, and find that which is lost.

CHAPTER ELEVEN

Prayed up and feeling good from listening to my gospel favorites, I returned home. My car clock had just changed to 7:18 as I turned the ignition off. I knew Raymond would be asleep, and Little Raymond and Francine would be up climbing the walls. Taking a deep breath and slowly exhaling, I exited the car throwing my purse on my shoulders as I locked the door. Relishing the last few moments of peace and tranquility, I slowly walked to the house. When I opened the door, I braced myself for what I knew was sure to come.

To my expectation, they were in the living room arguing. Little Raymond was standing up, hovering over Francine, who was sitting on the sofa braiding her doll's hair. They were so into their dispute, they didn't see me enter the house. However, I'm glad I did before their dispute turned into a scuffle.

"That's all you do is comb your ole nappy headed dolls," yelled Little Raymond, reaching for the doll.

"Don't you touch my doll!" Francine screamed, jerking away from Little Raymond's reach. "Move, or I'm gonna tell Daddy on you! You know he don't like you messin with me."

"I'ma tell him you toe up my wrestling man I bought yesterday!" Little Raymond said snatching the doll.

"I'm gonna tell Daddy you took my doll," Francine said getting up.

Little Raymond pushed her back down and grabbed her. "You're not going no where!"

"That's enough," I shouted from the door. "Raymond, let go of her right now! How do you expect your dad to sleep with all this racket going on?"

"But she broke my man."

"I did not," Francine quickly added, getting her doll back from Raymond.

"I'm gonna break your doll," he said, reaching for the doll's neck.

"Didn't I say that's enough?" I asked glaring at both of them waiting for a reply. Neither one of them said anything. Francine started braiding her doll's hair again and Raymond stormed downstairs. Normally, I would have gone after him to give him an attitude adjustment, but I was too tired to deal with him. All I wanted was peace and quiet, and that's what I had after he slammed the door.

By the time Raymond woke up, I was fully rested. The incident with the kids earlier had no bearing on the remainder of the evening. Little Raymond remained downstairs and Francine went back and forth. I relaxed on the sofa by having a lengthy Bible study. Reading God's Word always gave me solace and peace.

Raymond's alarm had gone off ten minutes before I entered our bedroom. Since the lights were off, I knew he was still in the bed. Sure enough, when I opened the door, his whole body was buried underneath the covers. Feeling mischievous, I took my shoes off, went to my side of the bed and eased next to him, putting my arm around his waist, being careful to keep a small distance between Raymond and our unborn daughter. I felt her move as I lay next to him. I guess, she wanted his attention, too.

"She moved!" I said excitedly. "Don't you want to feel the baby?" I asked moving closer to Raymond's chest.

"No, I want to sleep five more minutes," he said removing my arm from his waist.

"I've been gone all day. Aren't you glad to see me?" I asked feeling saddened from his rejection.

"No, I want more sleep. My clothes are hanging up. You can start ironing them to give you something to do," he sleepily replied.

As I got up, I rubbed my abdomen, comforting our daughter. I prayed she would have my personality and not be insensitive like her dad. Slowly, I put my shoes back on and ironed Raymond's clothes for work. To Raymond, ironing his clothes was my wifely duty, showing affection and trying to make love wasn't. Raymond got up as I finished ironing his clothes.

After unplugging the iron, I went back downstairs and continued my Bible study until he went to work. I read many Scriptures, but two really stuck- - they settled me down and gave me the peace of God that surpasses all understanding. God knew that I was hot under the collar with Raymond. Therefore, He had me to read these two Scriptures first: Galatians 5:13 & 14, *"For you, brethren have been called to liberty; only do not use liberty as an opportunity for the flesh, but through love serve one another. For all the law is fulfilled in one word, even this: 'You shall love your neighbor as yourself.'"*

God's Word let me know that I had to love Raymond regardless of how he acted. God was more interested in my love towards Raymond than He was with the lack of love Raymond gave me. Or in other words, God was more interested in my reaction than in Raymond's actions. I had liberty in Jesus. I was commissioned to love Raymond as myself.

Next, God directed me to two more Scriptures that really hit home. They were Ephesians 4:31&32, *"Let all bitterness, wrath, anger, clamor, and evil speaking be put away from you, with all malice. And be kind to one another, tenderhearted, forgiving one another, even as God in Christ forgave you."* After reading those Scripture, I was at peace again. They were what I needed to get my head back on straight.

About an half hour later, Raymond came down the steps dressed for work. I always loved how he looked in his blue, security guard uniform. It was something about how his small, firm buttocks protruded from his pants, showing off his thirty-two inch waist. His thirty-four inch chest stuck out a little as his light-blue uniform shirt caressed his well-toned body. My husband was fine! I always experienced electrical shocks whenever I looked at his body. I generally stopped whatever I was doing to get a full view - - a view that would be etched in my mind.

I was sitting at the kitchen table, watching him as he entered the kitchen with a glazed expression on his face. Every night, the last thing Raymond did before going to work was to take his blood pressure pill. Not saying anything, he robotically opened the freezer, where he kept his favorite red plastic cup, took it out and opened the refrigerator at the same time. Seeing his choices, he grabbed the large burgundy cooler with lemonade in it.

"Do you want to take something to eat?" I asked, realizing I had not fixed him anything to take.

"No," he answered, filling his cup with lemonade, popping the pill in his mouth facing me.

"I have a book signing next Saturday at Macon Mall from 7-9 p.m.. Would you and the kids like to go with me, then we can go to Dublin since it will be the second Sunday?"

"No," he said after taking a large gulp.

"It's supposed to be the largest mall in Georgia. I'm sure the kids would love to go."

"I said, no," he said looking at the wall clock. "I must go."

He walked over to me, gave me my goodnight peck, and headed for the door. "Don't you get concerned about your pregnant wife driving by herself to book signings out of town?" I asked as he picked up his briefcase by the door to leave.

"No," he said, opening the door. "I'm more concerned about my wife not being home to do her wifely duties," he said giving me a disdained look as he walked out the door.

I felt the baby move as her father closed the door. I'm sure she felt my heartache; she was letting me know she understood and everything was going to be all right. We were a team. I patted her gently. She moved again as if to touch my hand. My unborn daughter and God's Word helped me endure Raymond. Without them, I don't know what I would do.

The next morning, however, Raymond had changed his mind. He decided to go to the book signing and spend the night in Dublin, about an hour's drive away. I was glad he changed his mind.

When Saturday came, I was anxious to go to the book signing. Lisa said she and Alvin would be there, too. Todd, the manager of the Macon, B. Dalton Bookstore, said *Uncaged* was highly recommended by William, the South Dekalb Mall manager, who shipped him some of my books. I needed Todd's encouraging words; being an unknown author has few rewards and even fewer positive reinforcements.

I couldn't believe my eyes when I located the bookstore in the mall. Shelves of *Uncaged* were at the front of the store next to the book signing table that had more books displayed. I smiled then walked to the cashier's counter to tell them I had arrived. Raymond and the kids left to check out the mall.

A tall, white, middle aged man and two younger white females were behind the counter. One female with long, curly blonde hair was handing a customer her change. The other female with short dark-brown hair left the counter as I approached it to wait on a customer in the back.

"Excuse me," I said to the man, "I am Deeva Denez. I am here for the book signing."

"Oh, Miss Denez," he said grinning, "I have everything ready for you. Can I get you anything to eat or drink?"

"Water would be nice," I replied, squirming, desperate to go to the ladies room." "Where is the closest restroom?"

He pointed to his right. "You can use our facilities. It's in the back, to the right. I'll get your water while you use the restroom."

"Thank you," I said following his directions.

The restroom was small and clean. I was really in a tight, being pregnant. I was glad it was so close. When I finished, I went to the front. Todd came very shortly thereafter with a cold bottle of spring water.

"Can I get you anything else?" he asked placing the water on the table. There's a wonderful pastry shop next door. Would you like for me to get you something? They have excellent carrot cake."

"Not now, Todd. Maybe after the book signing," I said, sitting down, placing my things on the floor underneath the table.

"I read your book, Miss Denez. It was quite interesting. *Uncaged* is a perfect title for it. It's been doing well at this store. You should do well tonight if the storm doesn't keep the shoppers away. It was crowded in the mall before the storm came," he said walking to the display.

"Deeva!" I heard someone say to my left. I turned to the voice. It was Lisa and Alvin.

"Lisa!" I exclaimed excitedly. "I'm glad you made it."

"The weather's nasty, and we got lost, but we got here safely."

"I just got here myself, too. Lisa, this is Todd, the manager," I said introducing them. "Todd, this is Lisa, my publisher."

"Nice to meet you," they both said together. Alvin was standing from a distance, checking out the mall. He stood by Lisa after the introduction.

"Todd, this is my husband, Alvin," Lisa announced, sliding her arms into his.

"Nice to meet you, too," Todd said extending his hand for Alvin to shake before walking back into the store.

"My family's here, too," I said to Lisa, "they're in the mall somewhere."

"That's good. I'm going to look around myself while you have your book signing. Alvin and I plan to stay overnight in the hotel across the street," she said smiling at Alvin.

"Listen, Deeva, Alvin and I are going to run. We'll be back before your book signing is over. Good Luck!" she said as they walked off.

Customers started coming as soon as they left. Todd and his two female associates kept coming to me during the two-hour session to see if I needed anything. Raymond and the kids checked on me, too. Fortunately, the evening turned out to be a success despite the terrible weather. I sold twenty-five books, mostly to females who could relate to my story or who wanted to support me because I was a black author.

When I finished, Todd gave me a thoughtful thank-you card. He was the most considerate manger I had ever known. He made me feel truly appreciated. I will always remember him for his congeniality, and his readiness to serve me. I want others to know about him, too.

Lisa and Alvin came back ten minutes before my book signing was over. She and Todd went over the figures while I sat on a bench in front of the bookstore. I joined them after I made another trip to the restroom.

Todd thanked me again for coming. I told him it was my pleasure. As I left, I was tired and ready to go to Dublin. Although my body was in Macon, my mind was already in the bed with Raymond in a hotel in Dublin.

Since Raymond took a shortcut to Dublin, we were there in forty-five minutes instead of an hour. We talked to his mom for thirty minutes before leaving the kids with her and going to a hotel. We decided to stay at Days Inn. Raymond went inside to get our room while I stayed in the car. I felt myself getting excited when he entered the car.

"Our room is in the back on the top," he said as he drove off.

"Will this be a lovemaking night?" I asked, placing my hand on his thigh, smiling.

He stopped the car and looked into my eyes. "Do you want it to be?" he asked seriously.

"Yes, don't you?" I asked trying to retain my smile.

His eyes turned back toward the road as he drove. My heart skipped a beat as I waited for his reply which never came.

CHAPTER TWELVE

We rode in silence for the remaining short distance to our room. I held my breath as Raymond turned the ignition off. I prayed silently that he would not spoil this night.

"Well, we're here. Our room is 212. "I'll get the luggage from the trunk," he said opening his door.

I didn't move; I wanted to see if he was going to open my door. I heard the trunk close, and his feet walked to my side of the car. Reaching for my purse, I anticipated Raymond opening my door.

"Aren't you getting out?" he asked through the door holding our luggage.

"I'm waiting on you to open my door," I said looking into his eyes.

"You want me to do everything!" he exclaimed, opening my door.

"No, not everything," I responded, "I just want you to be the gentleman you used to be when we dated. You did everything right then. I'm still trying to make the adjustment of how you are now since we've been married. Believe me, it's harder on me than it is on you. I'm trying very hard not to mark our baby. Sometimes you act like I'm not pregnant," I said, walking toward the steps as he locked the car door. I heard him behind me as I walked up the steps. I told myself if this was any indication of how the rest of the night would be, I should have brought a good book to read.

Raymond unlocked the door and turned on the light before allowing me to enter. He placed the luggage on the floor next to the queen-sized bed. I rushed to the bathroom, admiring the dark-green, gold and lavender colors. I heard voices from the TV as I flushed.

"What are you looking at?" I asked while I washed my hands in the sink.

"Nothing. I'm just flipping channels," he answered switching the station. "I haven't found anything worth watching yet."

"You can watch me," I said drying my hands with a towel next to the sink.

"Watching you is not the same as watching TV," he replied scooting to the head of the bed, flipping the channel.

"You're right. Watching me is better. At least then you can direct your attention on one object instead of keep going from station to station. You know that TV can't hold your attention like I can," I said sliding next to him on the bed.

"Yes, it can. I just haven't found the right program yet," he said, flipping the channel again.

I reached for the remote, but he grabbed my hand. "Give me the thing!" I shouted. "I didn't come all the way to Dublin to spend the night in a hotel for you to look at TV all night!"

We wrestled for a few minutes before he decided I was right. He flipped the TV off. We showered together then had a very nice love making session, one I had been wanting for a long time.

The next morning we started where we left off before we picked up the kids. The morning session was even better than the night before. I think the hotel brought out the best in my husband. I was glad to have the best for a change. We checked out by 11 a.m.. By then, we were anxious to see the kids. Later we discovered, they were anxious to see us, too. Little Raymond always hated for us to leave him with his grandmother because he wanted to go with us. Francine didn't mind; she liked staying with her grandmother. Carrie spoiled them with treats. She never sent them away empty handed.

During the drive home, I reminded Raymond about my doctor's appointment on Thursday, August 13. Lately, he had stopped going with me, but I wanted him to go this time. I always liked having him there with me if nothing more than to hold my hand. The appointment was at 11:40 a.m., his sleep time. He said he would think about it and let me know before Thursday.

When Thursday came he decided not to go. He had had a hard night at work and wanted to get some sleep. I understood although I was disappointed. I knew how hard it was to work the night shift. I had worked it full-time for seven years. I thought about him as I pulled out the driveway to go to my appointment. Looking at my car clock, I was five minutes early when I pulled into the Kaiser parking lot. There was one space left in the front. I smiled as I pulled right in.

I always liked my prenatal visits because they gave me a chance to hear my baby's heartbeat, something I cherished dearly. Reassuring my daughter that everything was all right, I locked my door and went inside.

Ten minutes after I checked in, my name was called. The medical assistant first weighed me, then took my blood pressure. My weight was 175 pounds, 7 pounds more than last month and an all time high for me. My blood pressure was 96 over 60, its usual values. After giving a urine specimen, I was escorted to an examining room.

At Kaiser, they worked as a team. Since anyone on the team of doctors and midwives would deliver me, I never had the same team member all the time. My favorite, however, was Pam, a midwife. I hoped I had her today.

I undressed from the waist down as instructed and pushed the green light on the wall to signify I was ready to be seen. The door opened shortly thereafter. Since my back was to the door, I turned to see who it was. To my satisfaction, it was Maureen, another midwife. Maureen had examined me twice before. She was good, too. She just wasn't Pam.

Maureen was older, in her early fifties. She smiled a lot and was very friendly; I liked her personality. We hit it off right away.

"Mrs. Miller, I'm Maureen," she said as she entered the room, smiling. "How are you today?"

"I'm doing fine, thank you," I said shifting the paper sheet to make sure I was fully covered.

"Have you been having any problems?" she asked standing next to me.

"No."

"Well, let me take a look at how the baby is doing. Lie down, and I will examine you," she said pulling up my sheet.

Maureen placed her hands on my lower abdomen and probed with her fingers. Slowly, she worked her way up and to the sides.

"Everything seems fine so far. Now, I will listen to the heartbeat," she said walking to the table near the sink. She came back with a tube of ointment in her hand. "This is cold," she said spreading it on my swollen abdomen. "Let's hear his heartbeat."

"Her," I corrected.

"Excuse me. Her heartbeat," she said as she placed the stethoscope in her ears and at the other end on my abdomen. She glided the stethoscope across my abdomen until she heard the heartbeat. She listened intently while looking at her watch. "Do you want to hear the heartbeat?"

"Yes!" I replied excitedly. Maureen removed the stethoscope from her ears and placed it into mine. My baby's rhythmical beat filled my ears. "She has a good, strong heartbeat," I said giving Maureen back the stethoscope.

"Yes, she does. Her heart is beating at 53 beats per minute." Maureen added, smiling.

"I read somewhere that girls hearts beat faster than boys."

"That's correct."

"I have a friend who is having a son, and his heartbeat was 37. So, what you just told me confirms I'm having a girl?" I asked even more excited.

"Don't jump the gun, Mrs. Miller. Although your baby's heartbeat is higher than your friend's, they both fall within the normal ranges. I've been delivering babies for twenty-three years, trust me, anything can happen."

"That's the same thing my mother said her midwife said who delivered me."

"You can't be one hundred percent sure until the baby is born," she said walking to the table, picking up my chart. "Ultrasounds can be wrong as well," she added, writing in the chart. "I repeat. You can't be one hundred percent sure until the baby is born. Now, I'm going to ask you some questions before I do your vaginal exam."

I didn't care what Maureen said. I was having a girl. I answered her questions and completed the exam knowing my daughter would be here soon. During the questioning session, Maureen was concerned about my weight. I vowed to myself that I would do better next month. When my doctor's appointment came around the next month, on September 14, I had lost two pounds. Although I was proud of myself for keeping my vow, I was concerned over the weight loss. I prayed it wasn't' a sign that something was wrong.

For that visit, Pam examined me. She said everything was fine. She informed me that my lab work, including a fasting glucose test would be drawn the next visit. She instructed me not to eat anything after midnight. Since I was in my third trimester, my appointments were bimonthly or every two weeks. My next appointment was September 28.

Between my two September appointments, I completed my second manuscript *The Bearer of the Sign*, which was the sequel of *Uncaged*. It was forty-seven chapters and 278 pages long. I was very proud of myself because I wanted the book finished before my baby came. When she came, I wanted to give her all my attention since I had waited a long time for her arrival. I didn't want anything to rob her of my time.

I was stunned when I saw my weight for the September 28th visit. I weighed 171 pounds, two pounds less than two weeks ago and four pounds less than in August. I'm supposed to gain weight, not lose it, I told myself as I walked to give my urine sample.

Dr. Cordolus assured me not to be alarmed about my weight loss after my examination. She said the baby was doing well as far as she could tell and sometime weight loss does occur in the last trimester. If anything was wrong, the blood tests would detect it. She thought my due date, however, was wrong and wanted me to take another ultrasound next week to confirm to her the fetus was smaller than what she expected. She asked me if I had been fasting before she sent me to the lab to get TORCH titers, a fasting glucose, and a CBC drawn. Since I worked in the lab, I understood the tests she requested.

TORCH titers are for the following tests: toxoplasmosis, rubella, cytomegalovirus, or CMV, and herpes. All of these diseases would be detrimental to the fetus if the mother had an acute or new infection during pregnancy, but would be less threatening if the mother was immune or had been infected before the pregnancy, with the exception of herpes, which would warrant a C-Section instead of a vaginal delivery. The fasting glucose would detect diabetes mellitus or high blood sugar, which sometimes occurs during pregnancy. Lastly, the CBC or complete blood count, measures the amount of red and white blood cells; as well as platelets, clotting components; and a differential or different kinds of white blood cells such as neutrofils, lymphocytes, and monocytes.

After my blood was drawn, I was relieved my visit was over. My main concern now was the repeat ultrasound next week. I prayed my baby was all right. After praying, a peace came over me to verify my baby was fine.

The following day, Maureen called to tell me my fasting glucose was one point too high. I needed to come back to the office for a three-hour glucose tolerance test as soon as possible. I told her, I'd be in Thursday from nine to twelve.

On Monday, Maureen called me again when I returned home from my ultrasound to tell me the glucose tolerance test came back normal.

I told her the ultrasound moved my due date back one day. My baby was now due November 30, instead of the 29th. We were both relieved as we hung up the phone.

Lisa called as soon as I put the phone on the receiver. She wanted to meet me at the Chick-fil-A on Highway 85, Wednesday, at 10:30 a.m. to discuss our contract. I told her Wednesday was fine.

I arrived at Chick-fil-A by 10:25 a.m.. I looked for Lisa's silver Mercedes to see if she was there. Not spotting it, I shook my head, gathered my things and went inside.

Two empty wooden benches were nestled against the wall in the waiting area as I entered the restaurant. I looked in the dining area to make sure Lisa wasn't there before I took a seat on a bench in the waiting area.

Forty minutes passed before I went to the dining area to order something to eat. I told myself, if Lisa hadn't shown up before I finished my meal, I was going home.

I chose a big round table in the back. In case she did make it, we would have plenty of room to conduct business. I ordered my food as soon as the waitress came to the table. While eating my food, I heard Lisa and Alvin talking as they entered the dining area.

"Deeva!" Lisa shouted across the room, trotting to me with her arms full and her swollen belly swaying with each step. "I'm sorry I'm late, but I just became a new grandmother! Alvin's oldest son had a boy last night," she said placing her things on the table. "We were up all night! I'll sit on this end," she said sliding into the booth.

"Hey, Deeva," Alvin greeted with his deep baritone voice. "I see you started without us," he said sitting next to me.

I scooted to the middle, so they could occupy both ends. "I didn't know if or when you were coming, so I ordered my food," I said not trying to conceal my agitation.

"Oh, that looks good, Deeva!" Lisa exclaimed, ignoring my remark. "I'm starved! Are you ready to order, Alvin?"

"Yes, I am," he answered reaching for a menu on the table.

"I already know what I want," Lisa announced, "I don't need to look at a menu. "Waitress!" Lisa shouted. "We're ready to order."

The same waitress that served my food came to our table after she gave the couple two tables down their food.

"I'm not deaf, honey," the elderly waitress said, holding her pad, ready to take their order. "It's just two of us working, and I'm not Lois Lane. What will you have?" she asked Lisa.

"Hot tea with cream on the side, grits, two eggs fried hard and a chicken biscuit."

"And what will you have?" she asked turning to Alvin.

"I would like the same, except I want a large orange juice instead of tea."

"Can I get you more coffee?" she asked me, noticing my cup was half full.

"No, thank you. I don't need anymore," I said eating the last of my food.

"Let me get that out of your way, honey," she said reaching for my dirty dish.

I quickly placed my dirty fork on the plate as her hand grabbed the other end. "Your order should be ready in fifteen minutes. Our regular cook is out, and the one we have today is not Clark Kent," she said, walking off.

"Well, Deeva, let me give you the new contract," Lisa said, opening her briefcase on the table. "You can go over it while I eat." She handed me the contract, then closed her briefcase.

"Excuse me ladies while I go to the men's room," Alvin said as he slid from the booth.

I looked at the contract and couldn't believe what I read. According to the old contract, Lisa was responsible for the cost of re-publishing *Uncaged*. In the new contract, I was responsible, something I thought I wouldn't have to do again.

"Lisa, in this contract, you say that the author is responsible for re-publishing."

"That's right. You have 219 books left. If we had sold out or made more money before the contract expired last month, then I would have reprinted. But as it stands, we still have books. Therefore, it's up to you to reprint."

"Well, Lisa, if I have to pay again to reprint my book, then I will find another publisher, I said getting up as Alvin and the waitress returned to the table.

Lisa's mouth flew open.

"What happened?" Alvin asked as I walked out the dining area.

CHAPTER THIRTEEN

I felt good leaving Chick-fil-A. Although I had no idea who would re-publish *Uncaged*, I knew God would send the right person to do it. Whoever He sent, I would let them publish *The Bearer of the Sign*, also. The incident with Lisa let me know it was time for me to divert my attention away from *Uncaged* and concentrate on my daughter to come. I patted my abdomen to communicate to her my intentions.

I thought about my schedule for the rest of October and November. I wondered how I was going to concentrate on my baby before she was born. Tomorrow I was scheduled to be in Macon at the Conference Center for the Librarian Convention. In addition to having two more book signings, one in Macon on Halloween and the other one in Columbus on November 7, Carlos' 12th birthday. Thinking of Carlos' birthday made me think of Little Carl, who would be 17 on December 14.

When Madame Lee told me 18 years ago that I was going to have four children, two boys and two girls, I never dreamed my children would be so far apart in age. Neither did I think I would be so old, 42, having a child. Only God knew how old I'd be when the second daughter came. No, my thought, at that time, on that day, was that I was going to have four stair-steps for children. And at age 24, I was not ready for that much responsibility. Now, at age 42, 18 years later, I relished the thought of having my daughter.

By the time I got home, the meeting with Lisa and finding a new publisher seemed so insignificant compared to the baby developing inside of me. Instead, I thought about God's plan of salvation for mankind; how it paralleled with the birth of my daughter.

My daughter was first an image that I saw in '95. In seven and a half weeks, she will be a real person. God first made man in His and Jesus' image. I knew in Genesis 1:26-27, The Bible said, "Then God said, *'Let Us make man in Our image, according to Our likeness.'...So God created man in His own image; in the image of God He created him; male and female He created them.''* Then I thought about Genesis 2:7, *"And the Lord God formed man of the dust of the ground, and breathed into his nostrils the breath of life; and man became a living being."*

These Scriptures clearly reveal that we are made in the physical image or likeness of God, our Creator. But His plan of salvation transcends the physical realm. He also wants us to bare His spiritual image of righteousness. Since I couldn't remember the Scriptures pertaining to God's spiritual image, I grabbed my Bible from the table when I went inside.

As I picked up my Bible, God led me to John 3:3-8, *"Jesus answered and said to him (Nicodemus), 'Most assuredly, I say to you, unless one is born again, he cannot see the kingdom of God.' Nicodemus said to Him, "How can a man be born when he is old? Can he enter a second time into his mother's womb and be born?' Jesus answered, 'Most assuredly I say to you, unless one is born of water and the Spirit, he cannot enter the kingdom of God. That which is born of the flesh is flesh, and that which is born of the Spirit is spirit. Do not marvel that I said to you, 'You must be born again.' The wind blows where it wishes, and you hear the sound of it but cannot tell where it comes from and where it goes. So is everyone who is born of the Spirit."*

Clearly, it is God's plan for us to be born again of the Spirit. Only through the life, death, and resurrection of Jesus Christ is this made possible. His shed blood on the cross gave us atonement for our sins. With His sinless body, He bore our sins. God's plan for us is that although we are sinners, we take on the righteousness, faith, Holy Spirit and resurrection of Jesus and by doing so we become a new spiritual creation. Through Jesus' resurrection this new spiritual creation is made possible.

God then led me to I Corinthians 15:21-53, *"For since by man came death, by man also came the resurrection of the dead. For as in Adam all die, even so in Christ all shall be made alive....But someone will say, 'How are the dead raised up? And with what body do they come?...So also is the resurrection of the dead. The body is sown in corruption; it is raised in incorruption. It is sown in dishonor; it is raised in glory. It is sown in weakness; it is raised in power. It is sown a natural body, it is raised a spiritual body. There is a natural body, and there is a spiritual body. And so it is written, 'The first Adam became a living being.' The last Adam became a life-giving spirit. However, the spiritual is not first, but the natural, and afterward the spiritual. The first man was of the earth, made of dust; the second Man is the Lord from heaven. As was the man of dust; so also are those who are made of dust; and as is the heavenly Man, so also are those who are heavenly. And as we have borne the image of the man of dust, we shall also bear the image of the heavenly Man. Now this I say brethren, that flesh and blood cannot inherit the kingdom of God; nor does corruption inherit incorruption. Behold, I tell you a mystery; we shall not all sleep, but we shall all be changed- - in a moment, in the twinkling of an eye, at the last trumpet. For the trumpet will sound, and the dead will be raised incorruptible, and we shall be changed. For this corruption must put on incorruption, and this mortal must put on immortality."* As I finished reading, I thought truly God has great things in store for us if only we can believe it to receive it.

Raymond came down the stairs as I closed my Bible. My mind was still on the Bible study. God's Word always boggles my mind, especially His plan of salvation for mankind. His Word reassured me of how merciful, loving, kind and great He is.

"When did you get home? I didn't hear you come inside," Raymond said, walking towards me at the table.

"I haven't been here too long. I came straight to the kitchen to have a Bible study," I said standing up to get something to drink. Raymond gently grabbed my waist and pecked my lips. "Does this mean you missed me?" I asked enjoying his touch.

"No. But I am hungry. What's for dinner?" he asked releasing me and opening the refrigerator.

"The baby moved!" I shouted. "Here, feel her move!" I exclaimed, placing his hand on my abdomen. His hand rested there for a moment. "Can you feel your daughter moving inside your wife?" I asked smiling, waiting for his reply.

"No. What's for dinner," he asked again removing his hand from my abdomen and reaching for the lemonade.

"I wished you were as interested in our daughter as you are with getting something to eat."

I don't need a lecture," he said pulling leftovers out of the refrigerator.

"Raymond, our daughter will be here next month. You haven't done anything to get ready for her."

"I'm the father, I don't have to do anything before she comes. My responsibilities begin after she's born."

I reached in the cabinet for a glass to get some water. Raymond walked past me to get a plate for his leftovers to heat in the microwave oven. His words cut through me like a knife and left me totally speechless. However, he was right again. As a man, his role as a father begins after birth. Only mothers have the role of nurturing and caring for the unborn fetus. Suddenly, I felt truly blessed to be able to carry a child in my womb, feel it move, provide nourishment and love while it's developing to face this world. I patted her again to let her know her mother was there for her, today and forever.

Raymond reached for a mat on top of the refrigerator. Quickly, he placed his hot food on the mat and sat down. I glanced at his plate. The aroma suddenly made me hungry.

"Is there any more spaghetti left?" I asked wanting very badly to get some.

"No," he answered sprinkling Parmesan cheese all over the spaghetti.

My mouth watered as the white specks melted into the red sauce. "Let me have some of yours," I replied not taking my eyes off his food.

"No. Get you something else. There is some chicken and rice in the refrigerator," he answered, swirling his fork in the pasta, meat mixture.

"I don't want chicken and rice. Just let me taste a little of your spaghetti. All I want is a little taste."

"No. If I let you taste it, then you'll want more."

"Raymond, I'm pregnant with your child! Whatever happened to pampering the mother-to-be?"

"I don't know. You tell me, Mrs. Miller," he said smiling as he continued to eat.

"Well, Mr. Miller, tell me one thing. Do you love me?"

He stopped his fork in mid-twirl, looked up at me and said, "Yes, I love you, but I love this spaghetti more," he replied eating a big mouthful.

"Raymond Miller how could you say such a thing!" I screeched, wanting to leap across the table and smack him good.

"Easy. I opened my mouth and let the words come out."

I watched him as he ate the last of his food. I was too pissed off to continue the conversation. Feeling my baby move inside me gave me instant solace. I patted my abdomen again wishing that she would come soon.

The conversation with Raymond made me want to lie down. He had completely killed my appetite. As I left the kitchen, I wished Raymond would turn back into the kind, charming, loving man I dated instead of this cold, heartless, monster I was married to. At times like these, I tried not to think about Douglas and how caring, considerate and affectionate he was to me. I fought back the thoughts about being in his arms, drinking cups of coffee at the table, and eating jerk chicken at his favorite Jamaican restaurant.

However, my mind repeated the conversation we had concerning the daughter he said I would have for him. One evening while drinking a cup of coffee, Douglas said he dreamed I handed him our daughter, Righteous. He said she was dark like him, but she had my eyes. Our daughter seemed real to both of us. I wondered in my mind as I lay down on the bed, if she would ever be born? Would she be my second daughter? If so, then Douglas and I would somehow get back together. But when and how? I closed my eyes and smiled at the thought of getting back with Douglas. I prayed that God would give me the answers as I dozed off to sleep.

To my disappointment, none of my questions were answered as I slept. I was just as confused when I woke up, as I was when I went to sleep. The only difference was, I was rested and at peace. My eyes gazed at the picture of Raymond on our first date. He was smiling broadly holding a bouquet of white, lavender, and pink carnations, the only flowers he had ever given me.

After several minutes of staring at Raymond, my eyes shifted to the plastic white, yellow and purple bouquet of flowers Douglas had given me. I had placed them on what is now Raymond's dresser. They were one of two bouquets he had given me. The other one was in the living room. Douglas was good about giving me flowers and cards. He rarely came over empty handed.

Sometimes I wondered what my life would be like if I had married Douglas instead of Raymond. I imagined a life of comfort living in a big house he said he wanted for us. Also, I thought about how he loved to travel. Lately, I thought about how he would shower me with love and smother me with kisses everyday. Douglas was very affectionate. I missed that most of all. I missed Douglas, I thought as I climbed out of bed.

The baby moved, jerking me back into reality of my marriage with Raymond. I must let all thoughts of Douglas go. I was married to Raymond. I was his wife. I was carrying his daughter. He was my husband. He was my reality.

I was sitting on the side of the bed, wrapped up in thought, when the phone rang. I answered it on the second ring.

"Hello," I said, slowly.

"Hi, what are you doing?" Douglas asked on the other end.

"I'm just waking up from a nap. Why are you calling me?"

"I think about you all the time. I just wanted to hear your voice. Is that wrong? We can be friends, can't we?" He asked apologetically.

"You know that I'm married now. It's not right for us to talk anymore. Being friends have nothing to do with it," I said trying to sound convincing. My heart was saying something totally different. But I knew what came out of my mouth was right.

"I've been waiting to hear from you. You do still have my number?"

"No, I got rid of it after I got married."

"But you have caller I.D. You could have gotten it from there. This is my second time calling you since you've been married."

"I deleted your number, so I wouldn't be tempted to call you."

"Oh," he said with hurt in his voice. "I guess I was wrong about you. I thought you cared for me like I cared for you."

My heart sank to my feet. I tried very hard to compose myself. I couldn't let Douglas know how I really felt. I couldn't tell him, I still loved him and wished I were his wife. I couldn't tell him I missed him and thought about him sometimes although I used everything in my power to block him out of my mind. No, I couldn't tell him any of that. So I told him, "Douglas, I'm married now. What we had is over. It doesn't matter how I feel, or how I felt."

"It matters to me. Do you still have feelings for me?"

"Douglas, I'm Mrs. Raymond Miller. That's all that matters, now."

"Okay, Vanessa. I'll try not to call you again," he said with disappointment in his voice. "I won't bother you no more."

"Bye, Douglas," I said as he hung up the phone.

I stared at the phone for several minutes until Raymond walked into our bedroom. He went straight to the bathroom, not noticing me at all. Why couldn't he be Douglas? I asked myself.

CHAPTER FOURTEEN

The conversation with Douglas stirred me up the remainder of the evening. I kept thinking about him no matter how hard I tried not to. It was something about his cracking voice that I kept repeating in my mind. He still loved me; there was no doubt in my mind. But the question I kept asking myself was did I still love him? Could I think about him sometimes the way I did and still love him, or was he a good memory I didn't want to get rid of? Since I couldn't answer either question, honestly, I had to let the matter rest. I had to live my life as Raymond's wife no matter how I felt about Douglas.

My baby moved as I finished my last thought. She also confirmed my decision. She was Raymond's daughter, our beloved new arrival to come. She moved again to snap me all the way back to reality. I was grateful she did and patted my abdomen to convey my thanks.

The next several weeks hurried by with book signings and doctor appointments. On my November 11th, appointment, Pam, my favorite mid-wife told me the baby was breeched. She gave me instructions of exercises to do to possibly turn the baby around in the two and a half weeks left before my due date. She warned me that if the baby had not turned by delivery, a C-Section was inevitable.

The thought of a C-Section unnerved me along with my baby being breeched. I instantly prayed to God that He would straighten this situation out. Only He could change it.

When I told Raymond about the baby being breeched, it didn't seem to matter to him. I guess not since he wasn't the one carrying the baby, and he wouldn't be the one getting the C-Section either. Men! Once they plant the seed, their work was done. It was us poor women who had to carry the load to term.

My baby was not going to be breeched, I told myself. She would turn around and be delivered vaginally like her two brothers. "God, I'm counting on You for this. Don't let me down," I said aloud.

For my next appointment, on November 19, Dr. Benjamin told me the baby had turned around and was no longer breeched. I shouted with joy and praised God for His miracle and Divine intervention. I knew He wouldn't let me down, and He didn't.

Needless to say, I left the doctor's office feeling above the clouds. I was so happy, I treated myself to lunch at Checkers across the street. As I ate my food, I couldn't wait to get home to tell Raymond.

To my disappointment, Raymond's car was gone when I pulled into the driveway. My good news had to wait. I hoped he'd be home soon, but something told me it would be a while before he returned. To ease my hurt, my mind started to think about what to cook for dinner instead. Fried chicken, cabbage, macaroni and cheese, and cornbread sounded good. I would start cooking as soon as I got inside because the kids would be home soon.

The baby moved constantly while I cooked. I felt good knowing she was okay. Joy filled my heart knowing I had everything ready for her. Last week, I went shopping for the remainder of her things. Everything was ready except her crib and changing table, which Raymond had promised he'd buy. I told myself not to worry. He could get them while I was in the hospital if necessary. Besides, I had enough going on without having to be responsible for his end, too.

Just as I finished frying the last piece of chicken, Raymond opened the door. To my surprise, he had the crib in his hands. He carried the box downstairs to the storage room, then went back out the front door. Staggering through the door with a second box, he went downstairs again. I peeked at the cornbread, which was a golden brown and the macaroni and cheese that was bubbling along the edges. Turning the oven off, I trailed behind Raymond.

"So, you finally broke down and got the crib and changing table," I commented as I entered the storage room.

He was making room for the second box when I entered the room. I looked at the crib box. It was white like I wanted. However, the changing table was brown.

"Yes, the baby is due in a week and a half. I've put it off long enough."

"Did you know the crib is white and the changing table is brown?" I asked stepping closer to the crib.

"No. I thought I was getting the same color - - white."

"Well, that's okay. It doesn't matter to me if it is mix-matched. I'm glad to have them here in the house. How soon will you put them up? I need time to organize the baby's things."

"Probably, sometime next week when I'm off," he said leaving the storage room.

"Can you do it sooner? I hate to wait until the last minute. The baby might come early."

"I will have the bed up before the baby comes home. I have plenty of time to put the crib and changing table up. I don't need you nagging me, woman," he said grabbing me, spanking my butt hard with his hand.

"Ouch! That hurts! I'm not nagging you either. I just wanted enough time to get everything ready for our daughter," I said rubbing my butt.

"The only thing you need to get ready is my plate. Let me wash my hands, so I can eat," he said walking up the steps to the bathroom.

"Raymond, thanks for getting those things today. You don't know how good it makes me feel to know they are here in the house," I shouted to his back.

"Woman, go fix my plate! I'm ready to eat."

I thought about my good news as he turned going up the steps. It can wait until we eat, I told myself. Let me go and fix plates.

During dinner, I told Raymond my good news. His expression never changed. I guess it didn't matter to him one way or the other. He was more interested in getting some sleep before he went to work that night. The circles under his eyes told me he was tired. My heart went out to him. I was glad he only had three more nights to work this week.

When Raymond went to work Saturday night, I felt fine. But two hours later, at midnight, I felt a contraction. At first, I thought I was imagining the dull, aching pain that came then went away. Another pain came ten minutes later, just like the first. As the second contraction ended, I knew I was in labor. Luckily, my suitcase was already packed. All I needed was for Raymond to come home to take me to the hospital. Before calling Raymond, I called the emergency number for Kaiser. I told the nurse on the other end that I was in labor because I had a blood show. She instructed me to come to the hospital when I told her my last child came within four hours.

I called Raymond as soon as I hung up the phone with the nurse. He said he would be home right away. Raymond was home within the hour. By then, the contractions were seven minutes apart. Fortunately, Carlos was at the house. We left without waking him, or Raymond Jr., or Francine up. We figured Raymond would be back home before they woke up.

On the way to the hospital, the contractions were intensified. I squeezed Raymond's hand as he clasped unto mine. At that moment, I felt connected to my husband of eleven months. Despite our differences and rocky union, I hoped tonight would change all of that and get our marriage on track. I hoped our daughter's birth would signify a new beginning for all of us. As another contraction came, I squeezed Raymond's hand harder.

"We'll be there soon," he consoled me, looking into my eyes instead of on the road. "How far apart are the contractions?" he asked looking back at the road.

My mind was more on his driving than on my pains. The dark, lonely streets had a soothing effect that couldn't be explained. "About five minutes," I answered glancing at the car clock. "They're getting closer and stronger. She'll probably be here by three or four. I'm not anticipating a long labor because I had Little Carl in twenty hours and Carlos in four. Each labor gets shorter, thank God!" I shouted as another pain came.

"Try to relax. It will make the contractions easier."

"Thanks to Eve, relaxing won't help the contractions; they were meant to hurt like hell, and they do."

"Good ole Eve. She messed things up for man, too. All was well until she ate the forbidden fruit. Man would have been better off being alone."

"Maybe, Adam would have been better off, but it's too late for you, Raymond Miller, to say that, especially when I'm in labor with your child," I moaned as another contraction came. I placed my hand on my abdomen, hoping that would give me some relief.

"God was right for punishing Eve; she got just what she deserved. If it wasn't for Eve, we could all be living in paradise," Raymond said smiling. "You're just reaping what she sowed."

I stopped talking after Raymond's last comment. He loved the story of Adam and Eve. I knew no matter what I said, Adam would always come out on top and Eve on the bottom. I was not in the mood to defend Eve or debate about Adam. All I wanted were the pains to stop, and my baby to come. With each contraction, I knew I was getting closer to the final outcome - - the birth of my daughter.

Ten minutes later, Raymond pulled into Piedmont Hospital's parking lot. I couldn't help but think I was having my third child at a third hospital. Carl Jr. was born at Grady Hospital, seventeen years ago; Carlos was born at Doctor's Hospital, twelve years ago; now my daughter will be born at Piedmont Hospital.

Doctor's Hospital had a special dinner for the parents the next night after the new arrival came. It was a cozy setting complete with candlelights and champagne. I remembered sitting across from Carl, eating a chicken breast, salad, beans, and a roll. For some reason, it seemed like yesterday although it was over twelve years ago.

I smiled until another contraction snapped me back into reality, into today, into this moment with Raymond. I looked at him just to make sure of his presence. He smiled at me and reached for my hand, a hand that belonged to him.

Getting directions from the parking attendant, we went to the emergency room. Raymond carried my suitcase and held my hand as we walked side-by-side to the hospital. A warm feeling enveloped me as he walked next to me. He displayed a softness that I had never seen. Had I been wrong about Raymond, I thought? Is he really soft and gentle, or is he cold and hard? For the majority of our eleven months of marriage, he's been a cold-hearted, male chauvinist monster. I loved the soft Raymond. It truly was a refreshing change.

Upon arriving into the Emergency Room, a nurse quickly escorted me to the wheelchairs, nearby. A contraction came as I sat down. The expression on my face signified I was in a great deal of pain, and I was. Raymond gave the clerk information about my insurance and me. When he finished, I was wheeled to the labor and delivery area.

Minutes after entering my room, Sarah, my midwife, came inside. I was disappointed she wasn't Pam, but I hoped my facial expression didn't reveal my true feelings. Sarah asked me how I felt, and how far apart were the contractions? My reply was, "Okay and about five minutes." She washed her hands in the sink nearby, then put on gloves to examine me. To my disappointment again, I had only dilated three centimeters. I comforted myself by thinking at least I was really in labor. My baby would be here soon.

How wrong I was. Hours passed, and I had still not delivered. By three p.m., twelve hours later, I had grown tired and weary. This was my first natural delivery. Raymond and I wanted it that way. The pain, however, was getting more than I could bear. With each contraction, I felt a heavy weight pressing down on every organ in my body causing an excruciating pain like I had never experienced in my life.

Sarah came to check on me as the last pain subsided. She asked me if I wanted to take anything for the pain since my screaming was getting louder for the past two hours. I told her to examine me first before I answered. Raymond looked at me and gave his approval if I wanted it. He told me I didn't have to suffer any longer.

"Vanessa, you're nine centimeters. You're not there yet. Do you want me to get you something for the pain?" she asked removing her gloves and discarding them in the trashcan.

I glanced at Raymond, and he nodded approvingly. "Yes, please give me something, anything! I can't take these pains anymore. Oooohhhhhhh!" I screamed as another contraction came. "Honey, take me to the bathroom! I have to go badly."

Raymond got out of his lounge chair to help me out of bed while Sarah went to get something for pain. "Baby, it's going to be all right. The baby will be here shortly," Raymond said as we walked to the bathroom.

"Oooowwwlllllll, Ooooohhhhhhh!" I screamed to the top of my lungs. "Honey, I tried to make it all the way, but I can't take these pains anymore." I felt like everything on the inside of me was trying to come out.

Although my bladder felt full, only a trickle came out. "Ooooooouuuuuucccccclllllll!" I screamed as I finished. "Raymond, help me back to the bed."

He grabbed me by my waist and walked with me to the bed. A white female with an IV pole and an IV fluid were waiting for me. Sarah was also present. They helped me onto my bed, then put the IV into my left wrist with a butterfly needle.

"Vanessa, I want to examine you again," stated Sarah, pulling up her stool at the foot of my bed.

The time was now, 3:20 p.m.. A contraction was coming, and I wanted to push. "Sarah, I want to push! Can I push now!"

"Vanessa, I can see the baby, but don't push!" she yelled as she stood up running.

"I can't help it! I want to push now!"

"Vanessa! Don't push!" Instructed Raymond, holding my right hand.

A team of people came into the room. Sarah took her place at the foot of the bed. Someone on the team converted my bed from a regular bed to a delivery bed. A young, black female came to my right side and instructed me how to breathe.

"Mrs. Miller, blow out, blow," she said, showing me how to blow.

"I don't want to blow; I want to push!"

"Push! Vanessa push!" Sarah demanded. "You need to push the baby out!"

"I am pushing!" I shouted.

"Push harder!" Sarah demanded. "You have to push this baby out!"

Unfortunately, the anesthesia had already taken effect. It prevented me from pushing with all my might. I said a silent prayer for God to give me the strength I needed to push my baby out.

"Push! Vanessa, push!" Sarah screamed with urgency.

I knew I had to push my baby out this time or else she might not make it.

"Push, baby," Raymond said impatiently. "You have to push her out."

"Okay," I said as I pushed with all my might, and the strength of God.

"Good," Sarah said as the baby popped into her hands. "You have a fine baby girl."

Seconds later when Sarah brought the baby to me. I looked at her, and my daughter looked at me. Her eyes were wide opened. I've seen that look before, I told myself as Sarah rushed her away. The image! I exclaimed to myself silently. Those were the same eyes that looked at me through the windshield three and a half years ago.

CHAPTER FIFTEEN

Something was wrong with my little girl, I thought as the team worked on her on a table nearby. Everyone surrounded her except Sarah, who was pressing on my abdomen to expel my afterbirth. The pain I felt for my daughter, not knowing what was wrong, was greater than the procedure Sarah was performing between my legs. Suddenly, they left with my baby as if her life was in danger. Not being able to take the suspense any longer, I shouted to Sarah, "What's wrong with my baby? Why are they taking her away like something is wrong?"

"She had a bowel movement while she was inside of you. Unfortunately, she swallowed some of it while you were pushing her out. That's why I was insistent that you didn't delay any longer, so that she would not get an infection and have trouble breathing," Sarah replied.

"Is she okay?"

"She should be fine, Vanessa. She was suctioned immediately. That's what you saw them doing. They're running tests on her now to be sure."

"When will I be able to see her? I only saw her for a second. Honey, can't you go and be with her? I don't want her to be alone," I said turning to Raymond.

"I am staying with you," Raymond answered, holding my right hand. She's in good hands. Besides, there is nothing I can do for her."

"Relax, Vanessa, because I have to stitch you up. I gave you an episiotomy to facilitate the delivery."

"How many stitches are you going to give me?"

"I don't count them. As many as you need," Sarah replied pulling the needle through my flesh.

"Sarah, you never did answer me. When will I be able to see my baby?" I asked squirming from the pain of the needle.

"Be still, Vanessa, or I may sow the wrong thing."

"Baby, cooperate," Raymond interjected, "You don't want to interfere with what she is doing.

"By the way, Mr. & Mrs. Miller, what is the baby's name?" Sarah asked when she finished.

"Mya Kaliah Marie Miller," we both said in unison.

"That's a pretty name," Sarah responded. "How did you come up with that name?"

"We both liked Mya," I said. "And her name ends with an "a" like mine. We like the way Kaliah sound with Mya. And since Mya has two other sisters whose middle names are Marie, we wanted her name to be Marie, too."

"That's interesting," Sarah replied standing up covered in my blood. "Well, I'm finally finished down here. Let me get you some pads and undergarments, then you can leave this room and go to your other room where you have a nice meal probably waiting. I'm sure you're starved."

A nurse came into the room as Sarah finished speaking.

"Mrs. Miller, I need to take your vital signs before you leave," she said taking my blood pressure.

"Sarah, when will I be able to see my baby?" I asked desperately.

"As soon as they complete the tests. Probably, by the time you finish your dinner, they will bring her to your room. If you're okay and she's okay, she can stay in your room for the night. That's up to you, if you are up to it."

"Good. Take me to my room," I said as the nurse left. "I want to be with my daughter."

Raymond gathered our things, then stood beside me as I was wheeled to my room. Sarah and her assistant cleaned up as we left. All I could think of was being with my daughter, Mya. She was finally here. I prayed that she would be fine. I had been through this before with Little Carl. He suffered with pneumonia but pulled through beautifully. I prayed the same would happen to Mya.

About five minutes later, I was inside of my nice, private room. The blinds were opened allowing the afternoon sun to flood in. The brilliance of the sun enlightened my spirits. A smile spread across my face that I couldn't take off. It was a nice change from the drab birthing room. I was glad my labor was over, I told myself as I was helped onto my bed.

Raymond placed my suitcase inside the small closet at the window. After glancing momentarily out the window at another wing of the hospital, Raymond sat in the oversized rocking chair in the opposite corner. He slowly rocked back and forth watching the nurse take my blood pressure and check my pad for bleeding. Someone else came into the room to give me a pill that caused my uterus to contract. Next, my dinner came complete with a menu for breakfast.

I offered Raymond some of my food since he had not eaten either. He said he would eat when he picked something up on his way home because he needed to feed the kids. He said he would be leaving as soon as he saw his daughter and was sure I was all right.

I assured him I was fine, but I wanted to see Mya, too. The door opened as I finished my last word. It was a thin, white, older woman pushing an infant inside a small bed. It was Mya! She had finally arrived. I pushed my tray aside to get a good look at my daughter. She was beautiful lying in her bed, sleeping peacefully. Both Raymond and I stared at her as she slept.

"Here's your daughter, Mrs. Miller," the person pushing the bed said. "She's been checked out by the pediatrician, and she's fit as a fiddle. She has a nice set of lungs on her, too. She kept the nursery so lit up everyone was glad she could leave. She fell asleep on the way, but she's really ready to eat. Are you breastfeeding?" she asked reading my armband.

"Yes, I am. I hope I have something to give her," I said feeling my breast.

"Oh, don't worry. Your supply will meet her needs. God planned it that way," she said lifting Mya from her bed and laying her near my breast.

Holding my baby gave me so much joy. I enjoyed watching her sleep at my breast. Dark brown, curly hair covered her tiny head. It looked as if it was going to be "good." She was yellow like me, but looked a bit like Raymond. She definitely had his wide nose, mine was straight and pointed. "She's beautiful." I said aloud, removing her blanket to count her fingers and toes.

"She sure is," echoed Raymond. "And she looks just like you."

"You think so? To me, she looks like you. Look at her nose. That's definitely a Miller's nose. You can't deny this one."

Raymond smiled proudly as a peacock. There was only one Miller nose and he, Francine, and Mya had it. Raymond Jr. had his mother's nose.

"Let me hold her," Raymond said, taking her from me. I want to get a good look at her, too."

"I'll leave you alone now with your daughter," the person who brought her in said. "I'll leave you some formula in case you think you might need it," she said placing it on the counter near the sink.

"Thank you," I said as she closed the door. "Baby, what do you think of our daughter? Isn't she beautiful?"

"Yes, sweetie, she is. It feels good holding a little one again," he said putting her to his chest. "She's so small, I wonder how much she weighs?"

"That information is on her card inside her bed. I can see it from here." Raymond walked over to the bed to retrieve the card. He gently caressed Mya as he picked it up. By now she had awakened and was a little fussy. "What does it say?" I asked as he read silently.

"She weighs six pounds and fifteen ounces. She measured twenty inches long. The time of her birth was 3:33 p.m., November 22. I think you better feed her now. She is sucking on me," he said walking towards me.

"I see God answered my prayer about her weight."

"What do you mean? He said handing Mya to me.

"I prayed that she would weigh between six and seven pounds. I didn't want to work too hard during labor," I said putting my nipple into her mouth. "She's really hungry. Can you see how she's sucking?"

"I better get back to the kids. Do you need me to do anything for you before I leave?" Raymond asked smiling at Mya enjoying her first meal.

"Could you push my eating table closer, so I can get something to drink. You know us nursing mothers must drink plenty of fluids."

"Certainly," he said sliding it over, so I could reach my cup.

"When will you be back?"

"Probably tomorrow. I am too tired to come back today. I will call you later after I get settled in," he said bending over to give me a peck. "Goodbye, love."

"Goodbye, babe. I'm tired, too. As soon as Mya falls asleep, I'm going to sleep. It's been a long day for all of us," I said as he kissed Mya on her forehead, then walked away.

Mya nursed for a few minutes longer before dozing back off to sleep. I burped, changed, and cuddled her before making her a spot next to me. I loved having her close to me. We were inseparable. I had waited too long for her to get here. Nothing and no one was going to keep us apart.

Throughout the evening and night, someone came in to check on either Mya or me. Although I was tired, it was hard to get some sleep. It seemed as though every time I went to sleep, someone else came.

That morning, a person from the nursery staff came to get Mya to take pictures and to perform more tests. They assured me they would bring her right back as soon as they were done. I cleaned her up, brushed her hair and put her on a white sleeper, the smallest one I had.

While she was gone, I ate breakfast and cleaned myself up. A nurse came to check my bleeding, temperature, and blood pressure. Everything was fine. She said since I was doing well, I could leave today.

As soon as the nurse left, I called Raymond to tell him the news. He said he was up. He would come to get us after he fed the kids and got them ready to go. He was so tired from yesterday that he overslept and did not wake the kids up in time to go to school. But they were up now, so they would be there shortly. As I hung up the phone with Raymond, they brought Mya back. She was crying.

"She's ready to eat," the short, petite, black staff member said, as she handed Mya to me.

I exposed my nipple for Mya to nurse. She sucked as though she was starving. "How were her tests?" I asked while admiring my daughter.

"She's one healthy little girl," she replied smiling at Mya.

"Good."

"Since she is doing well, she can be discharged today. A nurse will come to your home tomorrow to evaluate her, to make sure she is still doing well after forty-eight hours. You need to schedule a doctor's appointment Friday for her. She needs more tests."

"What tests will be performed?"

"A PKU…"

"Oh, a phenylketonuria, which measures phenylalaine."

"Why, yes. And MSUD…"

"Maple Syrup Urine Disease, which measures leucine an amino acid."

"Yeah," she responded looking at me in amazement. "Also, CAH…"

"Congential Adrenal Hyperplasia, which measures a form of progesterone, a female hormone."

"That's right. Mrs. Miller you should be telling me instead of me telling you."

"Okay, I will. The other tests are hypothyroidism, where thyroxine or T4 is measured to test the function of the thyroid gland, which is responsible for growth and development; another test is galactosemia, which measures galactose. It's a sugar function test. I guess you also test for tyrosinemia, which measures tyrosine another amino acid. And of course sickle cell anemia since she's black."

"Wow, that's amazing Mrs. Miller. How did you know all of that although you did miss a test?"

"Let me guess, homocystinuria which measures the amino acid homocystine. I didn't forget. I was testing you. You see, Gail," I said looking at her name tag. "I work in the lab at Grady Hospital. I used to send out tests when I worked in Immunology, six years ago. I guess some things you never forget."

"Mya is a lucky little girl to have a mother like you," Gail said glancing at her watch.

"No, I am a blessed woman to have Mya, but that's another story," I said lifting Mya up to burp.

"I must go, Mrs. Miller. It was nice talking to you," she said turning away.

"Gail!" I shouted.

"Yes, Mrs. Miller," she replied facing me.

"Do you like to read?"

"Why, yes. I love to read. Why do you ask?"

"I am an author. I wrote a book called *Uncaged*. I will leave you and the other staff members a copy before I leave. It will give you more insight about Mya and me. My pen name is Deeva Denez."

"I would love a copy Mrs. Denez. I-I mean Mrs. Miller."

"Good. I'll tell my husband to bring some copies when he comes. I'll make sure I sign one for you."

"Thank you," she said as she left the room.

I called Raymond as soon as Gail left. He laughed when I told him to bring me some books for the staff. He said I called him just in time because he was getting ready to leave in a few minutes. He asked how we were doing, and I said fine.

The feeding put Mya to sleep. I dressed while she slept. About an hour later, Raymond and the kids came through the door. Mya was still asleep. Raymond helped me gather my things while Francine and Little Raymond took turns holding Mya. They couldn't believe how small she was. Francine held Mya as if she was one of her dolls.

Raymond brought ten books for me to give to the staff. I signed one for Gail before an attendant came to wheel me to the car. I held Mya and Gail's book. I was hoping to see her before I left. Fortunately, she was at the desk. I gave her the book and told her to pass out the rest. Gail smiled as I put her book in her hand. My smile matched hers as I went to the car with Mya in my arms.

CHAPTER SIXTEEN

Raymond nestled Mya between Francine and Little Raymond. Joy filled my soul at the sight of the carseat with Mya in the back. It was hard for me to keep my eyes on the road because I kept looking back at Mya. She cried a little before the ride home put her to sleep. The other kids seemed to have formed an instant bond with her. I noticed they kept watching her, too.

All of a sudden, tiredness engulfed me. Going forty-eight hours with about six hours sleep had caught up with me. Now, I couldn't wait to get home to get some sleep, too. Halfway home, I couldn't resist the urge to sleep any longer. I closed my eyes like Mya. We both had been through a lot. We both needed rest.

When we arrived home, Raymond helped me inside first. He took me straight to our bed. I know I must have fallen asleep as soon as my head hit the pillow. The kids waited in the car with Mya until he brought her inside, too.

Two hours later, I woke up refreshed. I smelled a sensual aroma as I lifted my head from the sheets. Raymond had dinner waiting for me. He brought my meal to the bed complete with a glass of cranberry juice. I smiled as I saw the chicken, mashed potatoes with gravy, fried okra, and a biscuit.

As I sat up in bed, still savoring my dinner, I glanced at Mya's crib; she was sound asleep. Raymond neatly placed my food in front of me.

"Thank you for dinner," I said, reaching for my cranberry juice.

"You're welcome," he responded, handing me a napkin.

"So, you do know how to pamper a woman?" I asked putting the glass to my lips.

When the occasion arises, which is not too often."

I silently said grace before I replied. I didn't realize how hungry I was until I tasted the mashed potatoes. "Mmmm, this is good," I said putting another fork full into my mouth.

"Yes, Church's Chicken makes good mashed potatoes," Raymond said, smiling.

"What did you do while I slept?" I asked eating my chicken.

"Oh, I watched the kids, cleaned the kitchen, washed some clothes, and went to get something to eat." He said sitting at the edge of the bed.

I almost choked on my chicken. I couldn't believe my ears. Raymond had never lifted a finger to do anything at home before. He considered cleaning the house, "women's" work. "I could easily get used to this kind of treatment. You get dinner, clean, wash, and take care of the kids?"

"Don't get too excited. This treatment is only temporary until you get back on your feet and do your job, woman."

"Dear husband, my job is not this house. When I married you, I promised to love, obey and cherish you all the days of my life. I didn't say anything about being a maid in the house," I said eating my biscuit.

"Mrs. Miller, we've been through this before. You agreed that everything inside the house was your responsibility and everything outside the house was mine. Your problem is, you don't think you supposed to do anything – inside or outside the house. Since I pay all the bills in the house, the least you can do is cook, clean, and wash."

"You know what? I work my tail off in this house, and no one appreciates it. Everybody takes what I do for granted. I'm glad you're getting a sample of what I do. Maybe after I recuperate, you'll appreciate what I do more," I said eating the last of my biscuit.

Mya started moving in her crib; she obviously was waking up. Raymond turned to watch her while I ate.

"I will keep her after you nurse her," he volunteered.

"Will you also take my dishes back down to the kitchen?" I asked smiling. "It is included in my room service, isn't it, dear?"

"Women! God should have stopped with Adam," he said reaching for my plate.

"God is the brilliant Creator, He knew man and creation were not complete without woman. You may disagree with me, but you can't argue with God," I said as he stood up.

"Women!" he jeered as he walked out the door with my plate.

Mya opened her eyes as Raymond left the room. She whimpered first before letting out a full-fledged cry.

She cried as I changed her soggy diaper. Her tiny body moved feverishly in the oversized sleeper. Raymond and the kids came into the room while I poured powder on her clean, dry bottom. Francine wanted to hold Mya, but I told her I needed to nurse her first.

Mya was anxious for me to put my nipple into her mouth. To be one day old, she had a good suction. She sucked on the right breast first since it was the last one she sucked on previously, then I switched her to the left breast. I could tell she was getting full because her sucking had ceased. Laying her over my shoulders, I patted her until she burped.

It felt strange having a baby again after twelve years. At least I knew what I was in for - - changing diapers, sleepless nights, broken sleep throughout the day, caring for the umbilical cord, and giving baths in the infant tub. This time, however, was different; I didn't have a circumcised penis to deal with. No, this time my baby had a vagina. I was only instructed to keep it clean and wash the mucus that would eventually go away.

I glanced at Mya lovingly then handed her to Raymond. She cooed as her father talked to her as he sat on the bed. Francine and Little Raymond watched eagerly waiting their turns.

"Can I hold her, Daddy?" Francine asked, not being able to watch any longer. She held out her arms as she waited for her dad's reply.

"Sure," Raymond replied, relinquishing Mya to her. "Sit next to me," he said smoothing out a place on the bed.

"Okay," she said as she sat down holding Mya. The two sisters eyes met instantly. Francine smiled as if she was the happiest child on earth.

Little Raymond walked towards them then sat next to Francine. He smiled and waited patiently until it was his turn. Raymond and I looked at our growing family.

The next day, a nurse came to the house as scheduled. Both Mya and I were asleep when Joanna Brewer arrived. I wanted to be up and have Mya ready when she came, but Mya had kept me up most of the night. It was all I could do to throw on my robe and wash my face before she entered the room.

I hated waking Mya up, she was sleeping so peacefully, but I knew it was for a worthy cause. I wished I could get her to sleep like that at night, I said to myself as Raymond lifted her from her crib. Joanna, a middle aged, vibrant, golden brown, average height, and average build woman walked over to the ironing board after introducing herself.

She neatly placed her long, black coat and multi-colored scarf on the bed before taking things from a large bag. Raymond gave me Mya to change, which distracted me from seeing what she took from the bag. Joanna instructed me to take everything off Mya accept a clean diaper, so she could be weighed.

As I followed Joanna's instruction, I noticed a small scale she had placed on the ironing board. I handed her my nearly naked daughter. Mya cried as her body touched the metal scale.

"She weighs six pounds and seven ounces," Joanna announced, laying Mya on my bed.

"You must be mistaken," I said, making room on the bed, "she weighed six pounds and fifteen ounces, Sunday when she was born."

"I'm not mistaken, Mrs. Miller. It is not uncommon for newborns to lose weight after they're born. You must realize they're not being fed through the umbilical cord. She's adjusting to being in the real world. Sometimes newborns lose weight making the adjustment," Joanna said, flexing Mya's legs.

"What are you doing?" I asked.

"Oh, I'm testing the strength of her legs and arms. You have nothing to worry about, Mrs. Miller, your daughter is perfectly normal. Don't let her weight loss bother you either," Joanna said putting a thermometer under Mya's arm.

"What all will you do to her today?" I asked as she read the results.

"Oh, I'm almost done. She's hungry. I'll let you feed her in a few minutes. By the way, are you breastfeeding?"

"Yes, I am."

"Good. How is it going?" she asked doing another procedure.

"Pretty well, I guess. My milk hasn't come in yet, so I don't think Mya is getting enough. She stayed up most of the night, probably because she was hungry."

"Don't you fret none, Mrs. Miller. Mya is getting colostrum; it's better than milk, right now."

"I know God is all wise and all knowing. He knows what she needs and when she needs it, but I still feel she's not getting enough. Maybe, if I had bigger breasts," I said feeling my hard, aching breasts. "I'm glad you're almost done. I need to get some relief."

"Here's your daughter," she said handing her to me. "I'm done. And don't worry about your breast size; supply equals demand.

Joanna left as soon as she gathered her things. I nursed Mya who enjoyed her mother's colostrum.

The next day, my milk, indeed, came in. I woke up to two enormous breasts. I couldn't believe how large and full they were. I even woke Mya up so that she could give me some relief.

Unfortunately, she wasn't very hungry. I ended up expelling most of it into a plastic nursing bottle for future use.

Thanksgiving was the following day. Mya was four days old. I had a lot to be thankful for, and she was number one on my list. My little Mya was a fighter, an overcomer, a blessed child predestined by God to be here at this appointed time.

For Thanksgiving, Raymond and I had a quiet meal together. Little Raymond and Francine went to Augusta to spend Thanksgiving with their mother and grandparents. My mom cooked for everyone at her house, but Raymond couldn't wait until someone brought us food to eat. Therefore, he went to the mall to get our turkey and dressing dinner with all the fixings.

Mom was livid when she came over and saw us eating. She felt we should have waited until she brought us our food. We kept on eating our meal while she ranted and raved about the matter. Finally, I couldn't take anymore. She was disturbing our peace. Besides, Raymond and I were perfectly content with our bought meal. We were still thankful all the same. It didn't matter to us if our meal was bought or homemade. A meal was a meal. I calmed my mother down by convincing her how we felt.

The day after Thanksgiving was Mya's first doctor's visit. Because of a long sleepless night, we were fifteen minutes late. After checking in, we went to the waiting area. Small children played with toys while parents watched. Raymond and I held hands and watched our creation, Mya, and occasionally glanced at the other kids playing, too.

About ten minutes later, Mya's name was called. A slender young, black woman escorted us to the weighing area. She instructed us to remove Mya's clothes, so she could be weighed. Nina, the physician's assistant, stretched Mya's legs out and marked with an ink pen where her head began and her feet ended. Mya measured twenty inches. Nina then recorded her weight, which was still six pounds and seven ounces.

When Nina finished, she escorted us to a back room to wait on Dr. Milburn, the pediatrician. Dr. Milburn, a tall, thick, white man with short, thick, auburn hair and an even thicker mustache. Everything about Dr. Milburn was thick – thick body, hair, hands, and big thick feet. He shook our hands before taking a seat.

"I see you came late for your appointment," Dr. Milburn queried opening up a chart. "That is to be expected when you have a newborn," he smiled. "So, how has Mya adapted to this world?" he asked as he wrote in the chart.

"She has her days and nights confused," I answered feeling a yawn coming.

"That's probably because her mother works the midnight shift," Raymond added placing Mya's blanket on her almost naked body.

"Don't worry. Most newborns get their days and nights confused. Really, the problem is not Mya adapting to the world, but the world, or shall I say, her parents, adapting to her."

"You can say that again," I replied. "I may never adapt if she continues," I said letting my yawn go.

"I won't hold you too long, Mr. and Mrs. Miller. I know you need to go home and get some more sleep," Dr. Milburn said standing up. "Now, Dad, if you will put Mya on the bed, I will start my exam," he said putting his stethoscope to his ears.

Mya cried as the instrument touched her chest. "I see she has an excellent pair of lungs," Dr. Milburn said, laughing. "No wonder, you're so tired," he said turning her on her back. "Her crying can wake the dead."

We all laughed as Dr. Milburn continued his exam.

CHAPTER SEVENTEEN

As I looked at my daughter, lying on the doctor's bed, being examined, I thought about God and His love for His children. He sent His only begotten Son, Jesus Christ, into this world to save us from our sins because He loves us so much. His child, Jesus, was a living sacrifice, so that we, His other offspring, can be righteous like Jesus although we are all sinners.

God loves each and every one of us in a capacity that we cannot fully comprehend. According to Isaiah 49:15-16 verses, God speaking to the children of Israel said, *"`Can a woman forget her nursing child, and not have compassion on the son of her womb? Surely they will forget you. Yet I will not forget you. See, I have inscribed you on the palms of My hands...`"* What God said to the Israelites applies to us today. His love never changes despite all that we do that are contrary to His ways.

In Luke 12:6-7, Jesus spoke to His disciples, *"`Are not five sparrows sold for two copper coins? And not one of them is forgotten before God. But the very hairs of your head are all numbered. Do not fear therefore; you are of more value than many sparrows.`"*

And, of course, most of us know John 3:16-18, *"`For God so loved the world that He gave His only begotten Son, that whoever believes in Him should not perish but have everlasting life. For God did not send His Son into the world to condemn the world, but that the world through Him might be saved. He who believes in Him is not condemned; but he who does not believe is condemned already, because he has not believed in the name of the only begotten Son of God.`"*

Just like how Dr. Milburn examined Mya to make sure she was healthy, God examines us through our thoughts, actions, words, and ways. He desires for us to be pure in heart, then our thoughts, actions, words, and ways will also be pure and a delight to our Creator. Without God, we are nothing and can do nothing!

As I continued to watch Dr. Milburn, I prayed this prayer:

Thank you Jesus for my daughter, Mya. She was born a healthy baby, and I pray that her health will continue all the days of her life. I give her back to You as a living sacrifice to do Your Will and Work in her life. I don't know how much time we will have together, here on earth, but let each moment we spend together as mother and child be special and beautiful. Keep her from all harm and danger. Guard her path at all times. Let her never forsake You, the One and True God. But direct her steps to righteousness. Never let sin have dominion over her all the days of her life. Help me to be a true and faithful witness of You and Your Son, Jesus Christ, so she will have an example to follow. Amen.

Raymond and I left the doctor's office with our bundle of joy, proud of the good report given by Dr. Milburn. I was very happy the Lord had blessed us with a healthy daughter – an answer to my prayers.

The days and weeks that followed were spent getting adjusted to having a little one again. I was somewhat out of practice since it had been twelve years between Carlos and Mya, but everything came back to me rather quickly. I guess, once a mother, always a mother. Some things you can't forget. I think the hardest part of being a new mom again was the sleepless nights. At twenty-five and thirty I bounced backed faster than at forty-two. Most days it was afternoon before I was fully functional. I spent most mornings in bed trying to recapture the sleep I lost the night before. By the time Mya's next appointment rolled around, I had adjusted.

Mya's second doctor's appointment was Friday, January 22, with Dr. Armstead. Since our insurance changed in January, we were no longer with Kaiser but had changed to Aetna because the hospital only offered Aetna to its employees after January 1. I was apprehensive at first about switching doctors but had no other recourse except to go along with the program. I was glad, however, that I didn't have to change during my pregnancy.

Dr. Armstead eased my apprehension as soon as she greeted me with her warm, caring smile. I liked her office as well as her staff. They were courteous, conscientious, and considerate- - three qualities I love and desire from my health care provider. I was also pleased when Dr. Armstead told me Mya weighed ten pounds and was twenty-one and three-fourth inches long.

As I admired Mya, all ten pounds of her, I couldn't help but think of how happy I was to be her mother. I was also glad that I was able to spend a lot of time with her since I only worked two nights. I remembered with my sons, I worked five to six days a week, only taking the Sabbath off most weeks. But thanks to Raymond, who believes in his wife staying home or working part-time, I would be able to be the mother I had always wanted to be.

My heart still sank as I thought about returning to work in less than a month on February 21. Twelve weeks of Family Leave was definitely not enough. I wished there was some way I didn't have to work the two nights. I didn't want to be separated from my baby for any length of time. Reality set in as I continued to think and watch my child. I knew I had to go back because I needed the money. But one day, I told myself I would be able to stay at home all the time. That was my goal, and I would achieve it one day.

Before I knew it, I was back at work. But thankfully, it was only for two nights. My first night back, I felt out of place. Luckily, Jenny was there, so I felt somewhat relieved. There were two things I could count on when I worked in the Emergency Clinic Lab: Jenny and lots of work. And I must add, my first night back was no exception.

I brought plenty of pictures of Mya to update Jenny and the rest of the staff. Jenny and Tia came by to visit Mya at home. I wanted to especially make sure I kept them current. Since Tia didn't work Sunday nights, I would show her my pictures Monday night.

During the Sunday night shift, Jenny and I exchanged pictures and stories. She told me about her only grandchild, Hannah, who had just turned three. Jenny had three grown sons. They were all in their mid-thirties. Two were married, and one still lived with her. Hannah was truly the joy of Jenny's life.

One story Jenny told me about Hannah was: Jenny had just returned from California to celebrate Hannah's birthday. She lived with her son and family. She also slept in the same room with Hannah since her son's mother-in-law lived with them, too. Hannah, who wasn't quite toilet trained, gave Jenny these instructions before she went to sleep. "Make sure you don't wet the bed. My mommy won't like it." Jenny and I both laughed. Jenny also said that one time when she was playing puppets with Hannah while she took her bath, Hannah was pretending to cook. So Jenny asked Hannah for her recipe. Hannah's reply was, "You can get it from Hannah's cooking dot com." That was Sunday night.

Monday night Tia and I exchanged stories about Mya and her two nephews. They had come from Boston over the holidays to visit. They were six and one. Tia couldn't believe how big they had gotten since the last time she had seen them. Her youngest nephew was active and especially rough with her dog, Peaches. Kyle was so rough with Peaches that she stayed under the bed until he went home. When I showed Tia Mya's pictures, it made her desire for having a baby increase.

"Mya has grown since I last saw her," Tia replied, looking at the last picture.

"You think so. She seems so small to me. She must sneak and grow," I answered, taking all the pictures back.

"I'll be glad when I have my child. The way Derrick's been acting lately, I don't think we will have any," she said with a troubled expression.

"When the right time comes, you'll get pregnant," I said trying to console Tia. "Remember, last year when I had the two miscarriages?"

"Yeah," she replied adjusting her glasses.

"I know now that, that would have been a terrible mistake if I had had my daughter during either one of those pregnancies."

"What do you mean?"

"Although I thought Raymond and I were ready for another child, we were not. I know that now, but I didn't know that then," I said, putting my pictures back in my bag by Becky's desk.

"Huh? I'm still confused," Tia replied, walking toward me.

"Last year, Raymond and I were not married because there were things that needed to be worked out in our relationship. It would have been a disaster to bring a child into the relationship before everything was straightened out between us. God knew we were not ready although we both thought we were."

"Oh, so you're saying something needs to be worked out between Derrick and me before I can get pregnant?" Tia asked with a quizzical expression.

"Yes, that's exactly what I'm saying. You may think you're ready now, but in actuality, you're not. God knows best. When everything is right, you'll get pregnant."

"I'm beginning to think something is wrong with one of us. I'm not using any birth control except the withdrawal method. Surely, that would have failed us by now," Tia said, taking her pregnancy specimens off the analyzer.

"Nothing has to be wrong with either of you. Look at Raymond and me. We are the same two people who tried and wanted to have a baby last year. Nothing changed with us, except God and His plan and purpose for our lives," I said walking to my station, passing Tia.

"That makes sense, Vanessa. I hope you're right."

"Trust me, Tia. God knows when the right time is. You have to wait on Him."

"Blood gas!" Jenny yelled from the accessioning station.

I did my blood gas while Tia finished her work. By the expression on her face, I could tell my words had sunk in. Now, her only recourse was to wait on God to give her, her heart's desire. I prayed as I ran my blood gas that He would.

For most of the night, I thought about Tia and her situation. I also thought about Mya, how God had shown His love and mercy toward us and gave her to Raymond and me. My mind drifted back to when she was just an image in March of '95, three and a half years before her physical birth. Then God showed me a second image of me being very pregnant before a large book came in front of the pregnant image of me. God said, "Your book will be published first before you deliver." Why did God show me, not one, but two images of what was sure to come? Why did God allow the two miscarriages before the actual birth occurred? When will the second daughter be born? More and more questions kept popping into my head as I worked. Since I couldn't answer them, I gave them to God to rest my mind.

However, the one question that I couldn't get out of my mind was, when will the second daughter come? I wasn't taking any birth control, therefore, I could get pregnant at any time. Ideally, Raymond and I wanted Mya to be six months old before I got pregnant again. But we were on God's schedule, not ours. Anytime would be fine. I guess I was in the same shoes as Tia was in with the second daughter. I had to wait on Him.

Leaving Mya for two whole nights in a row was very hard. I missed my baby and wanted to be with her every waking minute. It had taken her so long to get here I couldn't stand being separated from her for any length of time. When I arrived home, she was sleeping peacefully in her crib. Raymond was asleep, too. I watched her for a long time before I went to sleep. The sight of her gave me so much joy and peace. As I admired my daughter, I prayed for a bright future.

The following month, March, I also had work scheduled for Deeva Denez. I had a TV interview on TV 57, a Christian Broadcast

Station, and two book signings. My convalescence period was definitely over. It was back to business as usual. My time as Vanessa Miller, the wife and mother, exclusively, was over to be both Vanessa and Deeva Denez.

My TV appearance was Tuesday, March 16, from 7-9 p.m.. The interview went well, I thought. I always enjoyed telling people about *Uncaged*. My desire was for them to be free like me. I knew first hand about the power of forgiveness. I wanted everyone else who was a slave to their past to be delivered, too.

March 21, I had a book signing at the South Dekalb Mall B. Dalton Store. My book signing was from 2-5 p.m.. I always enjoyed book signings at that store since it was so close to home. It felt more like a homecoming because I saw so many familiar faces. I knew the manager and staff personally. They made me feel as if I were at home. When it was all over, I sold 14 books.

Saturday, March 27, was my second book signing. It was at The West End Mall in the Two Friends Book Store from 2-4 p.m.. Going there was like being with old friends. I knew the owner and staff there as well. As a matter of fact, I had arranged my own book signings since Lisa had dropped out of the picture months ago. God knew I was not going to let His work, *Uncaged* die. I didn't care what it took and how much money or effort. *Uncaged* would live up to His fulfillment of a movie. No one and nothing was going to stop me from reaching His goal for *Uncaged*. They may hinder me or temporarily delay me, but no one could permanently stop me; I wouldn't allow it. Sadly to say, however, I only sold three books.

At the end of the book signing, I wasn't discouraged. As a matter of fact, I was thankful for another opportunity to expose my work to others who had not heard of my book or me. I couldn't help but think of how my book signings would be at some future time. When people would stand in line for hours to meet me and get their books signed. No, that didn't happen today. But one day it would. Guaranteed!

CHAPTER EIGHTEEN

The Passover was the following week along with the Days of Unleavened Bread. Reflecting on Jesus' life, death, and resurrection always renewed my faith. My life as a Christian as well as an author was truly a faith walk. Faith - - that five-letter word which has so much meaning. Faith according to the Bible in Hebrews 11:1 means, *"Now faith is the substance of things hoped for, the evidence of things not seen."*

Looking back and thinking ahead, I recounted my acts of faith. By faith, I believed God was going to deliver me from my marriage with Carl before Carlos turned eighteen, so I could have my daughter(s) prior to menopause. By faith, I believed the image I saw of Mya before she was born. By faith, I believed God when He said my book would be published first before I delivered. By faith, I believed God when He said my name, Vanessa Lewis, would not be on my book. By faith, I believed God would choose the next man in my life by him giving me my sign. By faith, I married Raymond believing he was the one that God had chosen for me. By faith, I started writing *The Bearer of the Sign* before I received my sign. By faith, I wrote *Uncaged* because God had instructed me to do so the year before. By faith, I believed God would publish it and make it a movie.

God continues to say in Hebrews 11:6 regarding faith, *"But without faith it is impossible to please Him, for he who comes to God must believe that He is a rewarder of those who diligently seek Him."* God wants us to believe and trust in Him to do those things that we cannot see with our eyes, but know in our hearts that He will bring it to past. That's faith in action.

Faith is also the fruit of the Holy Spirit found in Galatians 5:22-23. *"But the fruit of the Spirit is love, joy, peace, longsuffering, kindness, goodness, faithfulness (showing faith), gentleness, self-control. Against such there is no law."* Jesus wants us to live by faith and not by sight (II Corinthians 5:7). Furthermore, God says in Romans 1:17, *"... 'The just shall live by faith.'"* I know beyond a shadow of a doubt that I have faith. God says we only need as little as a grain of mustard seed (Matthew 17:20). It's not how much faith we

111

have that matters, but the object of our faith – who we believe in to make what we don't see come to past.

By faith, Jesus became our Passover Lamb. He left us instructions to remember His death until He returns. Only by faith can we accept and believe His words in I Corinthians 11:23-26, *"...that the Lord Jesus on the same night in which He was betrayed took bread; and when He had given thanks, He broke it and said, `Take, eat; this is My body which is broken for you; do this in remembrance of Me.` In the same manner He also took the cup after supper, saying, `This cup is the new covenant in My blood. This do, as often as you drink it, in remembrance of Me.` For as often as you eat this bread and drink this cup, you proclaim the Lord's death till He comes."* My constant prayer is that I do not take Jesus' death in vain; that I do not profane His shed blood for me and my sins.

On the last day of Unleaven Bread, April 6, Mrs. Edna Crutchfield, the founder of The International Black Writers and Artist, Inc. died. She was eighty-four years old. Her organization helped me as a new writer to write *Uncaged.* I mention her here, so her life, like Jesus' life and death, was not in vain.

By faith, I started writing this book, *The Image: A Prophetic Birth* on June 30, 1999. During this time, *Uncaged* was almost out of print. Lisa had 219 books left, but would not give me any. I had a few in my possession. Consequently, I found another publisher, Paula Bowen, who said she could easily sell 5,000 books in one year. I believed her and signed a contract with her.

By faith, I started my own company, The Literary Connection, to facilitate and help other writers. I had learned a lot since I first started two years ago. I had also made many mistakes. I wanted other writers to benefit from my experiences. They didn't have to go the route I went. They didn't have to make the errors I made.

Faith is having complete trust and confidence in God. It means believing Jesus and His written Word totally and completely without any doubt. Faith is not something that you are born with, but you learn it and acquire it as you live. Faith is a fruit of the Holy Spirit. It is a gift from God.

Due to my lack of books, my last scheduled book signing was July 10, at Medu Bookstore from 4-6 p.m.. By faith, I believed that there would be many more book signings to come with large fans at each. Although I was out of books and the future looked bleak, my faith kept hope alive. I knew my present situation was only temporary because I was destined for greatness! I would succeed.

Two weeks after my last book signing, I discovered I was pregnant again. Mya was eight months old. The timing was also perfect because the baby would come before my 44th birthday in August of next year. Since I didn't have any book signings scheduled, I could use this time to concentrate on Mya and this unborn child.

Life at home was already demanding with Raymond, Mya and the other kids. When I recounted what I did by the end of the day, it seemed as if nothing was accomplished. Most of my time was spent with Mya, taking care of her and her needs. Dinner was my second priority. Sometimes that was the only other thing that was done. If time and energy allowed, I spent time with Raymond, but he was usually so drained from working the night shift that he slept most of the time. Raymond Jr. and Francine entertained themselves. All they needed was something to eat and drink to make them happy along with TV.

Even with my life presently the way it was, I looked forward for my second daughter to arrive. I had been waiting since September of 1980, almost nineteen years. Madame Lee prophesied her coming then when she told me I was going to leave Carl and have four children, two boys and two girls. Carl Jr., Carlos, and Mya were here. Now it was time for the fourth and last child to come. I smiled each time I thought of her growing inside of me. Now, I couldn't wait for her to come, too.

I must admit, nineteen years ago. I was sick at the news of being the mother of four children. All I wanted then was one or two. But now, nineteen years later, I was overjoyed at the thought of having my second daughter. Raymond was just as excited, too. I'm sure deep down inside he wanted another son. I wish I could give him what he wanted, but I had already filled my quota for boys.

I knew it would be a lot of hard work taking care of two small children, but I was up for the challenge. The positives far outweighed the negatives. I can still recall the conversation with Raymond when I told him I was pregnant.

My cycle was due, Saturday, July 24. I performed a urine pregnancy test that next night at work. I didn't tell Raymond about my missed period or the results of the pregnancy test until I arrived home Monday morning from work. Both Raymond and Mya were asleep when I entered the bedroom Monday morning. I admired Mya for several minutes before I crawled into bed next to Raymond. At first, I started not to wake him, but I was too excited to fall asleep without telling him the good news.

"Honey, wake up," I said softly, nudging him in his back. In mid-snore, he turned to face me. I thought he was awake, but he was still asleep. "Honey, wake up," I said again. This time I could tell I had gotten through because he stopped snoring and opened his eyes. "I have something to tell you, then you can go back to sleep," I said as he sleepily looked in my direction.

"What are you talking about?" he asked, closing his eyes again.

"No, baby, wake up. I have something very important to tell you," I said, shaking him.

"What is it?" he asked giving me his full attention.

"I'm pregnant. I did a pregnancy test last night at work."

"That's good," he said, rolling back over to go to sleep.

"Raymond, did you hear me? I said, I'm pregnant," I said shaking him some more.

"I heard you. You said you are pregnant. Congratulations."

I rolled over to my side of the bed. I was disappointed because I was expecting a different response. By the time I had gotten comfortable on my side of the bed, Raymond rolled next to me, held me in his arms, turned me towards him and said,

"You have made me the happiest man alive today, knowing you are carrying my child."

I smiled at his words and touch. They reached a special place in my heart. We kissed, then fell asleep. Raymond's arms not only enveloped me, but our unborn child. It felt good knowing he loved both of us. Mya would have competition. She already had a special bond with her dad that words could not explain. She was both a mommy and daddy's girl. I hoped this next daughter would be the same way.

Feeling refreshed from my sleep, I called my doctor to make an appointment. Their first opening was August 25 at 9 a.m.. After making my appointment, I went downstairs to check on Raymond and Mya. As I exited my bedroom door, I saw them in the living room. Raymond was reading the paper while Mya was on a mat playing with her toys. She still had her nightclothes on, and her hair had not been combed. Raymond felt like those were my duties. His duty was to watch her until I woke up. I didn't mind the division of labor. I was more than glad to take care of my daughter. I was thankful, however, I only worked two days a week.

At the sight of me, Raymond smiled as he put his paper in his lap. Mya smiled, too. "Ma, Ma," she said as she left her mat and crawled to me. My heart melted as I saw my daughter eager to come to me. I thought of my unborn daughter. Would she be like Mya, who seemed to be the perfect child? I hoped so. I couldn't imagine having another child who had Mya's temperament, which was exactly like mine – happy and carefree.

"I'm surprised you are up so soon," Raymond said, glancing at his watch.

"I know it's early. It's not even two o'clock, but I felt rested, so I got on up," I said reaching for Mya who was at my feet. "I even called the doctor's office to make an appointment before I came down," I said holding Mya in my arms. "Hey, booboo. You miss Mommy?"

"When is your appointment?" Raymond asked, walking toward me.

"August 25, at 9 o'clock. Booboo, are you ready to take your bath?" I asked Mya as she grinned in my face.

"She's probably ready to eat if you don't mind fixing her something. She ate earlier, but I think she's ready to eat again."

"What are you going to do when we have two little ones?" I asked going into the kitchen to fix Mya something to eat.

"I will cross that bridge when I get there. Now, that you're up, I'm going into my office to get some work done," he said walking to the steps.

"Suppose I have something I want to do?"

"You're holding everything you need to be concerned with right now. Since you're up, everything you need to do, you have to do it with your daughter. Excuse me, I'm going to get some work done," he said as he walked up the steps.

I looked at Mya, then opened the refrigerator to see what I was going to give her to eat. My next task was to give her a bath, then comb her hair. When she was done, I had to cook dinner, wash clothes and dishes. Forget Raymond. What was I going to do with two babies? I'd had to cross that bridge when I got there, too.

After completing all my tasks, I sat on the sofa with Mya and read her a book. She loved for me to read to her, especially her *Count with*

Teddy book. Next, I read *Snow White*. I could tell she was sleepy while I read. She dozed off as soon as I finished. I laid her in her crib then wrote on *The Image: A Prophetic Birth*. As I wrote, I was glad the second daughter was on her way. I didn't know how I was going to manage with two little ones. I would have to adapt somehow.

Sad to say, five days before my doctor's appointment, I started bleeding vaginally. I immediately called my doctor. He told me to come in for an exam. His examination confirmed I had miscarried again. He drew blood to determine my HCG levels. They were 700 mIU/ml. When he told me, I was too stunned to cry. All I could think of was I thought I had gotten off the miscarriage merry-go-round with the birth of Mya. This last miscarriage made me realize I had to face it again. My only consolation was by faith, I knew my daughter was going to be born. Wasn't she a prophecy from Madame Lee? Didn't everything else Madame Lee prophesied come to past? Wasn't my second daughter destined to come? Wasn't there more time on my biological clock to ensure another safe and normal delivery?

CHAPTER NINETEEN

The loss of my daughter made me feel empty inside. She was my fourth miscarriage. All of my hopes and dreams for my daughter had now disappeared just like her developing body from inside of me. Raymond consoled me as best he could. However, no words or kind gestures could ever substitute for my daughter who would never be born. By the grace of God, I had to get through this somehow.

Mya was my ticket to recovery. Watching her made me thankful for what I had instead of dwelling on what I didn't have or hoped for. I counted my blessings daily as I watched her grow. Her smile always melted my heart. Her life erased my hurts and turned them into joy.

Mya's doctor's appointment was on the same day as my OB/GYN for the child I just lost. My appointment was scheduled for 9 a.m., and hers was at 11:45 a.m.. I took her to her appointment. She checked out fine except for her weight of 15 pounds 13 ounces. She had only gained 9 pounds and 6 ounces in 9 months. The doctor was concerned about her weight. She wanted me to bring her back next month.

Mya was a busy child who wouldn't be still. She probably would gain weight if she wasn't moving all the time. She still nursed, so I was confident she was getting enough nutrients with my milk, and the small amount of table food she consumed. Her weight didn't bother me. I felt like she would be short and petite. Everybody was not meant to be big. I sure wasn't going to fatten up my daughter, so she could fit on the doctor's weight chart. Some people were not meant to be like everybody else. And Mya was one of those people.

When Mya and I returned home, Raymond was still asleep. He had worked the night before. He usually slept until 3 or 4 p.m.. By then, the kids were home from school. I waited until they came home before I cooked, so they could watch their sister. Mya was usually so busy, I couldn't get anything done. She took up all of my time and energy.

Mya was just as excited to see them as they were to see her. Francine usually played with her for a few minutes when she first came home. Raymond Jr. played with his sister, too. I always enjoyed seeing them interact together. Sometimes they took her upstairs to watch TV while I cooked. Most of the time they played with her in the living room, which was adjacent to the kitchen. Yes, we were one happy family, all five of us.

Dinner was almost ready when Raymond woke up. I fixed a quick meal – spaghetti. Spaghetti was a favorite at my house. I was glad since it was so easy to make.

"Hhmmm is dinner ready?" Raymond asked as he came into the kitchen. He went straight to the refrigerator for his red cup in the freezer to pour him some lemonade.

"It will be in ten more minutes. The noodles need to cook some more. Do you want a salad? I can fix it while the noodles are cooking," I said stirring the sauce.

"No, don't bother. Spaghetti will be fine," he said drinking his lemonade. "How was school?" he asked Francine and Raymond Jr. while going into the living room.

"Fine." Raymond Jr. replied, giving Mya a toy.

"My teacher gave me a reward for being good in class," Francine responded, reaching for her bookbag.

"What was your reward?" Raymond asked, picking up Mya.

"Da, Da," Mya said as he held her in his arms.

"I'll show you," Francine said, digging in her bag. She searched for several minutes before pulling objects from the bag. "See, Daddy!" she exclaimed. "Mrs. Sims gave me a pencil sharpener and two new pencils."

"Very good, sweetie," Raymond replied, looking at the objects.

"What did you do that was so good?" Raymond Jr. questioned.

"I was quiet in line, and I turned in all my homework."

"You're supposed to do that anyway," Raymond Jr. replied. "I do that all the time, and my teacher don't give me nothing!" he said getting up.

"Well, I can't help it if my teacher rewards me, and your teacher don't!" she yelled putting the objects back in her bag.

"That's enough!" Raymond retorted. "I'm glad your teacher rewarded you, Francine. Maybe next time your teacher will reward you, too, Raymond."

"Yeah, right!" Raymond Jr. responded.

"Dinner's ready!" I said as I started fixing plates.

"Go wash your hands," Raymond instructed. "I'm going to wash my hands, too."

They all left while I fixed plates. When they returned, the mood had changed for the better. I was glad because I love a house with peace, not confusion or contention. Those were two things that Raymond Jr. and Francine thrived on. I prayed daily that Mya would be different.

Before I knew it, Mya's first birthday had rolled around. I couldn't believe a year had already passed. I didn't have a big celebration, just ice cream and cake with the family. Carlos and Carl Jr. came over with his son, Davonte, to help celebrate. Davonte's birthday was six days before Mya's. They were both born last year.

I felt truly blessed sharing this moment with my family. We celebrated both Mya and Davonte's birthdays together. Neither one of them knew what was going on, but they enjoyed the occasion anyway. We all did. We said happy birthday as they attempted to blow out their candles. Raymond helped Mya, and Carl Jr. helped Davonte.

After we ate the cake and ice cream, Carlos and Francine opened Mya's piggy bank to count its contents. She had $72.36, which I planned to deposit the next day. I enjoyed that activity so much, I decided to make it a yearly tradition.

My sons and grandson stayed for another hour before we called it an evening. I always enjoyed having them over. At this juncture in my life, I felt full to overflowing. I had three sons, three daughters and a grandson. My life was truly full, but I still wanted my other daughter to complete the family. Seven was God's number for completion. I wanted the same number of children in my family, too.

Thanksgiving was three days later. Indeed, I had a lot to be thankful for in my life. My family was first on my list. My life, health, and strength were next. Everything else followed after them. God had truly blessed me, and I wanted Him to know how I felt.

When January came, I was also very thankful for my husband. Raymond and I celebrated our second wedding anniversary, January 15. I couldn't help but reflect on Raymond and Carl. My wedding date with Carl was January 10. I thought that was odd to have my two wedding dates five days apart. Raymond and Carl's birthdays were one day apart – Raymond's was June 29, and Carl's was June 28. They were one day and ten years apart and were different as day and night. Raymond was the exact opposite of Carl, and I loved the difference.

Raymond took me to one of our favorite restaurants, Steak and Ale. The thing I liked most about Steak and Ale, besides the food, was the cozy setting. The dimly lit rooms that were sectioned off to hold small groups, with burning candles, always added a romantic touch to the meal that I loved. I had a lot of fond memories at Steak and Ale. It was the perfect place to celebrate our anniversary.

Raymond and I exchanged cards while we waited on our food. We had gotten our salads and drinks before Raymond said grace, then we opened our cards.

"Here's your card," I said reaching into my purse. Raymond had already laid my card on the table when I went to the ladies room.

"Thank you," he said, carefully reading the outside before opening the sealed envelope. "To my wonderful husband," he said as he reached for his card. "So, you think I'm wonderful."

"Yes, I do. I mean every word of that. "You must think I'm wonderful, too, because that is how you addressed my card,."

"You are the joy of my life," he said opening his card. "You are wonderful to me."

I opened my card. We read silently. My card said: Please don't forget you're the joy of my life, And it means everything having you as my wife, Your voice cheers my heart and your smile lights my day. Your touch warms my world in a magical way. Please don't forget what I want most to do is to give back as much as I'm given by you… To show you each day that you're never alone, That I cherish your hopes and your dreams as my own, That whatever life brings we'll both face it together…Please don't forget that I'll love you forever. Happy Anniversary. With all my love, your husband, Raymond.

"This is a beautiful card," I said, smiling. "You make me feel so special."

"You are special. You're everything to me," he said reaching for my hand. "I'm so glad you are my wife."

"Baby, nothing can top this. Right now, I'm the happiest woman on earth."

"And, I'm the happiest man," he said putting his card down and picking up his tea.

"Did you like your card?" I asked picking up my tea also.

"I loved it. I hope I can live up to it."

"Let's make a toast," I said lifting up my tea.

"Okay. You first."

"To my husband of two wonderful years, may our marriage get better and better with each passing day. Our love has grown for each other to a height neither one of us has ever known. May God continue to bless our marriage and family all the days of our lives."

"I'll toast to that," Raymond said, hitting my glass with his then putting it to his lips.

"Your turn," I said after swallowing my tea.

"To Mrs. Raymond Miller, my lovely wife of two years, my God-given soul mate. The woman I cherish and love. May our marriage be filled with love and respect for each other. May we share in each others dreams and goals. But most of all, may we love each other with our whole being until death do us part. This is to you Mrs. Miller, the love of my life," he said as our glasses touched.

At the end of our toast, our waitress brought our food. Raymond ordered steak, and I ordered chicken. The food was great, but the conversation that followed was better. I thoroughly enjoyed my anniversary dinner with Raymond, and I prayed for many more.

A spark had been ignited at dinner that only a romantic evening could turn into a roaring flame. Raymond and I had few flaming evenings. Our marriage survived on a flicker every now and then. Tonight was sure to convert the spark into a fire.

The kids went to Augusta for the three-day weekend. Therefore, we had a golden opportunity for romance. Raymond held my hand as we entered the house. I hoped his mind was on sex like mine. If not, I would have to change his mind. Raymond's passionate kiss after he locked the door told me we were on one accord.

"Mmmmm, that was a great kiss!" I said as I opened my eyes after the kiss was over. (I love Raymond's fireball kisses. He only gave them to me on special occasions. The rest of the times I received pecks.) He pulled me to the sofa, in our favorite corner, to cuddle.

"It's been a long time since we sat on the sofa together," he said, resuming his position.

"Yes, it has, but I hope you have more than cuddling in mind for tonight," I said ready for the real action to begin.

"Relax, you'll get more later. We have the whole evening ahead of us. It's only 8:15," he said looking at his watch. "Sex is fine, but it's nice to cuddle sometimes. I enjoy holding you, too."

"You're right," I said laying my head on his shoulder. "We've both been so busy lately, that we haven't taken time out to just sit and relax with each other. It's especially difficult since Mya's been born."

"There are many days I want to hold you like this, but don't get the opportunity," he said, moving my face to kiss me again. "I'm a simple man. I like simple things," he said putting his lips on mine.

A warm sensation went through my body as Raymond kissed my lips. His real kisses always drove me crazy. He kissed me a second time when the first kiss was over. My body was now ready to explode. Just when I knew I couldn't take anymore, he suggested we go upstairs. I was more than ready for phase II.

Phase II was the best it had ever been. The love I had for Raymond went to a higher level. Our marriage was intact; it would last the distance. At last, I had found my soul mate. God had truly answered my prayer!

CHAPTER TWENTY

I think Raymond and I got carried away during our anniversary because my cycle did not come in February. When I looked back at my planner, I realized I was ovulating at that time. Our anniversary was at mid-cycle. What a perfect time to get pregnant! My pregnancy made our anniversary more special.

As soon as I realized I was pregnant, I made an appointment the following week, February 11, at 2:30 p.m.. My excitement grew with each passing day. By the time my appointment arrived, I was beyond myself.

After my examination, my doctor said, everything looked fine. But because of my history of miscarriages and my advanced age of 43, my doctor requested an ultrasound for February 29. The ultrasound results showed I was 8 weeks and 3 days pregnant. My baby was due in October.

I left the ultrasound excited. Seeing my fetus inside of me always made me happy. To be able to witness such a miracle taking place gave me so much joy. Being pregnant made me think about God and The Church – they parallel each other.

Allow me to explain. In human reproduction, an egg is fertilized with a sperm during or after intercourse at the time of ovulation. The fertilized egg becomes a zygote. The zygote divides and multiplies and later attaches to the uterine wall where it is nourished with blood that contains all the life giving nutrients such as oxygen, minerals, proteins, sugars and electrolytes. There it grows to maturity to become a newborn child.

God established The Church to reproduce Himself. In the Garden of Eden, He made Adam from the ground in His image. Adam, however, was physical flesh. Through Jesus, God wanted mankind to bear His spiritual image. He planned to bring forth spiritual offspring through the life, death, and resurrection of Jesus Christ. In John 1:12 & 13, the Scripture explains this concept.

I will now illustrate how human reproduction parallel's God's spiritual reproduction. For conception to take place, there must be a mature egg and sperm present. We as mature people, who hear and understand the Word of God concerning Jesus and repent of our sins, become an egg that God can impregnate with His Holy Spirit. We, plus God's Holy Spirit, become a new creation just like the fertilized egg in human reproduction. With God's Holy Spirit in us, although we are mature adults, we become a child of God or born again. John 3:3-6 *"Jesus answered and said to him (Nicodemus), 'Most assuredly, I say to you, unless one is born again, he cannot see the kingdom of God.' Nicodemus said to Him, 'How can a man be born when he is old? Can he enter a second time into his mother's womb and be born?' Jesus answered, 'Most assuredly, I say to you unless one is born of water and the Spirit, he cannot enter the kingdom of God. 'That which is born of the flesh is flesh, and that which is born of the Spirit is spirit."* In order to receive the Holy Spirit, God explains in Acts 2:38, *"Then Peter said to them, 'Repent, and let every one of you be baptized in the name of Jesus Christ for the remission of sins; and you shall receive the gift of the Holy Spirit."*

After receiving God's Holy Spirit, we must be joined to God through The Church by the blood of Jesus Christ. The Church is Jesus' body. He is the head. The purpose of The Church is to feed us with the Word of God – our life source – until we reach spiritual maturity. Colossians 1:18 says, *"And He is the head of the body, the church, who is the beginning, the firstborn from the dead, that in all things He may have the preeminence."*

Lastly, we will be born as children of God after our death or the great tribulation, which is God's labor pain for His Church. Revelation 7:14 &15, *"...'These are the ones who come out of the great tribulation, and washed their robes and made them white in the blood of the Lamb. 'Therefore they are before the throne of God, and serve Him day and night in His temple. And He who sits on the throne will dwell among them."*

Yes, God is reproducing Himself through Jesus Christ and The Church, our mother. In reproduction, there is always a time of gestation. During this time, the mother protects her unborn child as well as provides the right conditions for it to develop. God uses The Church to separate His people from this world and its ways. In Revelations 18:4, God tells us *"And I heard another voice from heaven saying, 'Come out of her (Babylon, the great false church or the mother of harlots), my people, lest you share in her sins, and lest you receive of her plagues."* The time of gestation for both my daughter and God's people is now! Thank God.

Speaking of my daughter, for my next OB appointment on March 13, I had an OB work-up. I also saw my fetus again because they did another ultrasound. A smile spread across my face at the sight of my offspring inside of me. Watching her heart pump gave me another thrill. As I viewed the screen, witnessing her every movement, I couldn't help but think how nice it would be to hold her.

I was so excited when I left the doctor's office; I praised God all the way home. He knew how much this baby meant to me. I was thankful He had answered my prayers and set this time for her to come. For the rest of the month, people said I had a glow on my face because I was so happy. I had experienced a lot of emotions in my life, but the joy I felt carrying this child had to exceed all the good feelings I had ever felt.

Needless to say, when my next appointment came, April 10, I was so happy, I couldn't contain myself. Dr. Glasser, my primary OB physician, was not there, but Dr. Manderville, a black female physician in the group, examined me.

"Hello, Mrs. Miller," Dr. Manderville said as she entered the examining room where I was lying on the examining table with my tissue gown on reading a magazine. Her long, thick, chestnut brown hair rested on her shoulders as she stood in front of me.

"Hi," I said, sitting up. "So you're the lucky one today."

"Yes, I will give you your examination if that is what you mean," she said looking at my chart. "I see your weight, blood pressure, and urinalysis are fine," she said placing the chart on the table nearby. "Let's see how the rest of you are doing," she said putting her stethoscope to her ears.

"We're doing great!" I replied.

"Take a deep breath," she instructed, placing the instrument on my chest as she lifted the paper gown up. "Now, exhale."

I did as instructed. Next she placed a gel on my protruding abdomen.

"I should be able to hear the baby's heart beat from the outside this visit," she said gliding the instrument through the gel. She kept moving it, not picking up a heartbeat. I wasn't alarmed because I had been through this before. She applied more gel and kept probing. However, the expression on her face told me something was wrong.

"Can you hear a heartbeat?" I asked, concerned.

125

"No. I know you have fibroids. They may be interfering," she said putting the instrument and gel down. "Let me examine you vaginally," she said reaching for gloves then going to the front of the examining table. "Come all the way down," she instructed, sternly.

I scooted down to the end of the table. The urgency in her voice sent chills through my body. She examined me for a few minutes before speaking.

"Mrs. Miller, you need to get dressed. I cannot find the heartbeat. Let me see if I can pick it up on the ultrasound. Melanie will take you as soon as you are dressed. I will join you shortly," she said removing her gloves to wash her hands.

Melanie and Dr. Manderville rushed out of the room. I quickly got dressed and waited for Melanie to return. Five minutes after I was ready, Melanie came back to get me. We walked to the ultrasound room, a few doors down the hallway. Dr. Manderville joined us almost immediately.

"You don't have to remove your clothes again, just get on the table and pull your shirt up and pants down to your hips," Dr. Manderville said as she took her place in front of the ultrasound machine. Melanie helped me onto the table. I didn't say anything. I was too busy praying for the life of my child.

Within seconds, the fetus appeared on the screen. I saw everything. Its heart was not beating. It was a lifeless mass on the screen. Although I could see with my own eyes that my unborn child was not alive, I could not accept it in my mind. Dr. Manderville's words snapped me back into reality, however, when she spoke.

"Mrs. Miller, I'm sorry, but you have miscarried," she said turning off the machine.

A second after her words penetrated to the soul of my being, I cried. I wept loudly. Tears ran down my face. Melanie handed me several tissues. I used them to cover my face. I cried for my child who I would never hold, for the child I would never have. A thousand thoughts went through my mind, but the one question I kept asking myself was: How could I miscarry again with no warning or symptoms? My abdomen was swollen, and my breasts were sore as if I had a viable pregnancy.

"Mrs. Miller, I am sorry," Dr. Manderville said. "I will leave and give you some time alone. You may leave when you are up to it," she said, getting up.

I nodded my head because I was unable to speak. As she walked to the door, I thought of one question to ask. I had to know before I left the office. "Dr. Manderville," I said as I heard her open the door.

"Yes," she replied, walking back to me.

"What happens next?" I asked somewhat composed.

"We need to take another ultrasound to see how far along you are. That will give us an idea how long the fetus has been…when the fetus stopped living," she paused to rephrase her sentence. "Depending on the results, we need to schedule surgery for a D & C to remove the fetal remains."

"This is my fifth miscarriage. "I've never had a D & C before. The fetal tissue always expelled on its own. I want to be absolutely sure I have miscarried before you do a D & C. I will have another ultrasound to be sure."

"That's good. I will decide what to do after the ultrasound results come back. I will schedule you one as soon as possible. Let me do that before you leave. I am concerned about your health, right now. There is nothing more I can do for the baby."

Dr. Manderville walked out of the room to return five minutes later with a date for an ultrasound. She scheduled it for the following Tuesday at 10:30 a.m.. She also informed me that she would call the hospital to get a date to perform the D & C because she felt confident I had miscarried although I wasn't fully convinced. She felt like the sooner the fetal tissue was removed the better for me. She respected my wishes, however, and would do what she could, so I could have a peace of mind. I also told her if the D & C was performed, I wanted my tubes tide. I wanted another child, but mentally and emotionally, I couldn't take another miscarriage.

The ultrasound proved the fetus had been dead for four weeks. My surgery was performed Monday, April 24. Dr. Glasser did the surgery. I had signed papers before the surgery that I did not want any blood. He told me when the surgery was over, I lost over 1200 ccs of blood. He honored my request, but he thought he was going to lose me on the operating table. Consequently, he stopped the D & C early, not being sure he removed everything. He said I scared him to death. I thanked him and Jesus for sparing my life.

The hardest part of my recovery was the incision from the tubiligation and knowing I would never have another child. I knew God could perform a miracle, but my hope disappeared with the dead fetus they removed from the surgery. That was my last and final pregnancy.

During my recovery, I couldn't help but try to put the missing pieces together of this last miscarriage, which signified there would be no second daughter and Madame Lee's prophecy had failed. I recounted her exact words that she spoke to me nineteen and a half years ago.

"I see you are a kind and gentle person. You've had difficulties in your life, but you have been able to triumph over them. God has been with you from the beginning of your conception. You don't yield to Him wholeheartedly now, but you will later. You have more hard days ahead, but they will pass. The end of your life will be better than the beginning. Continue to follow the path you are taking. Soon, you will be directed to a different path, one that is more fulfilling and God-centered." She stopped talking and added more incense to the ashtray. She pushed her chair back and walked over to the Bible on the podium. Her mouth moved as she read Scriptures to herself. She walked over to the tables with the candles and other things. Several of the powders, she mixed together. Her back was to me, so I couldn't clearly see what else she did. After several minutes, she returned to her desk with some things from the table. "I see a house," she continued. "You are having trouble with the financing, but you will get it anyway. Here, take this and sprinkle it in your yard," she said handing me a small, plastic, sandwich bag one-third full of a powder mixture.

"What is this?" I asked, examining the bag.

"It is a cinnamon mixture. Make sure you put it in the back and front yard. Here is an oil." She handed me a vial from across her desk. "Put this on you to make your husband madly in love with you."

I took the oil and placed it beside the sandwich bag. The vial was two inches high with a red and yellow oil combination inside.

"Take these and chew on them." She handed me several small twigs. "These will help change the course of your life."

I took the twigs and held them in my hand. "Madame Lee, what about children? Will I ever have any?"

"Oh, don't worry about children. You will have four, two boys and two girls. You will leave your husband. Eventually, you will get tired of him." She began writing on her notepad. When she finished, she tore the paper off and held it up for me to see. "Here are some initials of men who will play a significant role in your life." She handed me the paper. There were six initials in a vertical column. They were: B.C., L.C., Z.A., H.L., D.J., and R.M. whom I married.

Everything Madame Lee said was right on the money. Everything happened except the second daughter. Something else she said that stuck out in my mind. When she said, "The end of my life will be better than the beginning." Her prophecy of my end agreed with the prophecy of Laura Sims, who prophesied to me at a Women in Christ meeting, almost two years later when Little Carl was six months old.

Laura said, "I see another child. A young girl from out of town will live with you." She started waving her right hand. "I see a room in your house that is unfinished. I see it being finished. You will get a promotion on your job. I see where you will be greatly blessed financially." She ended and went to someone else, a woman in a red and white suit. Everything Laura said came to past except the last part, being blessed financially. Both she and Madame Lee agreed on that point although Madame Lee did not say it directly. She implied it.

It puzzled me then why they disagreed on the number of children I would have. Laura prophesied two children and Madame Lee four. Both were wrong, but in my heart, I felt like Laura was right. God originally was going to bless me with my two sons, as Laura prophesied, but then in '95 when I became uncaged, during a transition in my life, He decided on His own to bless me with Mya, my daughter. He showed me the image of her before she was born, and He showed me an image of me pregnant with her to confirm the first image. The pregnancy was centered on the book, *Uncaged,* that He told me to write in '94. Through my obedience to Him, He gave me Mya, the image and prophetic birth.

CHAPTER TWENTY-ONE

Because of the many changes in my church, which I had attended for seventeen years, I decided to discontinue my fellowship after my surgery. This time in my life was one of complete healing – physically, mentally, and spiritually. I had been dissatisfied with my church for some time. I felt now was the perfect time to make a change.

Since I didn't know much about other churches, I decided to let God direct me. He knew me and what I needed. He knew the right church for me. Of course, I wanted to go where the truth was taught. I wanted to attend a God fearing, Word teaching, Holy Spirit filled, Jesus Christ led church. Any church wouldn't do. I sat at home, not going to any church, waiting on His reply to my prayers for a church home.

Occasionally, Raymond's old pastor friend, who he had known for fifteen years, called the house to speak to Raymond. If I answered the phone, we talked briefly. On a few occasions, he invited me to his church, which met on the Sabbath. Repeatedly, I told Raymond, I wanted to visit his friend's church. I waited week after week for him to take me, but he never did. Finally, the last week in May, his friend, James Ware, called the house again. I answered the phone.

"Hello," I said as I answered the phone in the kitchen while cooking dinner.

"Well, greetings, Sister. How are you today?" Is your honey home? Pastor Ware asked.

I recognized his voice from previous conversations. "I'm fine, thank you. I'm glad you called. I've been trying to get Raymond to bring me to your church, but he won't take me. Give me directions since you're on the line."

"Sure. Take I-285 West and take the Hapeville exit after you pass the Jonesboro exit. Make a right when you get off the interstate. Make another right when you see The House of 10,000 Picture Frames. That will be Blalock St. The church is the second building on the right."

"What is the name of the church, and what time does services start?"

"The church is called, The Holy Temple of the Lord's Church. And we start prayer service at 10:00, Sabbath school at 10:30, and regular service at noon. All services start on time."

"Before I come, I need to ask you a few questions."

"Okay, Sister. What are your questions?"

"I know you worship on Saturday. I do too; otherwise I wouldn't be interested in your church. Do you celebrate Christmas?"

"No. Neither do I celebrate Easter or the other pagan days."

"Oh, that's just what I wanted to hear. I will come to your church this Sabbath."

"Bible Study is tonight at 7:30. Why don't you come to it?"

"I might take you up on that. I know you called to talk to Raymond. Let me get him for you since you've answered all of my questions."

"Listen to me on the radio at 5:30 p.m. on WGUN 1010 AM, Monday through Friday."

"I will. Hold on. I'll get Raymond for you," I said putting the phone down and going into Raymond's office. I didn't want to yell because Mya was asleep.

A few seconds later, Raymond came to the phone, and I finished cooking. As I cooked, I thought of my conversation with Pastor Ware. The more I thought about Bible Study, the more I wanted to go. As soon as Raymond got off the phone, I called Angie, my neighbor, to see if she wanted to go, too. She said she wouldn't be able to go to Bible Study tonight, but she'd love to go to church with me Saturday. I decided to go to church Saturday when Angie could go, too.

Angie and I decided to go to the regular service at noon. At 11:30, I pulled out of my driveway and drove to her house two doors away. She now lived in the same house my ex-classmate, Bobby Freeman and his wife Monique lived in. Angie ran to the car before I blew the horn. I could tell she was just as excited as I was to get to church.

Angie looked like a living doll coming to the car. She was five feet even and weighed 98 pounds. Since she was petite, everything looked good on her. Her long hair that was flipped up on one side and curled under on the other side made her look like one of Charlie's Angels. It also reminded me of my favorite Farrah Fawcett hairstyle. She wore a navy blue suit with matching heels. Angie and her husband were truck drivers. With her size, it was hard for me to imagine her driving an 18-wheeler. She often told me funny things that happened while she was on the road. Last month she stopped driving the truck to start a home care business. I was glad she was home more. It gave us more time to be together.

We arrived at church by 12:10. Church had started. The congregation was singing a song, "Can't Nobody Do Me Like Jesus." We went to the first vacant seats directly across from the door. The church was small. It appeared to seat about 100 people max. The church was three-fourths full and divided into two sections. One section, across from the door, and the other section at the door. There were six red pews. The other seats were light gray chairs with four chairs making a row. The pulpit was surrounded with dark-brown paneling. Red carpet covered the floor.

As we settled in our seats, a woman in front of us stood up and said, "Giving honor to God, who is the head of my life, and Jesus Christ, His Son. To Pastor Ware, Sister Ware, ministers, deacons, and everyone here to make up this assembly. I thank Jesus for my life, health, and strength. For being in my right mind. I thank Him for His goodness and mercy and His abundant love. I thank Him for keeping me another week from all harm and danger. I thank Him for food on my table and clothes on my back and a roof over my head. I thank Him for sanctifying me and giving me His Holy Spirit. All of you who know the words of prayer, pray that I will continue my strength in the Lord." Then she sat down.

Someone else stood up and testified followed by another song. Testimonies and songs were given for another hour, then the Sabbath Creed of The Ten Commandments was read by the congregation in Exodus 20:6-11. *"But showing mercy to thousands, to those who love Me and keep my commandments. You shall not take the name of the Lord your God in vain, for the Lord will not hold him guiltless who takes His name in vain. Remember the Sabbath day, to keep it holy. Six days you shall labor and do all your work, but the seventh day is the Sabbath of the Lord your God. In it you shall do no work: you, nor your son, nor your daughter, nor your male servant, nor your cattle, nor your stranger who is within your gates. For in six days the Lord made the heavens and the earth, the sea, and all that is in them, and rested the seventh day. Therefore the Lord blessed the Sabbath day and hallowed it."*

Following the Sabbath Creed, announcements were given by one of my former church members, Shirley Napier. She and Adam, her husband and my buddy, left my former church months ago. I was delighted to see them again. They sat two rows in front of us. Shirley also introduced Pastor Ware by saying, "Let me introduce to some and present to others, our pastor, James Ware. Would you please stand to your feet," she said as everyone applauded, and she left the podium.

"Praise the Lord! Praise the Lord," Pastor Ware said as he came to the podium. He was a dark-skinned, slender man with small gold-rimmed glasses. He looked to be in his late forties. *"Let us pray,"* he said as he bowed in front of the wooden podium and microphone. *"Father in the name of Jesus. I thank You for another day. Please guard my lips, so that I will say nothing that You will not have me to say. Let me speak only those words which come from You. Speak through me to teach Your people. I ask this in Jesus name. I pray. Amen and Amen,"* he said, lifting his head. "You may be seated," he instructed.

"Amen and Amen! I thank God for the testimonies. You know a lot of churches have cut out testimonies, but I refuse to get rid of them. Often times people get delivered from testimonies. Amen! When you hear what Jesus has done for someone else, you know He can do the same thing for you. I know coming up, testimonies is what got me through a lot of times. That's why I believe in testimonies. Someone testified today that their gas bill miraculously got paid instead of being cutoff. That's how the Jesus that we serve operates. It's time out for shuckin and jivin. It's time to get real! Everyday we need to thank God for what He has done for us. We need to give our bodies as living sacrifices for His plan and purpose in our lives," he said opening his Bible.

"Open your Bibles and turn to Luke 3:3. This Scripture is talking about the works of John the Baptist. How he fitted into the plan God. It says, *And he (John the Baptist) went into all the region around Jordan, preaching the baptism of repentance for the remission of sins.* You see the first step with God is to repent of our sins. John knew that, and that is what he preached. Let's continue. As it is written in the book of the words of Isaiah the prophet, saying: '*The voice of one crying in the wilderness: Prepare the way of the Lord;*' John was called to prepare the way for Jesus. Before Jesus was Moses and the Prophets, but they were all dead. Therefore, God used John, Jesus' cousin, who was also called a prophet in Luke 1:76. He was alive to prepare the way or proclaim the coming of Jesus. God couldn't use the Pharisees, who sat in Moses' seat, because they had perverted the way of God. That's why God says in the next verse, *'Make His paths straight.'* The Scripture is referring to the path of Jesus. Before John the Baptist, the path of Jesus that led to righteousness and eternal life had been perverted or made crooked by false teachings and traditions of men. That's why in verse 5 God says, *'...The crooked places shall be made straight and the rough ways smooth; And all flesh shall see the salvation of God.'* Through Jesus, God opened up salvation to everyone, not just a few select people," he said closing his Bible, reaching for the microphone, leaving the pulpit. Thanks to our Lord and Savior, Jesus Christ, we can be saved! That truly is good news. Salvation for everyone is the gospel or message of Jesus Christ."

Pastor Ware spoke for thirty more minutes. He also called those to the front who needed healing or prayer. Several people were truly hurting. They were first in line. He anointed their foreheads with olive oil then prayed. When he was finished he said, *"Let me pray. Father in the name of Jesus, I thank you for Your Son, Jesus Christ and His wonderful good news of salvation. I pray that You bless the hearing of this message. Let Your words be proclaimed throughout the earth. I pray that You bless those who seek healing and deliverance today. Amen.* He lifted up his head and went back to the pulpit, placing the microphone back in place. Now, Brother Dix and Copeland will take up the offering," he said then sat down in his chair behind the podium.

Two men from the front row stood up and grabbed two small beige trashcans from the side of the podium. The tall, young, dark man said he had the tithes and offering container. The shorter, older man said he had the speaker offering. A heavyset, female usher in the back asked everyone on her right side to stand. Then she asked the left side to stand, which was us. Angie and I stood to give an offering. The two men prayed over the collections after everyone had given.

Pastor Ware came back to the podium and stood over the microphone.

"At this time, I would like to acknowledge our visitors he said adjusting his glasses. I believe Sister Miller is here," he said looking at us. "Which one of you is Sister Miller?"

I stood up.

"Do you have anything to say?" he asked smiling.

"My name is Vanessa Miller. My husband is a good friend of Pastor Ware. This is my neighbor, Angie Welch. I told her I was coming to church today and asked if she wanted to come, too. I have enjoyed the service today and plan to come back again," I said as I sat back down.

"I've know Mrs. Miller's husband, Raymond, for over fifteen years. I met him when he worked at Sears. Ms. Welch do you have anything to say?" Pastor Ware asked.

Angie stood up. "I would like to say, it is good to be here today. I drove a truck up until last month and missed going to church since I was on the road a lot. But I have thoroughly enjoyed myself today. I agree with Vanessa. I will be back," she said as she sat down.

"I drove a truck for 23 years before I was called into the ministry. My truck is behind the building," Pastor Ware said smiling.

Pastor Ware went to two other people before church dismissed. After church, several people came up to us to talk. Angie discovered there were two other truck drivers in our midst besides Pastor Ware. I talked briefly with Shirley and Adam. They told me they found the church by listening to Pastor Ware on the radio and had been attending for six months. Angie and I mixed and mingled for another thirty minutes before leaving. I spoke a few minutes with Pastor Ware. Angie and I were excited when we left. We felt like we had found a new church home. Amen.

CHAPTER TWENTY-TWO

Angie and I went to Bible Study the following Tuesday. We loved it as much as Sabbath service. We were glad we had found a church home. We enjoyed reading our Bibles at home, but it didn't replace fellowshipping with other believers. Three weeks later, we joined the church. A month later, Angie was baptized.

I didn't feel a need for a third baptism. My first baptism was twenty-seven years ago when I was seventeen. I was young then and didn't fully understand what I was doing. I had not repented of my sins and wrongdoings. Therefore, my baptism was in vain. I wasn't transformed on the inside. I was only a teenager who got wet and thought I was doing the right thing.

My second baptism was ten years later when I was a grown woman. The church I just left baptized me. Although I did wrong after my second baptism, my heart was right towards God. I understood the purpose of baptism; it is an outward sign that inwardly I have accepted Jesus Christ as my Lord and Savior. Jesus now rules my life. Yes, I might stumble and fall, but I repent of my wrongdoings and pray that God will cleanse me with the blood of Jesus to right my wrongs.

Baptism is a watery grave where our whole bodies are immersed. We have buried the old person and come up a new creation in Jesus Christ. It is a burial of our sinful self. The new wet person's life belongs to God, the Father, Jesus, the Son, and the Holy Spirit, which is the Comforter and Teacher, who will lead us into all truths. Through baptism, The Holy Spirit is given to dwell within us to keep us clean in order for Jesus to live His life in us.

Briefly, the Scripture explains baptism in Ephesians 4-6, "*There is one body and one Spirit, just as you were called in one hope of your calling; one Lord, one faith, one baptism; one God and Father of all, who is above all, and through all, and in you all.* And in Colossians 2:11-13, "*In Him (Jesus) you were also circumcised with the circumcision made without hands, by putting off the body of the sins of the flesh, by the circumcision of Christ, buried with Him in baptism, in which you also were raised with Him through faith in the working of God, who raised Him from the dead. And you, being dead in your trespasses and uncircumcision of your flesh, He has made alive together with Him, having forgiven you all trespasses."*

Angie said she felt like a new person when I saw her again, dried and dressed. She said she had done a lot of wrong in the past, and today, she could truly start her life anew, being fully repentant and forgiven by God. We hugged then ate with other newly baptized and old church members. Angie's face glowed. She was the happiest I had ever seen her before. On the way home, Angie couldn't wait to get home to tell her husband the good news.

Soon after I returned home, Paula Bowen, my publisher, called to tell me she was test marketing *Uncaged* in Savannah and Augusta, Georgia. I asked if she had any copies for me since I was out. She said she sent 500 copies to each location. She didn't have any herself, but would give me some as soon as the test was over, which should take two months.

I was delighted to hear from Paula. I was also glad to hear *Uncaged* was published again and back into the market. I knew book signings would soon follow. I felt the timing was perfect because Mya was old enough for me to leave her sometimes to travel. I had not had a book signing since November of '98, shortly before Mya was born.

The drive home from church put Mya to sleep. I put her in her bed after Paula called. It was hard to believe she would be two years old in four months. Of course, she was walking and getting into everything all day long. I spent most of my days cleaning up her numerous messes and protecting her from herself. She was a fearless child who wasn't afraid of anything or anyone. A person's size or age did not stop her from retaliating if she was wronged or stop her from doing something she wanted to do. Her size, less than 21 pounds, and a size 18 months clothes contributed to her quickness for getting into things. During the day, I often forgot she was my miracle from God. I was too busy trying to keep my sanity.

Because of my time restraints with having a small child, I had not written much since I completed *The Bearer of the Sign* before Mya was born. I was using this time to enjoy my daughter, my new husband, my family and my life. I told myself, I didn't have to stay busy. I could relax and take it easy for a change. No, I didn't have to cram everything into every day. Therefore, I decided to take a break from writing. I was living on easy street by only working two days a week. The more I traveled the low road instead of the high road, the more I enjoyed the journey.

Not having any books and book signing made a difference, too. I was an author with no work. I paid Paula last July to publish *Uncaged*. I had no idea it would take her so long to re-publish my book. But being the person that I am, I learned a lot from both Paula and Lisa. I learned I could do it myself. I had been reading a lot during this down time. I knew now that I could publish my works and the works of others. God helped me to turn my lemons into lemonade by starting my own company, The Literary Connection. T.L.C.'s goal is to facilitate other writers as well as edit, evaluate, and publish manuscripts. I also offer a ten lesson creative writing course.

During a conversation with Pastor Ware, I told him about my business. He told me he had a book he was writing and information he wanted in a series of booklets for his ministry, Believers Walking in the Way of Righteousness. I told him I would be glad to publish his material for him. He felt like I was God sent, and I did, too.

The following week, Pastor Ware brought me his writings for the first booklet series. Some was handwritten on a yellow legal pad. Some was written on individual sheets of paper. I took his work home, edited, and typed it out on my word processor. I gave him the typed sheets to review before I passed it on to my typesetter. I called Tosh Fomby, my cover person, to create a design. I drew out what I thought was appropriate. But Tosh was so talented the final cover was awesome. When I saw it, I was breathless. She had the title and Pastor Ware's name in bold, yellow letters on a black background. In between the title and his name was a lighted road with yellow lines, one in the center and two on the sides. Paths coming off the lighted road, on the black background, written in red letters were: Stealing, Deception, Unholiness, Lying, Sinning, and Addiction. For $100 I had thirty copies made, plus the typesetting and the cover. Pastor Ware loved the cover and the booklet. He was now ready to start his Believers Walking in the Way of Righteousness Ministry. I delivered his booklets on October 18. We were very pleased with the results.

Five days later, Paula came by the house and brought me 16 copies of the new *Uncaged*. It had a yellow background with a mixed female model that had a sensual expression on her face. She had on a dark-green, sleeveless, vested pantsuit. It was an improvement over the first cover of a black woman coming out of a cage with an orange background. Paula said she wanted my book appealing to all races.

Having books again, inspired me to write. I started back writing on my third book and last of this series, *The Image: A Prophetic Birth* on November 1, 2000. I had written nine chapters.

Life was great! I had books, my family, and my business running. I even had help around the house and with the kids because Brandi, Raymond's seventeen year old daughter moved in with us this summer. Having her in the house made a difference. Raymond Jr. and Francine loved Brandi being with them again. They had all lived together before Brandi lived with her mother six years ago. I could tell Raymond loved having Brandi around, too. It was obvious he missed her.

Since Brandi had her own church, I didn't bother her about going to mine. She went on Sundays to her mother's church. On Saturday, November 11, however, Brandi decided she wanted to go to church with us (Raymond always stayed at home). Angie stopped attending months ago, therefore, I had enough room in my car for all of us. During service, Brandi testified and sang a song. She loved singing. The congregation joined in and gave her a warm greeting. Shirley Napier announced earlier that the choir was having a concert that evening at 7 p.m. We planned to come back.

After church, we went home, so we could eat then return to church. Around 6:30, when we were planning on leaving the house, Mya went to sleep. While she slept, I decided to write on *The Image*. Her nap times were usually when I wrote anyway. It was the only time I could concentrate. Fifteen minutes into my writing secession, the telephone rang. I answered the phone.

"Hello."

"What are you doing?" a male voice asked.

"Writing," I replied, thinking it was Pop, my sister's husband wanting me to keep their kids.

"What are you writing?" he asked.

When he asked the question, I knew it wasn't Pop although they sounded alike. I answered anyway. "I'm working on my manuscript."

"What do you do?" he asked excited.

"I'm an author. I write books."

"That's incredible! I'm a movie producer."

"You're kidding."

"No, it's true. My name is Ronald Butler. My company is R. B. Productions. Tell me about your work?"

"Who were you calling?"

"That's not important. I want to know more about you."

"Okay. My name is Deeva Denez. When you called, I was working on my third book. It's called *The Image: A Prophetic Birth*. My first book, which is published, is called *Uncaged*. My second book, which is written but not published, is called *The Bearer of the Sign*. All of my books are about my life."

"That's interesting."

"Tell me more about you and your company."

"Certainly. I helped produce the movie *Remember the Titan* with Denzel Washington. I just finished a movie about Dr. Martin Luther King. It will be featured next year. I also do plays. Tell me more about your books. Maybe, I can turn them into a movie or a play. That is my business."

"Before I wrote a word, God told me *Uncaged*, my first book, will be a movie. He never said anything about a play."

"I think starting out with a play would be best. And depending on its outcome I can turn it into a movie. Now, tell me about your book?"

"*Uncaged* covers the first thirty eight years of my life. It begins shortly after my conception when my parents wanted to abort me. They were young and poor, a bad combination. Well, as you can see, the Grace of God spared my life. The rest of the book tells of my unhappy life at home followed by a roller coaster twenty-year marriage, the end of which was filled with depression and mental abuse. The last year of my marriage, however, I was delivered or uncaged by forgiving both my father and my ex-husband for mistreating me over the years."

"Listen, I would love to read your book and see what I can do with it. Give me your address, and let me call a cab on three-way, so I can get a copy."

"You would do that?"

"Yes. Give me your address, so I can call the cab."

"Where is your business located?" I asked, skeptical.

"My office is at 6275 Memorial Drive. Do you have pen and paper?"

"Yes."

"Good. My cell phone number is 404-555-9087. My office number is 404-555-3756. If you don't want me to call a cab tonight, I will be in my office tomorrow from 2-6. You're welcomed to bring your book then."

"I'm going out of town tomorrow. I won't be able to come by."

"Do you want to call my secretary next week and make an appointment? It's up to you."

"You can call the cab," I replied.

"Okay, what is your address?"

"8956 Lockheart Drive, Decatur?"

"What's your phone number?"

"404-555-9663."

"Deeva, I'm going to call the cab right now. You can listen." He dialed and someone answered.

"Atlanta Cab," said a deep baritone voice.

"I need a cab to pick up a package," Ronald said as I listened.

"I'm sorry, but we don't have any cabs available at this time."

"Thank you," Ronald said as he hung up. "Deeva, are you still there?"

"Yes."

"I'll call another cab company. It's something about you that I want to get my hands on your book." He dialed another number.

"Blue Dot Cab. How may I help you?" said a friendly female voice.

"I need a cab," Ronald responded.

"I'm sorry, sir, but we don't have any cabs at the moment. You can call back in thirty minutes or an hour."

"Never mind." Ronald said before clicking the cab company off. "Deeva, I don't know what's going on, but these cab companies are crazy! I really want your book. I tell you what. Since it's late and I can't get a cab tonight, I'll send someone by your house tomorrow to get your book. If that's all right with you?"

"I'll leave it in the mailbox. Give me your zip code, so I can mail it in case nobody comes."

"30032. Look, Deeva, I really do look forward to doing business with you. You have my numbers and address. And I have yours."

"Yes. I will make sure you get a copy of my book, one way or another."

"Okay, Deeva, I will talk to you later. I feel good about calling you tonight."

"I do, too. Goodbye," I said as he hung up the phone. As I put the phone on its cradle, a thousand thoughts filled my mind. It was no coincidence that Ronald dialed my number, a "wrong" number. God had to be behind this. There were too many factors involved. First, I answered the phone. The kids could have easily answered it. Secondly, I was here to answer the phone. If Mya had not fallen asleep, I would have been on my way to church. Thirdly, I was writing. I could have been reading, cooking or who knows what. Fourthly, I have a book in my possession to give Ronald. I had just received 16 copies three weeks ago. Lastly, he sounded genuinely interested in my work.

All I could think of for the rest of the night was: God works in mysterious ways and this was one of them.

CHAPTER TWENTY-THREE

Before I went to Dublin the next day, I left a copy of *Uncaged* in a brown envelope inside the mailbox. I wasn't sure if Ronald would send someone or not. But just in case, I wanted my book to be available. I told myself if it was still inside the mailbox when I returned, I would mail it Monday.

On the way to Dublin and on the way back, I wondered if Ronald would pick up my book. It was hard for me to concentrate on anything else the whole day. Besides the book, I kept reliving the conversation with Ronald. It sounded too good to be true. I prayed that he was the answer to make *Uncaged* a movie.

To my disappointment, my book was still in the mailbox when I returned home at 8 o'clock that evening. I retrieved it then went inside. I looked up Ronald's address and typed it on the envelope along with my return address. I didn't know what happened today, and it was too late to call the office to find out. Whatever happened, I was not going to let that stop me from getting my book into Ronald's hands.

First thing Monday morning, I mailed *Uncaged* off. I still couldn't believe the conversation Saturday night. All week long, it stayed with me. Now, I couldn't wait to hear from Ronald again.

Saturday, I told Pastor Ware about Ronald and our conversation. He told me to pray about it, and check him out by calling the Better Business Bureau. He had dealings with people before who had offices and everything, and they turned out to be crooks. I took his advice and called the BBB Monday morning. I found out R. B. Productions had been in business since 1998 with no complaints. After the called, I felt good about Ronald and R. B. Productions.

Two weeks passed, and I had not heard from Ronald, so I called his office on Monday, November 27. He said he had gotten my book and loved it, and he wanted us to do business. We made and appointment for Friday, December 1, at 11 a.m..

At first, I got lost trying to find his office in the complex. Since I didn't see his building number A, I decided to park the car and walk. I went up the first set of steps that matched the number he gave me. The office suites on my side were from C-E. I figured A was close by.

My walk took me to the side of the building where I spotted more suites. After passing two doors, I saw suite A. On its door was written R. B. Productions on a black sign with white letters. A large glass window with vertical blinds was next to the door. Nervously, I rang the bell.

The door opened a few seconds later. A young, medium brown, heavyset female dressed in black pants and a white shirt was on the other side. She looked at me with a blank expression.

"My name is Deeva Denez. I have an 11 o'clock appointment with Ronald Butler," I said as she opened the door.

She smiled. "Come in. Have a seat. Ronald is in a meeting. He will be with you soon," she said closing the door.

I stepped inside. There were two baby-blue fabric seats across from the door. A water cooler was two feet from one of the chairs. A dark-brown table was on my right with an open book on it. Several plaques were above the table. A desk with a computer and telephone was to the left of the door. The person who opened the door sat behind the desk. The phone rang as I sat down. She answered it. A small table separated the two chairs. A photo album rested on it. I opened it up to find pictures and a brochure of a play called "The Lord Answered My Prayer". While looking through the album, a door opened next to the water cooler and two tall, thin young females came out with a middle aged dark-skinned man. He walked them to the door. As it closed, he smiled at me.

"That's Deeva Denez," the female said as she hung up the phone, and the door closed.

"Deeva! It's nice to meet you. I'm Ronald Butler," he said walking towards me. "Did you sign in?"

"No. I didn't know I was supposed to sign in," I said getting up closing the album.

"Please sign in," he said putting his hands on the book.

I walked to the book and signed my name.

"Good," he said still smiling. "Come into my office. Veronica, hold my calls."

We walked to the opened door. "Have a seat, Deeva," Ronald instructed as he closed the door.

His office had two brown leather high-back chairs facing a brown desk with a computer on it. Several pictures lined his wall. A long table was across from the door and next to the second chair. It had several elephants on it of various sizes and photographs of himself with other people. I sat in the first chair. Ronald went to his desk and sat down.

"I'm glad we finally got a chance to meet," Ronald said sitting back in his chair.

"Me, too."

"Look, Deeva. I'm real excited about working with you. I passed your book around to several people, and they all had good things to say. I get my excitement from hearing them. They are young people, too. I get junk all the time, like these two pieces of shit," he said throwing a manuscript on the floor. "You won't believe some of the stuff that comes across my desk. That's why I get excited when I get my hands on something good," he said smiling, sitting up. "I want to take your book to another level. First, it needs to be changed into a play format. Renae Hill is just the person you need. Her fee is $2500. Once we have a script, I can screen actors to perform. Today is December 1st. I will give Renae until January 14th to complete her part."

Can we make it January 16th? My anniversary is on the 15^{th,} and I plan to be out of town on the 14th."

"Certainly. Then we can have your play the end of February. Let me see my calendar," he said looking at a calendar on his desk. "How does February 23, 24 and 25 sound. That's a Friday, Saturday, and Sunday."

"That sounds good to me. Are you sure you can produce a play in such a short time?"

"Trust me. Your play is top priority. Let me call Renae to see if she can convert it by her deadline," he said picking up the phone, dialing. "Hello, Renae. I have Deeva Denez in my office. How much will you charge her to convert her book to a play, $2,500? Okay, that's what I told her. I need it ready by January 16. Can you have it ready by then? Fine!" He said hanging up the phone. "Deeva, she said her fee is $2,500. How soon can you have it?"

"Today is Friday. I will need until Wednesday."

"Good. You can come back to the office Wednesday and pay Renae, so we can get this show on the road. I have been in this business for a long time. I know your play will be a sell out!" he said reaching for his calculator. "Look, you can make a lot of money with your play. Don't worry about the $2,500. That's peanuts compared to what you can make. What I want to do is take it to The 14th Street Playhouse. Then, depending on its success, I want to take it to different cities and to The Fox. Do you know how much money you can make if it goes to The Fox?"

"No."

"Let me show you something," he said punching numbers onto the calculator. First, let me show you how much you can make at The 14th Street Playhouse. It holds 400 seats. The tickets would sell for $18. There will be 5 shows: one Friday, two Saturday, and two Sunday. That's 400 times $18 equals $7,200 per show times five shows equals $36,000. Since this will be your play, you will get 77 percent and R. B. Productions will get 23 percent. Let's see. You will get 77% of $36,000 equals $27,720. How does that sound to you?" he asked sitting back, smiling.

"It sounds good. Who pays for the cast?"

"I do. Now, if we take it to the Fox, we're talking about a gross income of close to a million dollars. Do you see why I am so excited about your play? We're on to something big. You've heard of *Beauty Shop*?"

"Yes."

"I helped produce it. It has grossed over several million dollars. *Uncaged* can be the next *Beauty Shop*." All I need you to do is pay $1,776 for advertising, and I will pay for booking The 14th Street Playhouse."

"How soon will you need your money?"

You can pay me on January 16, after your book is converted. That is when our business starts. I will have a contract drawn up by then. Everything will be in writing. What time did you want to meet with Renae, Wednesday?"

"Eleven o'clock is fine."

"Okay, Deeva. I will see you next Wednesday at eleven," he said getting up walking to the door. I want to take your picture before you leave, so I can have it with your file. Step outside. I want to take your picture by the door," he said walking me to the table by the book. He picked up an instant camera from his desk. I posed, and he took my picture. Seconds later, I was out the door, walking to my car. As I walked the numbers kept churning through my head. I liked the idea of my book being a play. I also liked the idea of having more money than I'd ever had in my life!

On the way home, I kept rehashing Ronald's words and the numbers on his calculator. The concept of my book being turned into a play was mind-boggling, to say the least. I thought for once in my life, I could have a nice nest egg put away, be debt free, and give to love ones and friends like I have wanted to do in the past, but never had the means to do. Yes, the play was great! It could change my life forever, I thought. Maybe, this was God's way of turning *Uncaged* into a movie.

When I got home, I made the necessary phone calls to have the money to give to Renae by next Wednesday. I was so excited! I couldn't believe what was happening. I also couldn't quite phantom *Uncaged* as a play. I could visualize it as a movie, but a play was an altogether different animal. The more I thought about it, the more I couldn't wait for Wednesday to arrive to meet Renae.

Promptly at 11 o'clock, I was knocking on R. B. Productions' door. Veronica greeted me while Ronald was waiting by his door.

"Come on in, Deeva!" Ronald said as I crossed the threshold. "Renae is in my office waiting on you."

"Do I need to sign in first?" I asked not sure what to do.

"No. Come on in my office. We have to get this show on the road."

I quickly walked past Veronica and went to Ronald's office. A young dark-skinned woman with short black hair was sitting in the second chair. As I entered the room, Ronald closed the door.

"Have a seat, Deeva," Ronald said walking to his desk.

I sat down, resting my coat and purse.

"Deeva, this is Renae. Renae, Deeva Denez," he said introducing us.

"It's nice to meet you," we both said.

"Deeva, Renae has read your book. She is ready to get started. Did you bring the money?"

"Yes," I said reaching for my purse.

"Good. I will let the two of you handle your business first. Deeva, what you and Renae do has nothing to do with me. Our business comes later," he said opening his top desk drawer. "I have a receipt book for your records," he said handing it to Renae.

I gave her the check, and she gave me a receipt.

"Now, that that's settled, let's get started," Ronald said, sitting up in his chair. "Renae, I have a deadline to meet. I am giving you until

January 16th, to give me a script of Deeva's play, so I can do a casting call and produce her play by the end of February. Can you do it?" he demanded.

"Yes. Since I have already read the book, I have ideas in my mind. I feel like that's enough time for me to complete my part."

"I want you two to exchange phone numbers, so if any questions come up, you can easily be reached. Make sure you include cell phones. Do that right now!"

We wrote down our numbers and gave them to each other.

"Deeva, the last play Renae wrote grossed two million dollars. Your play is in good hands. Renae is damn good! That's why she's working for me. I have an outstanding crew. You'll see. I don't want to take up too much time today. Renae needs to get to work. Renae, do you have anything you want to say to Deeva?"

"Yes. Deeva, I just want to say, I love your book. It has great potential. While I was reading it a lot of ideas came to my mind. I want us to work closely. I will call you if I need your input on something," she said facing me.

When she turned, I saw that she had one bad eye. It was gray as if she could not see out of it. The other eye was dark-brown. I liked Renae. We had good vibes together. "I'll do whatever you need me to do. We probably need to get together before the January 16th deadline, so I will have a chance to go over the play with you. Call me when you're done."

"I will," she said smiling.

"Okay, now that that's settled. Renae, you can leave. You have work to do. I want to talk to Deeva for a few minutes."

Renae left quickly. I saw that she was short and stocky.

"Deeva, I travel all over the world. When I called you the first time, I had just gotten back from Africa. I had prayed that God would send me something big for my company, and He did through you. Your play will be a success! With the talent that Renae has, your play will be another multi-million-dollar baby that's been born," Ronald, said as he leaned back in his chair, put his hands behind his head and smiled.

CHAPTER TWENTY-FOUR

Renae called me several times in the subsequent weeks to discuss the play. She told me it would be ready, Friday, January 5. We planned to meet in the office at 1 p.m.. She wanted my approval before she presented it to Ronald, who was only interested in the finished product, not the draft.

As I drove to the office, I was anxious to see the script Renae had written. I still couldn't imagine *Uncaged* being a play. How could she take the first thirty-eight years of my life, which took me a year and a half to write, and turn it into a play format? The thought of something I wrote being acted out with real people to portray the actual people's lives that I wrote about was beyond my wildest dreams.

Renae was waiting on me as I entered the office. She was alone. Both Veronica and Ronald were not there. Renae led me to her office down a small corridor behind Veronica's desk. Renae explained how she shared an office with Paul, the photographer, who was also absent. Paul's office space was behind Renae's desk. They each had a desk and chair. Renae's desk had a computer and printer on it. Paul's desk had pictures everywhere – in baskets, on the wall, in boxes, and in envelopes. They were neatly arranged, which gave his desk an organized appearance.

Renae pointed to the chair in front of the printer for me to sit in. She handed me a stack of papers as she turned her computer on. I glanced at the first page. It read:

Uncaged

Plot – Vanessa Lewis got married for all the wrong reasons. He's handsome, supportive, seems understanding, and he is a great lover. But, he's the wrong man! Her Mr. Right, the man she thought wanted her too, is having an affair with her best friend. Talk about bad timing. Well, so much for that fairytale... and all the other stories about living happily ever after.

Character Bio

Vanessa – Vanessa is a Christian woman somewhere between the ages of 25-30. She works in a corporate office. She is attractive and must be able to sing!

Carl – Carl is a very manipulative and verbally abusive man. He's between the ages of 28-30. He's irresponsible but does have a humorous side.

Cynthia – Cynthia is an attractive, flirtatious backstabber. She works with Vanessa. She maintains to be a friend of Vanessa, but we later find out she's a foe. Cynthia is 25-30.

"You can read the script while I read it to you from my screen," Renae said as her screen matched my first page.

"Okay," I said, sitting back, getting relaxed, holding the papers, so I could get a good view of both the papers and the screen.

"Deeva, before we begin, let me explain what I have done. Your play is two and a half hours long. Having such a short time frame to work with, I couldn't write everything that happened to you in your book. However, I tried to keep the main points. And since the play will be held soon, I wrote your sons out of the play. I didn't want to have to deal with children for the rehearsals. You must also understand that you are limited in what you can do on the stage. For instance, Carl smokes in the book, but he can't do that on stage. I have substituted drinking a beer instead."

"I see," I said, trying to let her words sink in.

"Another thing. You have three generations in your book. I can't have all those characters on stage, so I cut Big Mama, Pop, your mom and dad out of the beginning. Instead, I bring out the point about your parents wanting to abort you with you and Carl. I have expanded Cynthia's role, so you won't be on stage alone, and I'm still using the point of how she double-crossed you."

"I see as part of Cynthia's bio on the first page that she works with me. That's not in the book."

"That's right, Deeva. There are more things about Cynthia that's not in the book that I bring out as well."

"Do you still have Zakee and Bryson in the play?"

"Yes. If you would look at the second page, you will see the list of other characters."

I quickly looked at the second page. It read:

Zakee – Zakee is a Muslim guy. He is a friend to Vanessa. Zakee speaks life into Vanessa. His words hit harder than a bag of bricks. Zakee is somewhere between the ages of 35-40.

Bryson – Bryson is a repairman. He's a smooth operator. He's a confidant to Vanessa. Bryson is 30-35 years old.

Xavier – Xavier is Vanessa's father. He is an older man. He's between the ages of 50-55. Xavier has a warm and forgiving character. He must be able to sing.

Betty – Betty is Vanessa's mother. She is between the ages of 50-55. She is a loving and wholesome mother. She must be able to sing.

Madame Lee – Madame Lee is a psychic. She speaks with a Jamaican accent. She's a very spiritual woman. She is between the ages of 35-45.

"So these are the characters?" I asked, pleased.

"Yes. They are all you need. The play has eleven scenes, five are in the first half and six in the second."

"How does it end?" I asked curiously.

"Aren't you interested in how it begins?" Renae asked staring at me with her good eye.

"Not as much as how it ends. I'm just curious how you wrote Bryson's part."

"You'll have to wait and see. I don't want to spoil the ending by telling you now. Let's get started with the beginning, so we can get to the end."

"Okay," I said as she read the play.

"Act One. Scene One. Vanessa is sitting on the couch talking on the phone. When there's a knock at the door. Deeva, can you guess who is at the door?" Renae asked talking to me, but still looking at the screen.

"No, who?"

"Cynthia."

"Why is Cynthia knocking at my door?" I asked puzzled.

"Cynthia is distraught and she needs your help."

"What? I can't wait to hear what happens. Read!" I commanded, wanting to hear more.

"Vanessa says, "Okay honey, someone's knocking. I'll see you when you get home. [She hangs up the phone and walks to the door] [Another knock] Okay, I'm coming! [She opens the door] What brings you here? You're usually with John at this time of day.""

151

"John! You have Cynthia and John together?" I exclaimed, cutting her off.

"That's right."

"Girl, I can't wait to hear the rest. I'm going to put my papers down and let you read to me. I know this is going to be good," I said, putting my script on my lap and relaxing while Renae read the rest of the play. We laughed most of the time because Renae had a canny sense of humor. I made a few changes along the way. But overall, I felt like the play was very entertaining and well written. I liked how she brought out the main points. It also seemed as if she emphasized minor things, such as Cynthia's role, and made them major while eliminating major roles such as Little Carl and Carlos, my sons. I especially liked how she wrote Mom and Dad's parts. They really brought out the main point of *Uncaged*, which is forgiveness. We must forgive those who hurt us, so we can be freed or uncaged from the mental and emotional bondage of unforgiveness. Yes, I felt like Renae and R. B. Productions were on to something.

After Renae finished reading the entire play, I was thoroughly entertained as well as pleased with the results. She and I had a lot of good laughs. I loved Renae's sense of humor, and the way she had the characters interacting. I liked Zakee's role although it was different from the book. I thought she brought out the point well about how much he meant to me. Because of him, I know one person CAN make a difference in another person's life. Also, because of him, I want to impact as many lives as I can. I know I can make a difference, too.

I told her to re-write Bryson's part because although it was small in the book, he played a big role in the second book, *The Bearer of the Sign*. He had to end the play in such a way to leave the audience wondering who I would end up with – either Zakee or Bryson. I loved to leave my audience hanging, wondering and wanting more.

She said she would make all the changes I requested and suggested we meet the following Friday at 1 p.m. to discuss them before the January 16, deadline. I agreed with Renae. Friday would be fine to meet again. Neither one of us wanted to delay Ronald.

The following Friday, I met with Renae. There were more changes to make – minor changes, nothing major. She said she could have them corrected by Tuesday. I was glad because although they were minor, they added to the cohesiveness of the book and play. One change was to make sure Vanessa prayed about a sign to identify the next man in her life. That prayer was very important because it introduced the second book. I wanted Renae to work the image of either the baby or me being pregnant, but she couldn't figure how to do it on stage and didn't think it would be relevant to the play. She reminded me again about the time restraints. It was then I saw clearly that the play was a different animal. An animal that I didn't know much about. I would stick to writing books, an animal I recognized.

Our session lasted two hours. I wanted to be sure everything was to my satisfaction for Ronald on Tuesday, and it was. Renae had four days to make her revisions. She assured me that she would have the play ready on time.

I went home confident that Renae would keep her word. It was no longer my concern, but hers. I focused my attention instead on my third wedding anniversary, which was three days away. I wanted to plan something for Raymond. He deserved the best. Our relationship had really blossomed over the last few months. It was on a higher level.

The more I lived with Raymond, the more I realized we were just alike. We both were studious. We spent most of our time either reading or writing. We were both business minded. I enjoyed being an author and having my own business, The Literary Connection. He stayed in his office, across from our bedroom, most of his waking hours working on his business. Actually, he incorporated his business last July, but with his work schedule he was unable to fully implement it. Therefore, he had given his two weeks notice to leave Grady's Security Department to finally work his own business, Raymond E. Miller Asset Management, Inc. His last day at Grady Hospital would be Friday, January 26. Afterwards, he would be free to do all the things he had been planning to do with his business for over five years.

Raymond was the type of man that I fully respected and could submit to. He was very level headed. He called himself a realist. I am an optimist. Sometimes we didn't see eye-to-eye, but it didn't cause any problems in our relationship because we respected the other's opinion. Neither one of us voted, which eliminated any upheavals during elections. Because of my Christian belief of being under God's government, I have chosen not to participate in man's government. Sure, man's government governs me, but I don't have to endorse it.

Let me give you a few Scriptures to shed some light on this point. When God took the children of Israel from Egypt, He ruled over them through Moses. Later judges were appointed to keep them on the right path. They were chosen by God to save the people from foreign oppressors. They were also military leaders with both legislation and executive authority. In Judges 21:25 God says, *"In those days there was no king in Israel; everyone did what was right in his own eyes."* When you are a born again, spirit filled Christian; God and His ways, which are higher than man's ways, govern you. God's ways will allow you to keep every law of man if they do not conflict.

Other Scriptures are: I Samuel 8:1-7, *"Now it came to pass when Samuel was old that he made his sons judges over Israel. The name of his firstborn was Joel, and the name of his second, Abijah; they were judges in Beersheba. But his sons did not walk in his ways; they turned aside after dishonest gain, took bribes, and perverted justice. Then all the elders of Israel gathered together and came to Samuel at Ramah, and said to him, 'Look, you are old, and your sons do not walk in your ways. Now make us a king to judge us like all the nations.' But this displeased Samuel when they said, 'Give us a king to judge us.' So Samuel prayed to the Lord. And the Lord said to Samuel, 'Heed the voice of the people in all they say to you; for they have not rejected you, but they have rejected Me, that I should not reign over them."* Man's government today is the same as having a king back then. I choose to let Jesus reign over me.

Our anniversary, January 15, finally arrived. Beverly, my sister, kept the kids while Raymond and I went out to eat. Since we usually went to either Red Lobster or Steak and Ale, we decided to try something new – Houston's. I had been to Houston's several times, but not with Raymond. I loved their food and atmosphere. After a thirty-five minute wait, we were seated at our table. He gingerly held my hands as we scoured the menu.

"Everything looks so good!" I said as I continued to read the menu. "Have you decided what you want to eat?"

"The steak sounds good," he said closing the menu, looking at me smiling.

"I think I'll have the barbecue chicken with slaw," I said closing my menu, too. "I can't wait to get the cheese toast. It's delicious! It's the best part of the meal," I said looking into his eyes.

"Being with you is the best part of the meal to me," he stated holding my hands tighter.

"I have something to read to you," I said reaching for my purse. "I was going to wait until after dinner, but I think this is the right time while we wait to order our food." Raymond smiled more, waiting to see what I was up to. I pulled out a copy of *Uncaged*.

"What are you doing?"

"I am going to read you something from my book that I think is fitting for us," I said opening the book, turning the pages. "Relax, dear. Listen to this. I read the first two paragraphs of Chapter Twenty-Eight, 'Reaching our twentieth anniversary gave me an unsurpassing thrill. However, after the candles were blown out and the champagne was gone, the excitement disappeared like the smoke and the fizz. Another photograph, of a once joyous occasion, was the only permanent reminder of the event.

I asked myself, the next night, would we be together in '96 to put another candle on the cake? My answer was, only if our cake of marriage is frosted with love, decorated with roses of happiness, joy, respect, balanced financial support, and hope for a better tomorrow. It must have candles of communication that illuminate light over our aspirations and dreams. Their light must increase in time and never wean. Then and only then will this marriage survive another year.' I said closing the book. I feel like our marriage has all the ingredients to survive another year and many more to come. It is the cake of marriage I just read."

Raymond smiled. "I am glad you think so. You make me very happy, Mrs. Miller," he said grabbing my hands again.

"Good. I hope it will always be that way."

"Me, too. Ahhh. Here's the waitress now. I'm starved," he said as he gave her our order.

CHAPTER TWENTY-FIVE

Raymond and I enjoyed each other as much as we enjoyed the meal. He kept telling me how much he loved me, and how much I meant to him. I kept telling him the same. Raymond made me happy now although our marriage was a little rocky at first. The major difference was his disposition, which had changed for the better. I was wife number three, which made my position even harder because I was constantly judged by what wives number one and two had done. I was different from them, but to him I was just another woman who did the same things.

I noticed toward the middle of our second year, Raymond finally realized I was different. I was not like his other wives. Every woman was not the same. Some women could be trusted and faithful. It was good I understood his dilemma. I was determined to be a part of the solution and not create another problem.

Raymond turned out to be everything I wanted in a man. I even noticed, I had stopped thinking of Douglas because I was now truly in love with my husband. I'm sure Raymond felt the difference. Raymond was strong, yet sensitive. I am insensitive. Sometimes my insensitivity clashed with his sensitivity, but I had learned through Carl, who was also a sensitive man, how to handle myself. Most of the times just keeping quiet was all I had to do to keep the peace. Raymond was not argumentative. He kept quiet like me, but thoughts filled my head of what to say, of which I dismissed. I learned a long time ago not to say anything that I would want to say I'm sorry for later.

Raymond was an excellent provider. That is where he differed from Carl, the most. The more I lived with Raymond, a real man, the more I loved the difference. No longer was I concerned about being the breadwinner. That was my husband's role. I was now the homemaker, the mother, the wife that I had always wanted to be.

That night, I prayed that we would always be together and that our union would be happy, no matter what happened in our lives. He was my soul mate. I felt it with all my being. I knew it with all my heart.

The next day, I went to R. B. Productions. I arrived at one o'clock sharp. I was anxious to meet with Ronald again. I wanted to get this show on the road. Veronica let me in. She informed me Ronald was in a meeting. I sat in the chair by his door.

Ten minutes later, Ronald's door opened. He came out with an older man and a young girl. I heard from where I was sitting that the girl wanted to model, and the man was her father. The father handled the business transactions. They looked happy as they left. I guess Ronald gave them a good deal.

"Deeva, come on in," Ronald motioned as the pair left.

I quickly stood up and followed him into his office. He had on blue jeans, white shirt and a blue and white tie. His jet-black skin contrasted with his shirt. I sat in the first chair, and he sat at his desk.

"Did you bring the money?" he asked as I took off my coat.

"Yes," I replied, reaching for my purse.

"Good. Let's get the money out of the way first, then we can begin."

I put the money, $1,776, on the table. He counted it.

"Here's your receipt," he said writing me one in his receipt book. "Here are two copies of our contract. You sign both, and I will sign both. We will each keep a copy. As you can see, I have everything in writing. Your money will be used for advertising. I will be responsible for securing The 14th Street Playhouse. I will do that today since you have given your money and signed the contract. We can start casting this weekend. I want you to take part in the selections. Are you available this weekend?"

"I go to church on Saturdays. I'm available after church around four o'clock."

"I will video the whole thing, so you won't miss anything. I don't know what time I will start, I definitely want your input since this is your production."

"Do you have the finished script?" I asked, sitting back in my chair.

"No. Renae is still working on it. She told me today, it wouldn't be ready until Friday. I told her that was the absolute latest because I have to make the casting call this week in order to make our February deadline for the play. Our schedule is tight. We don't have any time to waste," he said leaning forward putting both elbows on his desk clasping his hands. "We HAVE to get our cast this weekend. That leaves five weeks to get ready for The 14th Street Playhouse.

"Is five weeks enough time?"

"Damn right. But we don't have a minute to waste. We're done here, Deeva. I need to book the playhouse and begin the casting call. I'll see you this weekend," he said getting up.

I gathered my things and left.

Saturday at church, I announced the play and the casting call for the weekend. As soon as church was over, I planned to go to the office. Immediately after church, Shari, a member approached me asking to be in the play. She said she performed. I gave her the address to the office where the casting was taking place.

Shari was in her late twenties. Her identifying features were long, thick hair and a pretty face. She had a nice body as well. Although she had a baby last August, her figure was almost back to her pre-pregnancy state. Shari and I shared few words at church. We mostly spoke and went our way. I was delighted she was interested in trying out for my play. I had never seen her act but wished her well. I wanted the best actresses and actors to get the roles, regardless if I knew them or not.

By the time I got to the office, Shari was already there. Ronald was taping and giving instructions on what to do. I sat in a chair next to Ronald, who was standing with the camera on a stand. I had a copy of *Uncaged* in my hand. We were in the room next to the second chair as you entered the office. It was small with a stage, chairs, and water cooler. About twelve people were present, which filled the room.

"Act like you are taking a trip to outer space, and you are the only human left," Ronald instructed a young female on stage with a nose ring, big silver loop earrings, a tight black leather skirt, tall black boots, and a white shirt.

"I don't know who you think you are, but I am better than anybody in here," she said, sitting in the chair on stage talking to us. "I detect attitudes, but I know I'm good," she said getting up, showing her big legs. "No planet can contain all of this," she said placing her hands on her hips. "I must see what else this world has to offer," she said walking away.

Everyone clapped.

"Listen, everyone, we have the author of this play in our midst, Ms. Deeva Denez. Deeva read something out of your book for them to act out," Ronald instructed.

I turned to the end of Chapter Nine and read; "Carl was sitting in the living room when I came home with pills sprawled across the coffee table.

"Hi, honey, I'm home," I said as I rested next to him on the sofa. He sat lifeless with a forlorn look on his face. Something was up. "What's wrong with you?"

"I have VD," he said in a low audible whisper. He lifted his head up slightly and pointed to the pills on the table.

"You have what?" I asked shocked, not believing what I thought I heard. This must be a joke or a very bad dream. Certainly, this was not the truth, not my reality.

"You heard me right. You need to go to the clinic to be tested," He said as he buried his guilt-ridden face in his hands.

"How did it happen? Who was she? Why Carl? Why!!!" I demanded as tears flooded my eyes.

"She was some white girl I met walking down the street," he said as he stood up with his back to me and walked to the sliding glass door. "I'm sorry, Vanessa. It just happened."

"It just happened! Bullshit Carl! Some white whore was walking down the street, your dick smelled pussy, and y'all started fucking? Is that what happened? Mother fucker start packing your shit now!" I screeched as I scattered the pills everywhere with a quick swipe of my hand.

He turned towards the bedroom. "I'm sorry. I'll start packing. It won't take me but a few minutes, and I'll be out of your life." With his head still hung, he walked to the bedroom. I heard drawers opening and closing. Finally, he came out with one suitcase and a bag full of stuff. "Good-by, Doll. I didn't mean to hurt you," he said as tears streamed down his face. "I love you," he said as he reached for the doorknob.

"Wait! Don't leave," I said, running to the door to close it. "Don't go. I love you so much. Please don't leave me." I wrapped my arms around him and his things.

He dropped the suitcase emptying his arms. We embraced. No words were spoken. Only the sound of our hearts beating in rhythm was heard. We cried, holding each other, not wanting the other to let go.

"I love you, Vanessa. Please forgive me," he whispered between tears that choked his words.

"I love you, too, Carl. I forgive you. I love you too much to lose you. You mean too much to me. Although this whole incident hurts like hell, the thought of losing you is more painful."

We kissed. The passion flowed. The realization of almost losing each other enhanced the lovemaking that followed. He was mine, and I was his. We were one. When we exchanged vows, we took each other for better or worse. This was the worst, so it had to get better."

After I read, Ronald told several of the performers to get on the stage and reiterate the scene. He had different combinations to play Carl and Vanessa. Shari was my first choice for Vanessa. She was really good. However, I didn't see a Carl I liked. Maybe he would show up later at another time. Ronald left the camera to concentrate on the characters. A tall dark-skinned guy took his place.

Later I read the scene with Madame Lee in Chapter Twelve and Cynthia and Vanessa in Chapter Six. The performers acted out those as well. Two women played Madame Lee. They were older and heavy-set. One was light-skinned with braids and the other woman was dark-skinned with a short brown wig. I really liked the light-skinned actress. She played an excellent Madame Lee. Overall, I liked the first performer for Cynthia – the one with the black leather skirt. I could tell, Ronald did too, because he kept calling her to do the part of Cynthia.

So, in my mind, when the casting was over for the day, I had selected a Vanessa, a Cynthia, and a Madame Lee. The other roles were all male except one – Carl, Zakee, Bryson, Dad, and Mom. I prayed tomorrow would be more promising to select those roles. Monday afternoon I was to meet with Ronald to discuss the final decisions. He said, he had a list of other people if we did not find anyone we liked this weekend. I told him before I left that I would not be there on Sunday because I had to work. But I would see him Monday afternoon.

Late, Monday afternoon, at 4 p.m., I went back to see Ronald. We discussed our cast. He liked whom I liked for the female roles. Shari definitely stood out from the rest of the females who tried out. He told me he had the other cast members selected. They would be at rehearsal tomorrow. Since he didn't have his new place yet, rehearsals would be held at a friend's gym on Glenwood Road. We were to meet at the office at 7 p.m. then go to the gym.

While I was there, Renae wanted to see me to go over the script for the last time. They would be handed out at rehearsal tomorrow. I went to her office as soon as Ronald and I finished our business, which took forty-five minutes. As I was sitting, listening to Renae read the script, a young, attractive female appeared at her door looking for Paul, who was not there. Ronald had just hired her for the understudy for Vanessa. She came to the office in response to an ad to do some modeling. When Ronald saw her, he hired her on the spot. Renae asked her if she could sing because Vanessa's role was a singing role. She said her name was Janil, and yes, she could sing.

Renae then went into the room across from her office. Janil and I followed her. She put in a tape after searching for several minutes in a drawer under the tape player. She told us this song would be in the play, and Vanessa would sing it solo. The song was by Yolanda Adams. Janil said it was her favorite song, and she began to sing, "Alone in my room. Just you and me…"

Renae and I listened. Janil was a good singer. She said singing was one of her strengths along with acting. During our conversation after she finished singing, I discovered she attended the same high school as Brandi, my daughter. Come to find out, they knew each other and were good friends. Janil left shortly thereafter.

After Janil's departure, Renae and I went back to her office to go over the script for the last time before rehearsal. We wanted the play to be a success. We wanted everything to be right for the cast members tomorrow. When I left Renae, I felt good about the play. I couldn't wait to see my characters on stage. Once I had to pinch myself because it seemed too good to be true.

CHAPTER TWENTY-SIX

I arrived at the office the next night at 6:50 p.m.. Shari, Janil, Renae, and Ronald were the only faces I recognized. About two minutes later, the dark-skinned woman came, who played Madame Lee, with two other men I had not seen. A tall young guy with long dreadlocks was present as well as the dark guy who worked the video for Ronald. It was good to see some males. It seemed as though we had a full cast.

Before we left the office, twenty minutes later, several more people appeared. Renae counted the heads to make sure she had enough scripts to pass out. She gave me two copies in the office, one to keep and one to be submitted for copyrighting. Ronald was in and out of his office with different people before he told us it was time to go to the gym. Some people rode the MARTA train, which was located across from the office complex. Those of us who had extra space in our cars gave them rides. Ronald led the way with Renae, her three-month old son and two other cast members as his passengers. Janil ended up being my passenger.

The gym was located next to the Glenwood Lanes Bowling Ally. Most of the six cars parked directly in front of the gym. A few had to park in front of the empty adjacent building. As we entered, a karate class was taking place with five men participating. Ronald approached the instructor while we sat in tan folding chairs in front of a baby-blue stage in the rear of the room. The stage had weights on one end.

A thick, dark-skinned guy with braided hair, who was at the office, stood on the stage. He announced that he was the director of the play, and his name was Pele. Ronald joined Pele when he finished talking.

"Listen up everybody!" Ronald shouted. "I am the producer of this play, and here is your director, Pele," he said placing his hands on Pele's shoulders. "Do everything that he tells you. We have a full cast. I expect you to work hard because this play is scheduled to be at The 14th Street Playhouse in less than five weeks. Renae make sure everyone has a script. We also have the author of the play with us, Ms. Deeva Denez. This is where we will rehearse Monday through

Friday from 7:30 until 9:30 until I get my place, which will be soon. Deeva do you have anything to say?"

"No."

"Renae?"

"I will be here every night to assist Pele. If you have any questions about the script, please direct them to either Pele or myself," she said rocking her son who was crying.

"Pele, it's all yours," Ronald said as he left the stage.

Pele stood in the center of the stage, smiling. He had on blue jeans with an oversized black T-shirt. "I want to thank everybody for coming out. Rehearsals will start on time every night, so make sure you are here so that we don't waste time. I like to start rehearsals on time and end on time. I believe we have a full cast with some understudy parts," he said looking at his script. We will place two chairs on stage to be our sofa. Greg, will you do that for me, please?"

The guy who worked the video for Ronald took two chairs and placed them in the center of the stage then walked off.

"For Vanessa, we have Shari Lewis. Her understudy is Janil Harris. Shari, will you please come to the stage?" Pele asked.

Shari entered the stage wearing a semi-short, red skirt and white blouse with a wide black belt. She looked nice.

"For Carl, Vanessa's husband, Greg Johnson will be playing the main role. Jason Miles will be his understudy. (An unattractive short dark-skinned guy raised his hand.) The person who is playing Cynthia is not here. Shari brought an associate, Linda Mosley to play her part." (A slim, light-skinned woman with short brown hair raised her hand. I had never seen her before.)

"Thelma Jones is playing Mama. She doesn't have an understudy." (The dark-skinned fat woman, who played Madame Lee, raised her hand.)

"Dad will be played by Carlton Fuller. He doesn't have an understudy." (A tall, young heavy guy stood up.)

"Madame Lee will be played by Donna Jacobs. She is unable to make rehearsals due to her job situation. I'll let Thelma rehearse her part as well. Robert Taylor will play Zakee. (The cute, tall guy wearing dreadlocks waved his hand.) He doesn't have an understudy. Lastly, Darius McKnight will play Bryson. (A medium size, framed guy with small dreadlocks stood up.) He doesn't have an understudy. I believe that is everybody. The play has eleven scenes. We probably won't be able to go through all the scenes every night, but you need to be present in case we go over your scene. Let's get started. Shari is already on stage. Does anyone have a telephone?"

Greg threw a karate foam shoe he found on the floor on the stage. Everybody laughed, but Pele used it as a phone, placing it on a box he found in the corner.

"Act One, Scene One!" he shouted as rehearsal began.

Linda knocked on the make-believe door. Shari pretended to have a conversation with Greg, and the action started. I loved Shari as me. She was really good. They read from the script while Pele would interrupt to tell them where to "block" – the way each character interact to either say their lines or move to the next part. Greg was funny. He would do anything to get a laugh. He kept us laughing most of the night. Linda was strictly business. She read her lines, as written. She was okay, but I think the other Cynthia would have been better. She was more devilish, which was how Cynthia's role was written.

They managed to get to the second scene before calling it a night. I had more fun laughing at them than I had had in a long time. It was pure entertainment, to say the least. I enjoyed seeing the actors perform. A feeling came over me that's hard to explain. Just watching them act out my life made me feel as if I were living it all over again. I couldn't wait until we got to the part with Zakee. I hoped I could contain myself.

It took three days of rehearsals to finally get to Zakee's part. Robert was smooth as silk. He had Shari and me eating out of his hands. There was definitely some chemical vibes being emitted on stage. A match was lit on stage. Sparks were flying in my chair. Watching Shari and Robert playing Zakee and me was more than I could take. My feelings and emotions resurfaced for Zakee as if it was only yesterday.

The days of Zakee happened seven years earlier in '94. His good looks, perfect 10 body, charm, intelligent wit, and breathtaking smile swept me off my feet. Then Bryson came along, in '95 after my divorce from Carl and mopped me to the floor with what Zakee left behind.

I thought about Raymond as they continued to rehearse. He was different than any man I had ever known. He was what I needed in my life at this time. Raymond was the most chauvinist man I knew. His chauvinism was the only hard part about living with Raymond. He was from the old school – a man was a man and a woman was a woman and there was nothing in between. By him being all man, I felt like a total woman. I couldn't be accused of trying to wear the pants in my house because Raymond was not having it. No woman was going to rule him. He made his position very clear. He also fulfilled his role as the man of the house by being the breadwinner, the sole provider. My place indeed was as the helpmate as God had ordained from the beginning. I loved being Raymond's helpmate and mother to our children. Finally, I was living my God given role. A role, I enjoyed every minute of living.

As I tuned back into rehearsal, I realized Raymond would be the last man in my life. This marriage will go the distance. It will take me to my grave. Men like Zakee and Bryson will only be played out on stage as men of my past. Raymond was both my past and present. He would be with me until the end.

Zakee first appeared in the play in Act One, Scene Five towards the end of the scene. Vanessa had just lost her baby, and the only thing Carl had on his mind was getting a hundred dollars out of Vanessa, who eventually gives it to him after his persistence in asking for it. He feels his need for her money is more important than her using it to buy her prescription. Shari, Linda and Greg were into the scene.

Cynthia (Linda) walks seductively over to the table next to the living room where Vanessa (Shari) and Carl (Greg) are talking.

Carl - - [hurriedly hugging on Vanessa when Cynthia walks in] Come on baby give it to me. Don't make Daddy beg!

Vanessa - - [trying to talk as Carl kisses on her] Carl I have got to get my prescription filled.

Carl - - [seductively] You don't need a prescription. You have the doctor right here. [playing with her] Dr. Feel Good!

Vanessa - - [laughing] Carl stop! Go and get my pocketbook, so you can leave me alone.

Carl - - [going to get the purse] That's my girl. [handing Vanessa the pocketbook] Come on, baby. Daddy has got to go.

Vanessa - - [handing Carl the money, smiling] Take this money and get out of here.

Carl - - [giving Vanessa one last kiss and smiling at Cynthia as he takes the money] Okay, baby, I'll talk to you later. [grabs his coat and EXIT the front door]

When Carl leaves, Cynthia and Vanessa exchange words. A knock on the door keeps them from getting into a verbal confrontation. Zakee, a Muslim in the neighborhood selling fruit and bean pies, puts ice on the fire that has gotten started between Vanessa and Cynthia. Before Zakee leaves, Cynthia is right under him checking out his buns. He leaves shortly thereafter making it known that he approves of Vanessa's goods.

Pele walks onto the stage when the scene is over. "Well, we had a great rehearsal tonight," he said, sitting in one of the chairs that was the sofa. Since tomorrow is Friday, we won't have rehearsal. I want you to study your lines over the weekend. You have to wean yourself off the paper before we go to The 14th Street Playhouse. Mom, Dad, and Bryson, I didn't get a chance to get to your parts this week, but I will first thing next week, so study your lines. Let's all stand for a moment of silence, so we can be dismissed," he said bowing his head. (He ended all rehearsals with a moment of silence.)

We all stood, bowed our heads and closed our eyes. When a minute passed, we stopped. As I gathered my things, I overheard Janil say that she needed a ride to Agnes Scott College. It was fifteen minutes from the gym. Darius was standing beside her. They rode the train to the office then got a ride to the gym. I offered them a ride. I would drop Darius off at the train station beyond the college then take Janil to the college. Although it was out of my way to drop them off, I felt like it was worth it; it was the least I could do since they were in my play. They both gladly accepted my offer to take them where they needed to go.

We were next to the last ones to leave. Janil sat in the front, and Darius sat in the back.

"You can put your things on my daughter's carseat," I instructed as Darius opened the back door. Janil had a small purse and a large bag. Darius had a bag also.

"Miss Deeva, I didn't know you had a baby," Janil said as she placed her bag in the carseat. Darius held his bag in his lap.

"I have a two year old daughter. Her name is Mya. I saw her as an image before she was born. She is the subject of my third book, *The*

Image: A Prophetic Birth, I said backing out of my parking space in front of the gym.

"I liked *Uncaged*," Janil said, putting her blue jean jacket on, which concealed her shapely figure. "I'm only eighteen, and I haven't been in a lot of relationships, so I can't relate to what Vanessa went through. But I know a lot of older women who have, like my aunts and one cousin."

"I meet a lot of women myself who have had similar experiences. My goal is to help them through their situations. Sometimes when you read about someone else's problem, it helps you to solve or work through your own," I said putting a tape of The Mississippi Mass Choir in the tape player. "Darius I know you like your role. You get to kiss Vanessa. It's the only kiss in the whole play."

"Bryson is cool. I like his part. I can't wait until I get a chance to rehearse it," he said putting a piece of candy in his mouth.

"Do you have some more candy?" Janil asked, turning around.

"Sure," he said opening a small bag. I have gummy bears and Starburts."

"I'll take some gummy bears. They're my favorite."

"Here, take the bag," he said giving her the bag. "Get what you want."

By now, I was turning right on Candler Rd. "Have you been studying your lines, Janil? I know it's hard to watch and not get on stage," I said, stopping at a light.

"I have fun watching Shari, Linda and Greg on stage. That Greg is so funny. You never know what he will do next. I had a lot of impromptu training when I was in school. He won't catch me off guard if I get a chance to perform," Janil said putting another gummy bear in her mouth. "Mmmmm, these are good," Janil said giving Darius the bag.

"Would you like some more?" Darius asked, reaching into the bag.

"Yeah. I want some more of the red and yellow ones."

"Ya'll act like my two year old," I said laughing. "I guess some kids never grow up."

"I'm not a kid," said Darius, who looked to be about twenty-six, "but I still enjoy candy, especially, gummy bears."

"I'm not a kid either, Miss Deeva, but some things you just don't out grow."

"Candy keeps my mouth lubricated," added Darius. "It's my way of being ready for my big moment with Vanessa."

"Oh, so you plan to give her a big, wet, juicy kiss?" Janil asked.

"That's right. If you get on stage, then you'll be the recipient," he said laughing loudly.

I laughed, too. Janil popped another gummy bear in her mouth.

"Miss Deeva, if I get to play Vanessa, we will have to re-write the script."

We all laughed as I reached the train station.

CHAPTER TWENTY-SEVEN

Darius gave Janil more gummy bears before he exited the car. He seemed like a nice guy, but he definitely was not Bryson. Darius was short, small framed, wore dress shoes and slacks. He was more of a square although he wore dreadlocks, which didn't seem like the right hairstyle for him. A short natural cut was more his speed. Bryson, on the other hand, was tall with a wide chest, short hair, gold wire rimmed glasses, and a devious disposition. He usually wore a navy blue uniform or odd color casual clothes such as different shades of brown, green, beige or black. I understood Janil's position on not wanting Darius to kiss her. I wouldn't want him to kiss me either.

Janil ate the rest of her gummy bears as I drove to Agnes Scott campus, which was less than five minutes away. I really liked Janil. She seemed like a good person. In some ways she reminded me of myself. She had a certain innocence that I, too, possessed at her age. She seemed just as naïve, too. I hoped she wouldn't end up like me - - wasting most of her life with the wrong man, who would make her life a living hell.

Janil gave me directions to her drop off point. I stopped at the designated spot. I drove through a parking lot and was facing to go out. A big brick building was a few feet away. It was well lit with trees, grass, and a walkway surrounding it.

"That's my dorm, Miss Deeva," Janil said as I stopped.

"This is a nice campus. I've passed by it many times, but I've never actually been on it."

"I love it!" Janil said, picking up her purse.

"You don't mind going to an all female college?"

"No. Being around females all day does not bother me. I have met some really good friends. Besides, I have a male friend. He goes to Morehouse."

"That's good."

"It was prophesied to us before we graduated from high school, last year, that we were going to get married. He also goes to my church. We sing duets together a lot in church," she said smiling, opening the door.

"Don't forget your bag," I said reaching in the back to get it.

169

"Oh, I wasn't going to leave it. I was going to open the back door to get it. Thanks," she said as I handed it to her.

"You're welcome."

"Thanks, Miss Deeva, for bringing me home."

"My pleasure. I can bring you home every night since you don't have a way. I don't mind," I said as she closed the door.

"Okay. I'll see you Monday at rehearsal," she said as she walked off.

I watched her enter the well-lit building. She waved as she opened the door. I drove off after the door closed, and she was out of sight. Janil was a good person, I kept telling myself on the way home. I was glad Ronald selected her although she was just an understudy and may not have a chance to perform.

I thought about Janil on the way home. I think she thought of me as a second mother. Somehow, I thought of her as another daughter. Shari was great portraying me. I'm sure, Janil would be just as good although I couldn't imagine anyone but Shari playing Vanessa. She had stolen my heart playing that part.

When I got home, Brandi was up with Mya. They were watching TV. Francine and Raymond Jr. were asleep since they had to go to school the next morning. I took Mya and went into my bedroom, so Brandi could go to sleep since she had school tomorrow, too. As I opened the door, Raymond was putting on his black dress shoes. He was completely dressed with a white shirt, navy and white tie, and navy dress pants. I looked at my watch. He had less than five minutes to leave for work. Tomorrow night, January 26, would be his last night at Grady. I sat with Mya at the head of my bed, so that I wouldn't be in his way.

"Well, this is the countdown," I said, putting Mya next to me on the bed. I could tell she was sleepy. I would get her ready for bed as soon as Raymond left. "You only have two more nights to work."

"Yeah, I'll be glad when this is over. I look forward to getting a good nights sleep," he said, brushing his hair.

"It will be good having you in the bed with me at night. We've been married three years and have only slept together maybe ten times at night with our work schedules. We still won't have our complete privacy since Mya will sleep in the bed with us, but it will be better having you here at home instead of at work."

"I look forward to sleeping in my bed, too. This midnight shift is getting the best of me. All I do is sleep. I don't have any time or energy for my business."

"Dad-de," Mya called.

"Yes, love," Raymond, replied, coming towards us.

He pecked me on my lips and kissed Mya, too. "I gotta run," he said rushing out the door.

"Come on, Mya," I said scooping her up. "Let's see Daddy leave, then we will go to bed.

By the time Mya and I went downstairs, Raymond was out the door into his car. We watched as he warmed up his car. We waved as he pulled out the driveway a few minutes later. I told Mya as I closed the door we were going to work with Daddy tomorrow night to his going away party. She smiled as I took her upstairs to get ready for bed.

Mya was a good child. She had my disposition - - bubbly. Raymond was moody, so was Francine, Raymond Jr. and Brandi sometimes. I was glad to have another child in the house like me. It helped when everyone else were going through their moods, which generally consisted of non-communication. I gave Mya her bath before we went to bed. She always liked bath time. Usually, I put toys and bubbles in her water. Her favorite toy was a water frog she had gotten at her baby shower.

After her bath, we went to sleep. We slept soundly until Raymond returned home from work the next morning. He quickly took off his clothes then joined us in bed. I smiled at Raymond as he gave me a peck before he went to sleep. About ten minutes later, I dozed back off until Mya woke me up an hour later. I wished she would go in Brandi's room and watch TV while I slept some more. But I knew Mya was not the type of kid to leave alone.

Groggily, I fought the desire for more sleep and got out of bed. My first order of business was coffee for me and hot chocolate for Mya. We would eat something solid around lunch time.

"Mommie, get up," Mya commaded as she threw her clothes on the floor from her changing table next to my bed. She was selecting her outfit for the day, which was her daily ritual.

"Mya, Mommie's up," I said as I stood up to go to the bathroom.

"Mommie, look!" she exclaimed with an outfit in her hands.

"Okay, you can wear that today," I said approving of the purple pants and purple top.

"Can I watch TV?" she asked leaving the room with her outfit going into Brandi's room.

"I have to use the restroom first, Mya, before I can turn the TV on," I said going into the bathroom. I heard the TV playing by the time I reached the toilet. Undoubtedly, she had found the remote.

The rest of the morning was uneventful - - we followed our normal routine of coffee and hot chocolate. I read the newspaper. We watched TV for about an hour. We cleaned up, ate lunch, read a book, put on Mya's clothes. I then combed her hair. I couldn't put on my clothes until Raymond woke up since I had to take my bath and get my clothes ready. Raymond usually woke up between one and two o'clock.

At 2:15, I heard the toilet flush - - a sure sign Raymond was up. He still looked tired when he came downstairs. It seemed that no matter how much rest he got, it was never enough. I was glad for his sake that tonight was his last night to work. I was tired of seeing my husband always tired. With his present work schedule, he was working, and sleeping his life away, not having time for anything else. That's why he decided he had wasted enough time. If he continued to work, he would never fulfill his dream of having his own company and being a multi-billionaire like Warren Buffet, his role model. Being an author, I fully understood his position. I knew one day both our dreams would come true - - he would be a successful businessman, and I would be a well-known author. I also knew that neither would happen overnight.

I was also glad that tonight was his last night to work, so I could work one day a week - - 16 hours on Sunday. Having six days off would give me more time to go to the rehearsals and pursue my dream. It was a perfect plan for us. All we needed was time, energy, and an act from God to make our dreams become reality. I know with God all things were possible. With Him on our side, we could not fail.

Raymond went straight to the refrigerator when he came downstairs. Mya and I were in the living room on the sofa. I had just finished combing her hair. She had fallen asleep shortly after I started. I saw Raymond pour himself a glass of lemonade as I lifted Mya up to take her upstairs.

"I'm glad tonight is your last night to work," I said looking into his tired eyes.

"Me, too," he said closing the refrigerator, drinking his lemonade. "This night shift is not for me."

"I know. It's a hard shift to work. But God put you on that shift to meet me. If you continued to work days instead of nights five years ago, we would not have met," I said placing Mya's head on my shoulder.

Raymond laughed. "I guess you are right about that. You won't let me forget it either," he said walking into the living room.

"No. I think it's worth remembering, so you can count your blessing in having me for your wife. I'm not here by accident, but by Divine intervention of God. Therefore, don't ever take me for granted, Raymond Eugene Miller," I said going up the steps.

"Mrs. Miller have YOU forgotten that you were engaged to someone else when we got married because you had kicked me, God's Divine intervention, to the curb?" he asked laughing, sitting on the sofa.

I put Mya on Brandi's bed and placed some cover on her before I returned to the living room to answer Raymond. I wanted to make sure he heard me loud and clear. He watched me come down the steps with a smirky grin on his face. "Get your information straight. You kicked me to the curb, not the other way around. You ended the relationship to hurt me, but you ended up getting hurt instead. God had to show me you in your weakest state to reveal how much you truly love me. No matter what you say or do, I know you love me with your whole being. And for that reason, I will never leave you, but take whatever you dish out because I know how much you really love me, Mr. Miller!" I exclaimed sitting next to him.

"You have me all wrong. I'm just waiting for the day that I can hire a young, French maid with a short, tight skirt to keep me happy. That's why I'm leaving Grady and starting my own business, so I can really be a happy man," he said grinning even harder at me.

I pulled my hair back in a French twist. "This is the closest you will get to anything French. And as far as a young thing with a short, tight skirt, living in my house, NEVER! I'm all the woman you'll ever need or get while I'm alive. We're in this marriage until death do us part.

"Okay, Mrs. Miller," he said looking at his watch, "we have one hour before the kids come home from school. Let's see how well you can make me forget about my maid."

"Come on," I said, getting up, pulling him up by the hands. "I will not only make you forget about your maid, but you won't even remember your name when I finish with you."

"Oui, Oui, Madame," he said with a French accent as he left the sofa.

"Mademoiselle, to you, Monsieur," I replied as we went up the steps.

CHAPTER TWENTY-EIGHT

Raymond and I enjoyed that afternoon as well as that night at work. Mya and I went with Raymond to work to help celebrate his going away party. We drove separate cars because I could only stay until midnight since I had to pick Brandi up from work at 12:30 a.m. from Magic Johnson's Theater.

When we arrived at the Security Department, thirty minutes early, only Captain Lindsay and another female officer were present. Supposedly, Raymond's party was to start at ten o'clock, thirty minutes before the night shift began. I guess the other officers either forgot or were trying to get their last minute naps. Whatever the case, they were not there. Captain Lindsay, who also provided security for W. K. Wings, had two trays of wings on the table. The more I looked at the wings, the more I wanted the party to get started!

Raymond was all smiles as he sat in a brown chair in front of the officer and diagonal from Captain Lindsay at a long, dark-brown table in the conference room across from his office. Mya and I sat next to him. Captain Lindsay was preoccupied with papers in front of him. The female officer just smiled as if to say she was ready for the party to begin as well.

The conference room had a long table, which we were sitting, and a long green blackboard that was on the wall behind Raymond. Four cubicles were behind Captain Lindsay. Another table was behind me. There were about twenty chairs, twelve at the table, four at cubicles, and four at the table behind me. Also perched in a corner was a TV.

"How is everyone?" Raymond asked as he bounced in the chair, looking at Captain Lindsay and the officer.

"I'm fine," the female officer replied, "I'm just tired. I came early for the party. I have a gift for you," she said handing Raymond a large box wrapped in gold paper.

"That was very thoughtful of you, Officer Haney," Raymond responded, taking the box.

"I don't have a gift. I just brought wings," Captain Lindsay replied laughing, looking away from his papers.

"That's okay, Captain. I'm not mad at you," Raymond said taking the paper off the box. Inside was a desk size planner.

"I thought you might need that for your business," Officer Haney said, smiling as Raymond took it out the box.

"Thank you, so much. I can certainly use it," Raymond replied putting the planner back inside the box.

Meanwhile, Mya had left my arms to sit next to Captain Lindsay. "She's not bothering you?" I asked because she had grabbed a piece of his paper and a pen.

"Oh no. She's fine," he said giving her a marker. "I am around kids all the time. That's how I spend most Saturdays with the kids in my complex. Hey, Miller, that's a nice planner. I wish you well with your business. I'll be calling you to help me with mine. I can't believe the other officers are not here," he said looking at his watch. "They know about your party."

"Don't worry about it. This is my last night to work. Nothing and no one can bother me tonight," Raymond said, smiling, sitting back in his chair.

We waited twenty more minutes before the other officers came. Everyone came with food, drinks and gifts. It was a good turnout and a great party! I took pictures of everyone, so Raymond would have memories of his ex-coworkers. Raymond said a brief speech before the party ended. After Raymond's speech, Mya and I went to the lab before I left to pick up Brandi.

Time slipped away. It was 12:15 before I exited the hospital. The drive to the theater was twenty minutes away. When I pulled up at the theater, Brandi came out. The cold air made her quicken her steps to the car. Her long, thick hair covered her shoulders, which rested on her long black coat.

"Hi, Mom," Brandi said, as she entered the warm car.

"Have you been waiting long?" I asked, looking into her tired eyes.

"No. I got off a minute ago. It sure feels good in here," she said putting her purse down.

"I know. It was cold when we left your father's party. The drive here has made the car nice and toasty. I thought I was going to be late picking you up. You know tonight is the last night for me or your dad to pick you up. He said when he stopped working, we were not going to make this trip anymore because it's too far from the house."

"I put my two weeks notice in tonight. I've put applications in at other jobs closer to home. I haven't heard anything yet," she said placing her head on the headrest, closing her eyes.

Minutes later, she was fast asleep. I turned my gospel tape down and sang along all the way home. One of my favorite songs was on, Shirley Caesar's *Go*. Some of the words were, "Go, ye therefore and teach all nations. Go. Go. Go! Baptizing them in the name of the Father, the Son and the Holy Ghost. Go. Go. Go! Lo, I will be with you forever and ever until the end of the world. Go. Go. Go! If you love me, really love me feed my sheep." I felt like when she sang that song, she was singing directly to me. I took it personally as if God Himself was commissioning me to teach the gospel through my work, which is really His work that He is doing through me.

As I drove and sang, I thought about the three F's that Jesus had told me to write. *Uncaged* deals with the first F – Forgiveness. We must forgive others because God has forgiven us. Forgiveness heals both past and present hurts. Forgiveness is the first step for God's plan of salvation for us. Through the death of Jesus Christ and His shed blood on the cross, our sins are forgiven. With our sins forgiven, we become righteous before God because our sins no longer separate us from Him. Colossians 1:13-14 says, *"He (the Father) has delivered us from the power of darkness and conveyed us into the kingdom of the Son of His love, in whom we have redemption through His blood, the forgiveness of sins."*

The Bearer of the Sign deals with the second F – Flesh. As born again children of God, we must crucify our flesh. But we can't do it on our own. Again we need Jesus and the indwelling of the Holy Spirit to conquer our flesh. Galatians 5:16-17 says, *"I say then: Walk in the Spirit, and you shall not fulfill the lust of the flesh. For the flesh lusts against the Spirit, and the Spirit against the flesh; and these are contrary to one another, so that you do not do the things you wish."* The flesh is evil. It needs to be overcome. Only through Jesus Christ can it be held into submission.

The Image: A Prophetic Birth deals with the third and last F – Faith. It takes faith to please God. Since we can't see God, by faith we must believe that He exists, and that, *"He is a rewarder of those who diligently seek Him."* (Hebrews 11:6) My daughter, Mya, was an image in '95. By faith, I knew that one day she would be flesh and blood. By faith, we must believe that although we are now flesh and blood, one day we will be spirit beings like God, our Heavenly Father, and we, too, will bear His image. Thus this book is about both the birth of Mya, which occurred in November of '98 and our spiritual births into the literal kingdom of God. I Corinthians 15:42-53 says, *"So also is the resurrection of the dead. The body is sown in corruption it is raised in incorruption. It is sown in dishonor it is raised in glory. It is sown in weakness it is raised in power. It is sown a natural body, it is raised a spiritual body. And so it is written, 'The first Adam became a living being.' The last Adam became a life-giving spirit. However, the spiritual is not first, but the natural, and afterward the spiritual. The first man was of the earth, made of dust; the second Man is the Lord from heaven. As was the man of dust, so also are those who are made of dust: and as is the heavenly Man, so also are those who are heavenly. And as we have borne the image of the man of dust, we shall also bear the image of the heavenly Man. Now this I say, brethren, that flesh and blood cannot inherit the kingdom of God; nor does corruption inherit incorruption. Behold, I tell you a mystery: We shall not all sleep, but we shall all be changed — in a moment, in the twinkling of an eye, at the last trumpet. For the trumpet shall sound, and the dead will be raised incorruptible and we shall be changed. For this corruptible must put on incorruption, and this mortal must put on immortality."* God has an incredible plan for mankind, but we must believe in Jesus to receive it as part of the first fruits.

Brandi woke up as I pulled into the driveway. Mya was asleep. Brandi got out, not offering to help me with Mya as she customarily did. I grabbed my things and Mya and went inside, too. I told myself as I entered the front door, I was glad tonight was the last time to make the hour-long trip for someone who was so unappreciative. I never heard a thank you or any sign of gratitude. I was also never compensated for my gas, which was costly. From now on, Brandi would have to use MARTA to get back and forth to her job.

I placed Mya in my bed as I crawled next to her. Within minutes, I was out like a light. I had had a tiring week with rehearsals in the evenings. The last thought on my mind before I went to sleep was something funny that happened Thursday in rehearsal between Shari and Greg. I laughed at the thought of them playing Carl and me. Greg was harsh, something the real Carl never was. The real Carl was soft and funny - - the two things I loved most about him. If he was harsh like Greg portrayed him, we would have never made it twenty-five years.

Raymond returned home the next day by 1 p.m.. His shift ended at 7:30, but he had a lot of loose ends and last minute paperwork to complete before he came home. My husband was very efficient. He left no stone unturned. He took pride in his work and was a stickler that everything be done right.

His expectations were the same at home, but I let him know that I was no machine, nor was I a perfectionist. Therefore, don't expect a spotless house with four nasty children living in it because I was not going to kill myself trying to keep everything clean. The kids helped, but they did a half-hearted job. My main priority was Mya. My next priority was cooking dinner. If Mya was taken care of and dinner cooked, I fulfilled my obligations for the day. Everything else was a bonus. Often he complained about dust hanging from the ceiling fan or other parts of the house. I told him I had a high tolerance for dust and dirt. My well-being was more important than anything in the house. His problem was he wanted me to be like his mother, who kept a clean house. Mrs. Simmons stayed busy. Raymond was her only child, and she did everything for him. He didn't have to do anything for himself. As his wife, he expected the same treatment from me. He expected me to do everything, including ironing his and the kids clothes, who were 12 and 10. To me they were old enough to iron their own clothes and do some chores, which I delegated to them such as vacuuming, cleaning their bathroom, folding clothes, and keep their rooms clean. Brandi helped me with Mya some and washed clothes, but the bulk of the load fell on me.

As usual, Raymond slept most of the day. I spent my day trying to keep the kids quiet while he slept. Luckily, we went to church part of the time. That helped to relieve some of my stress. I was glad for that reason alone that he was coming home to work. Anyway I looked at it, it was all good. Next week and the weeks to follow, he could watch Mya while I went to rehearsal. I was thankful I could go to rehearsals with a peace of mind.

Monday night, I went to rehearsal tired from working Sunday night. I had to go back to work that night, too. Since I went to rehearsal, I wouldn't have time for a nap before I went back in at eleven. This was the last week that I worked Sunday and Monday nights. Beginning next Sunday, my new schedule would have me working sixteen hours on Sunday from 2:30 that afternoon to 7:30 Monday morning. On second Sundays when we went to Dublin to attend Raymond's church, I was scheduled to work Sunday night and Monday night to work my sixteen hours.

At 7:30, all were present except Linda, who played Cynthia. Shari said Linda was sick with food poisoning. Pele asked Janil to play Cynthia. As I watched Janil on stage, I knew she was excellent for the role. No longer could I have Linda to perform. The interaction with Shari and Janil was better, too. Janil had to perform. When rehearsal was over, I talked to Pele about Janil. He agreed with me that Janil played a better Cynthia than Linda. Since this was my play, Janil was in and Linda was out.

Linda's sickness proved to be a blessing in disguise. If she had been well, I never would have known how good a performer Janil was. God knew, but I didn't know. Now that I knew, Janil would perform. Both Pele and I discussed the change with Ronald. It was a unanimous decision – Janil would play Cynthia.

Linda was out for three days. By then Janil was really getting into her character. There was no question that she was the best. When Linda returned to rehearsal Thursday, and she was not asked to play Cynthia, she had a hurt expression on her face the whole evening. Not wanting her to be in the dark, I told her of the change. She cried and left the gym. By the time Janil, Darius and I left, Linda and Shari were still in the parking lot talking. I could see the hurt on Linda's face as we drove off. I was sorry her feelings were hurt, but I wanted the best actress for my play, and I had the best actress in the front seat of my car.

CHAPTER TWENTY-NINE

Janil was all smiles as I drove to the train station. Darius was in the back seat eating candy. Twice he had a chance to play his role as Bryson. Twice he gave Shari one of his juicy kisses, which Shari quickly wiped off. Luckily for Janil since she was playing Cynthia's role she didn't have to worry about Darius' kisses. I was glad for her sake because I wouldn't want to be subjected to him either.

Pele gave them the weekend off since they did so well this week. He instructed them to study their lines while they were off. Next week was the last week they could use them. Before we left, Ronald told me he wanted to see me in the office tomorrow. I told him I would be there at 1 p.m..

The next day, I went to the office at the designated time. Ronald let me inside. There was no sign of either Veronica or Renae. He quickly led me to his office. I sat in my usual spot, the first chair by the door and he sat in his, behind his desk. He reached inside a top drawer and pulled out a folder.

"Deeva," he said placing the folder in front of him. "I need some more money to buy the props for the stage," he said taking a sheet of paper from the folder and putting it in front of me.

"I thought I only had to give you the $1776 for the play," I said looking at him.

"It costs more than $1776 to produce a play. This is your play and you have to pay all of the expenses."

"Why didn't you tell me that at the beginning. I was led to believe that $1776 was my only expense."

"No, there are other expenses, too. Like you need to pay for the backdrop, where pictures will be taken. Let me show you the backdrop for the last play," he said as he got up and went out of his office. A minute later he returned. 'See, this is what I'm talking about," he said showing me a picture from the photo album in the lobby. "Yours needs to be bigger than this one because it was a tad too small for the pictures."

I had seen the picture before. I closed the album and gave it back to him. "How much does a backdrop cost?" I asked apprehensive.

181

"Santrice does our backdrops. Here's her number," he said writing a number down and handing me the paper. "She charged $100 for this one. But yours needs to be bigger."

"Okay, I'll call her," I said taking the paper. "Now how much do you need for the props?"

"It's right there on the paper. I have everything written down for you. It's all itemized. There are no hidden costs," he said touching the paper.

I studied the paper. The cost was $3,198. "When do you need the money?"

"Now."

"I will have it Tuesday. Is there anything else I need to pay?"

"No, this should do it. If anything else comes up, I can take it."

"You should have had everything written down in the beginning. This is my first play. I don't know all of the expenses. You're the one who has done plays before," I said getting the paper and putting it in my purse.

"Oh, yeah. I've done plenty of plays," he said sitting back in his chair.

Something is not right here, I thought to myself as I left the office. The way Ronald conducts business leaves much to be desired. I went home to make a phone call to get the money Ronald needed. I would have his money on Tuesday. I also called Santrice. We made an appointment for Wednesday afternoon. I planned to give her a copy of my book to make the backdrop from.

Sunday, I started my one-day a week. Time flew at home as I did everything I needed to do before I left at 2:15 p.m.. First, I washed and pressed Francine's hair. Second, I had to wash Mya's hair and plait it. She started daycare Monday for one day a week. I wanted to do as little as possible to get her ready Monday morning when I returned home. This arrangement worked perfectly. Mya could play with children her own age, Raymond could work on his business, and I could get some much needed sleep from being up all night. Last, but not least, I had to cook dinner. I couldn't go to work and leave my family hungry. By the time I did leave, I was tired. I needed to go to work to rest.

The more I thought about working one day a week and having six days off, the happier I became. My God is an awesome God. All things are possible through Him! The timing was perfect. I'd have more time to go to rehearsals, which I planned to go to all of them except the ones on Saturday during church and Sunday.

Monday night at rehearsal, everyone was present except Shari and Linda. Without Shari, there could be no rehearsal because she was in every scene. Janil could have taken her spot, but she was now playing Cynthia. After waiting thirty minutes, I called Ronald on my cell phone, thinking that maybe Shari was stuck in traffic and had called the office. He said Shari and Linda had just left the office five minutes ago. They should be there soon. Shari had given him an ultimatum to either let Linda perform or she was out. I told him I would talk to him after rehearsal to discuss the matter. He agreed.

Fifteen minutes after I hung up with Ronald, Shari and Linda entered the gym. They both had devious smiles on their faces. I knew then, Shari had too much power in this play, power that she would misuse. I decided then that she had to go. I didn't care how good she was. Her actions tonight told me that it was not the end, but the beginning of trouble – something that I didn't need.

Shari performed well the remainder of rehearsal, but the conversation with Ronald coupled with expressions on their faces let me know this was the last night I would see them. Good riddance! I'm glad I found out now, than later what was in their hearts. Getting rid of Shari would definitely affect the play. But the play will go on! She and no one else would stop the play. In my mind, it was ordained of God. It will happen, and it will come to pass!

When rehearsal was over I dropped Janil and Darius off before I went to the office. Ronald was alone as we went to his desk.

"Have a seat, Deeva," he said as we entered the room.

I sat down as he sat in his chair. He had on a black, brown, and white leisure suit. "Ronald, I don't like what I saw tonight. Shari held up rehearsal tonight and when she did come, she had a smirky grin on her face that spelled trouble," I said sitting up in the chair, still agitated.

"Deeva, she came in here with Linda and stayed for over an hour. I told her she needed to get to rehearsal, but she didn't care. She threatened to quit if I didn't put Linda back in. Damn it, she can quit! I have other people who can do a better job," he said sitting back in his chair.

"Ronald, she's out! That's all to it. You have to replace her. Right now, she has too much power. She may pull something else the closer we get to the play date. I don't trust her anymore."

"Are you sure, Deeva?"

"Yes, I'm positive."

"If we replace her, then I have no other choice but to postpone the play. I've put money into it already, but we have to do what's right. We can push it back another month, the end of March. I won't know for sure until I call tomorrow to see what dates are available."

"That's fine with me. We really don't have any other choice but to change the date. It wouldn't be fair to the new Vanessa to keep the same date."

"I want to get a new Dad and Mama, too. The two we have are not working out. I'm not satisfied with their performances. I have some more people lined up. They will be at rehearsal, too, tomorrow. I've been in this field a long time, I know good and bad talent when I see it."

"That's good because I'm depending on your expertise."

"This play will meet your expectations. All of this happened at a good time before I printed up flyers and tickets."

"Good," I said reaching for my purse.

"Tomorrow, I'll have Shari's replacement. I still need you to bring the money tomorrow, so I can buy the props.'

"I'll have your money tomorrow. You don't have to worry about that," I said standing up.

"I'll see you tomorrow at one. I should have a new date by then. I'll make some calls before you come," he said walking me to the door.

"Okay, Ronald, I'll see you tomorrow," I said as he closed the office door.

The next day, I went back to Ronald's office. I signed the paper he had prepared for the props and gave him the money. He said the next play date would be Saturday, March 31 and Sunday, April 1. There would be two shows each day. These dates would give us plenty of time to get ready with the new cast changes. He said he had all the new cast members selected. They would be at rehearsal tonight.

I felt good leaving Ronald's office. I was glad he had everything under control. I couldn't wait to see the new cast members. I'm sure they would be to my satisfaction. I trusted Ronald and his professional opinion. I went home to get some things done, so I could be ready for tonight.

At six o'clock, Ronald called me to come to the office. Shari was there. She had been there for an hour. He wanted me present to clear this matter up. Luckily, when he called, I had finished doing everything I needed to do at home. I was spending time with the family just waiting to go to rehearsal.

When I arrived at the office, Veronica led me to Ronald's door. She announced to him that I was there. I went inside. Shari was in the first chair, so I went to the second chair and sat down. Ronald was behind his desk sitting up.

"Thank you, Veronica," Ronald said as the door closed. "Deeva, I have told Shari of our decision to replace her, but she doesn't believe me. Will you please talk to her? She's been here an hour, and I'm not getting anywhere," he said leaning back.

"Shari, Ronald and I have decided to let you go and find someone else to play your part. Your behavior yesterday greatly disturbed me. I feel like you will cause problems later," I said talking directly to her. She was sitting back with her hands clasped in her lap. Her long hair was hidden underneath a white hood. She had on a white sweater and black pants. Dark circles accented her eyes. She looked as if she had not slept at all last night.

"Miss Denez (She calls me Sister Miller at church)," she said pausing to collect her thoughts. (Shari never had been one to shy away or struggle to speak her mind. Watching her made the moment awkward.) "I realize my actions yesterday were wrong. I have thought about it all night and day. I lost a lot of sleep last night because of what I did. That's why I came to the office early to talk to Ronald. I asked him to call you, so that I can talk to you. Yesterday, I said some things, which I now know were wrong. Linda is my friend, but she has nothing to do with my work. Our friendship does not come before my performance or professionalism. I am an actress first, friend second. Besides, we're not that close anyway. What I am trying to say, Miss Denez, is… will you give me another chance? I quit my job today to play this part, so I can learn my lines," she said looking into my eyes.

"I am sorry, Shari. What I saw yesterday was not a pretty sight. You and Linda held up rehearsal. Then the looks on your faces told me it was over. I don't want trouble. I feel as if you will cause a problem later. I can't have that. Therefore, my decision stands. You must be replaced. This is my play, and I have the last say so."

She looked at me then at Ronald. "I'm sorry," she said standing up to leave.

"Ronald, do you have anything to say?" I asked.

"I agree with you, Deeva. I've said everything I wanted before you came."

"I won't take up anymore of your time," Shari said as she left.

Ronald and I looked at her as she walked out. My eyes met his as the door closed. "What did ya'll discuss?" I asked sitting back in my chair taking a deep breath.

"She's evil, Deeva, and she calls herself a Christian! She came in here flirting with me. I told her I was not that kind of man. I am around females all day, and I am straight with them all. I can't believe you go to the same church. You are different as day and night," he said flabbergasted.

Dazedly, I looked at Ronald. It hurt me to hear him put down my church sister. I didn't know Shari the way he described her. I felt remorse, but I had to shake it off. "So, do you have a replacement for Shari?"

"Yes, she will be at rehearsal tonight," he said smiling.

"Do I know her?"

"Yes."

"What's her name?" I asked in suspense.

"Janil."

CHAPTER THIRTY

Janil playing Vanessa was ingenious! How did Ronald come up with that idea? I loved it. But, who will play Cynthia? Janil was an excellent Cynthia. I can't wait to see her playing Vanessa. Also the new Mom and Dad would be present.

Ronald told Janil and Pele of her new role. They were both happy. That meant everyone was in agreement over the change. Janil was a good person. I wished her the best. It was strange how when I talked to her on the trips to the college that she seemed a lot like me. She possessed an innocence that I once had, too. This whole play business had a way of making me re-live portions of my life all over again. Not everyone has a chance to do so. I was thankful for the opportunity.

Janil came to rehearsal all smiles. Pele gave the announcement of the change. He also introduced the new Mom, Dad and Cynthia. I had seen Mom in the office on several occasions. She sang with three other people. Her name was Janice Mays. Janice was dark-skinned with short, dark-brown hair. She and my real mom had one thing in common - - they were both short. Dad was short, too, just like my real dad. He was about the same complexion as Janice, maybe a little lighter. I had never seen him before or the new Cynthia, who was young and slim with long braids. Her name was Dana. Dad's name was Casey Banks. Our cast was in place. Let the play live on!

The new people made the play better. Janil was outstanding as Vanessa, and Dana was the best Cynthia yet. She was even better than Janil as Cynthia because she was sexy and sleazy - - two of Cynthia's most prevalent traits. Both Dad and Mom were better because they worked well together. Their chemistry worked.

After rehearsal, I asked Janil if she would be interested in going to her old alma mater, North Atlanta High School. Brandi was a senior there, and I had planned to go Thursday to talk with her English class about the play. Her teacher, Mrs. Singleton, often took a group of students to plays around town. Brandi went each time. I looked forward to talking to Brandi's class. Janil said she would be delighted to go with me. I told her I would pick her up at 8 o'clock because I was scheduled to be in the classroom by nine.

Deeva Denez

At 7:55, Janil was waiting at the designated spot. We both smiled as she entered the car. She looked really nice with long, fitting pants and a red turtle neck sweater. The outfit showed off her shapely figure. Janil was fine as aged vintage wine. By her mannerisms, I don't think she knew how stacked she was. I know when I was young I was straight up and down. It wasn't until I became uncaged that I realized I was shapely with curves, including bust. I hope it doesn't take Janil thirty-eight years to enlighten herself about her body.

"Thanks for coming to get me, Miss Deeva," Janil said as she entered the car. I just came outside, but I was getting cold," she said placing her purse by her feet.

"The car is nice and warm. You will warm up fast," I said turning the heat up hotter. "It's a nice day. I'm glad it's not raining like the weatherman said it would today."

"I gave up on the weather people a long time ago. I just take the weather as it comes."

"Me, too. But sometimes I like to see how far off the mark they are, and how they try to glaze over it the next day."

"I'm really looking forward to seeing one of my teachers, Mrs. Fuller. We use to pray in her class all the time. The bell would ring, and we would still be praying. She's the one who told me I was going to marry the guy I'm seeing now. We were both in her class. I talked to her last night, so she knows I'm coming."

"Maybe, I can meet her, too. I've never seen you so excited before."

"She's like my play mama. Sometimes she got in trouble with the principal because of her religious practices at school. Whenever the principal would give her any heat, she'd say that she was on God's time. She didn't care what he did. She knew what she had to do. She was great"! Janil exclaimed, bubbling over.

"How do you feel about Mrs. Singleton? She sounded nice over the phone."

"Oh, Mrs. Singleton is a nice person, but Mrs. Fuller is the bomb!"

"Good. I can't wait to meet both teachers. We will be there soon," I said driving on the surface streets anxious to get to the school.

The remainder of the drive was just as pleasant. Janil and I talked the whole time. Janil was such a pleasure to be around. She was like the daughter I never had, but always wanted. She reminded me of my relationship with my own mother - - a relationship I will cherish all of my life. I was thankful God blessed me with Mya, Francine and Brandi, three daughters of my own. Sometimes I talked to Brandi the way I talked to Janil, but it was not the same. Janil was truly special. I was glad God placed her in my life.

We checked in at the office when we arrived at the school. Janil took us to Mrs. Singleton's room. Mrs. Singleton, an elderly, stocky, white teacher, was sitting behind her desk, in the front of the room, when we entered the classroom. Several students were sitting down. Brandi and Marlon, her boyfriend of three years, were among them.

"Mrs. Singleton, I'm Deeva Denez," I said as I entered the classroom.

"Ms. Denez, it is a pleasure to have you here," she said getting up. "Please have my chair."

"Thank you. I brought Janil with me. She's in my play. She's playing me, the leading role."

"Janil, it's good seeing you again," Mrs. Singleton greeted her cheerfully. "How is Agnes Scott?"

"It's great, Mrs. Singleton. I really like it! Hey, Brandi and Marlon," Janil said waving.

"Mrs. Singleton, before I sit down, I need to go to the ladies room," I said putting my coat on the chair.

"Sure. Janil can you take Ms. Denez to the teachers' lounge?"

"Yes. Miss Deeva, follow me," she said leading the way.

"I'll meet you back in the classroom, Miss Deeva. I have some more people I want to visit while I'm here," she said as she disappeared.

The lounge was down the hallway from Mrs. Singleton's classroom. I had no problem finding my way back. The bell rang seconds after I went back inside. A few students came in after the bell. I could tell Mrs. Singleton did not want to address the matter at that time. The students acted like it was no big deal that they were late as if it was an everyday occurrence. I smiled trying not to think about the latecomers, but on what I was going to say.

"Class, we have a visitor today, Ms. Deeva Denez, Brandi's mother. She is an author, and her book will be a play next month. She also brought along, Janil, who is starring in the play. I'm sure most of you know Janil. She graduated last year. Now, if you will please welcome, Ms. Denez," she said as she sat on the front row in a vacant desk.

I received a lot of blank expressions on all of their faces except Brandi, Marlon, and Samantha, Brandi's friend. They were smiling. The class was half and half – half white and half black. Janil came back as I stood up to speak. She was all smiles, too.

"Good morning, class," I began to speak while searching for the right words. "My name is Deeva Denez. I wrote a book called, *Uncaged.* It is a story about my life. Next month, March 31 and April 1, it will be a play at The 14th Street Playhouse. The book begins with my parents, who just found out that I was on the way. They wanted to abort me because they were young and poor. Well, as you can see, I made it by the grace of God. But it was a real issue with them at that time.

Growing up, my father slapped and punched me in my face all the time until I was eighteen years old, about your age. It was at that time that I fought my dad and left home. Eight days later, I got married. I want to say to you don't make the same mistake I did. Don't leave home then get married right away. That's just like jumping from the frying pan into the fire. I understand you may be having problems at home. My advice to you is to either work out your problems while you're at home or work them out when you leave. But don't use your problems at home as an excuse for getting married because you will only carry your problems into the marriage. It may take you the rest of your life to work it out. It took me twenty years to realize that some of the troubles I was having in my marriage were due to issues from my childhood.

Also, it is important to choose the right mate the first time. You can marry the wrong person for the wrong reasons. When I got married at eighteen, I was young. I did not know how to judge a person by character. Godly character is important in a mate as well as in you. My criteria was how much fun I had when we were together. Let me tell you, fun and good looks don't pay the bills. You need someone who can manage money, hold a decent job, spend time with you, and take his or her commitment seriously. Marriage is serious. Don't get married if you are not willing to pay the price and endure until the end.

Uncaged covers the first thirty-eight years of my life. God told me to write it in '94. He told me to write the book the end of April or the beginning of May of '95. I started writing *Uncaged* April 21, 1995. I completed it November 13, 1996. *Uncaged* deals with forgiving those who have mistreated you. It took me thirty-eight years and six years of depression to forgive my father and husband at that time. Forgiveness is important. It releases the person who has hurt you, thereby getting rid of all the hurt, anger and pain that is associated with their actions. When you truly forgive someone, it frees you. Thus, you become uncaged or set free from your past. You are now able to live your life to the fullest, the way God intended for us to live. Our past should be our past and not part of our present. If you have something against someone, forgive him or her today. Don't let the sun go down on your wrath. Forgiveness changed my life. I know it will change yours, too.

I would like to read briefly from my book. Something that I think you will find interesting. But before I read, let's hear what Janil has to say. Janil it's your turn," I said, sitting down as she came to the center of the room.

Janil gave her childlike smile as she walked to the front of the room. She captured the whole class' attention as she found her place. "Hello, everybody. I'm Janil. Looking at the faces, I know most of you. I just want to tell you that I got a role in Miss Deeva's play by being in the right place at the right time. When I was here at North Atlanta, I was told I couldn't act. But I didn't let what other people said about me stop me from doing what I love - - acting. My love for acting and the training I received here helped me to do what I'm doing now. Actually, when I went to the producer's office, I went for a modeling job, but he recruited me for the play. I want to encourage each of you, who is interested in acting, to pursue your dreams. Have faith in yourself even if no one else does. Fortunately, I have the support of my family. My mother is very supportive of me, and I'm glad of that. Some of you may not have your family backing you, but don't let that stop you. Rely on God. I hope you can come and see me and the other cast members perform. Maybe one day you'll be on stage, too," she said as she closed.

The students and Mrs. Singleton asked both Janil and I questions before I read Chapter 6 from *Uncaged*. I tried to pick something they could relate to. Chapter 6 dealt with my teenage years when I first became involved with Carl. I read The Varsity scene. "...Are you

191

hungry? We can go to The Varsity," Carl asked, looking at me smiling.

"Yes, I am. The Varsity will be great! I've never been there before." I suddenly remembered I hadn't eaten a thing all day. I looked at Carl while he was driving. He was cola brown with golf ball shaped eyes. His nose and ears were large, but somehow, they went well together. His teeth were yellow and uneven with some kind of golden-yellow stuff on the front, bottom tooth that completely encircled it. If it was plaque, it had been there all of his life. It was definitely not your ordinary plaque buildup.

He was a nice guy, I told myself, a Christian. That counted for something. Carl was a talker. He talked the whole way to The Varsity. He was funny, too. I've never heard anyone put words together the way he did. He had me cracking up the entire time. I've never laughed so much in all my life. Boy, did it feel good. Thirty minutes later, we finally reached The Varsity. He went to the curb side service.

"What do you want to eat?" he asked as he slipped his right arm around my shoulders.

"What's on the menu?"

"Chili dogs, hamburgers, French fries, onion rings, fruit turnovers, sodas, shakes and ice cream."

"I'll have one of everything you named," I said smiling at him.

I noticed his smile disappeared after I placed my order. He ordered ice water for himself.

"Aren't you hungry?"

"Not anymore. I suddenly lost my appetite. But yours is big enough for both of us. When was the last time you ate?"

"Everything sounds so good on the menu. I want to try them all. I may be thin, but I eat like a horse."

"You mean a herd of horses. At this rate, you'll be as big as a house, and I'll vanish into thin air."

"I'll let you have some of my food if your appetite comes back. I don't want you to be hungry."

"That's very kind of you, Miss Piggy. Or should I say, Mr. Ed. Monday afternoon, I'll definitely start looking for another job. It takes a week's wages just to feed you for a date."

When the food came, the waiter placed my order in front of Carl. Carl told him only the ice water was his. All the food was mine. The waiter brought the food to my window and looked at me in disbelief.

"When is the baby due?" he asked, handing me the ice cream. I get pregnant customers all the time, and they always order ice cream."

"I'm not pregnant. I'm hungry."

He looked at Carl. "More power to you, brother. You must be a good man," he said, walking away shaking his head.

"I hope I impress you as much as I impress him," Carl said, gazing at me and giving me a golden plaque smile.

"You don't have to impress me."

"Oh, no? Since that's the case, you really don't think I'm gonna let you eat all that food in front of me, do you?" His long arms reached past my nose to retrieve the food at my window ledge. He centered the food between us.

Before I finished my fries, Carl had eaten the hamburger, onion rings, shake and apple turnover. When I realized what was happening, I stuffed the chilidog in my mouth whole! A race was on, and I was losing. I squeezed the ice cream in my lap, hoping it was not his next target. I put my soda between my seat and the door. I leaned toward the door and turned my head to eat my chilidog in peace. The way he was eating, I wasn't sure it was safe. The only thing that was safe was his ice water, which was untouched.

After the last morsel disappeared, I heard a loud burp and an earth-shaking fart. I thought to myself, this Negro is crazy. Not once did he say excuse me or anything. Does he think I'm deaf? "Aren't you going to say excuse me?" I asked in complete disgust.

"Why? It's only natural to burp and pass gas after you eat...."

I finished the rest of the chapter. The class laughed most of the time. They wanted me to read some more, but I ran out of time. The bell rang as they asked. Before they left, however, Mrs. Singleton gave them last minute instructions for their next assignment. Janil and I said our good-byes before going to Mrs. Fuller's class.

Mrs. Fuller was slender, medium height and medium build with salt and pepper short hair. Janil said she drove a Mercedes and went to World Changers Church. Mrs. Fuller's eyes lit up when she saw Janil, who quickly introduced me. She talked to me as if she had known me for years. The conversation of course was centered around Jesus - - something the three of us loved to talk about. Forty minutes later, we left. I dropped Janil off at the campus and told her I would see her tonight at rehearsal.

CHAPTER THIRTY-ONE

Everyone was at rehearsal that night except Robert, who played Zakee. Pele didn't wait on him to start because his first scene was the last scene before intermission or Act One, Scene Five. Pele was busy teaching the blocking with Janil as Vanessa and Dana as Cynthia. Greg just fit right in. He played his role well no matter who performed.

Brandi had started going with me to rehearsal. It was entertainment for both of us. She laughed as much as I did. Renae was especially funny when she made snide remarks about Dana, an old friend of hers. Sometimes we laughed so much, I don't see how anything was accomplished, but it was. Each night the performance got better.

The following week, Robert came late some days, some days he didn't come at all. That Thursday, we left the gym and went to Ronald's new place on Columbia Drive. I volunteered to go to the gym and direct anyone who had not gotten the news of the new location. Dana and Dad showed up by rehearsal time. I waited thirty more minutes before going to the new location myself. I was hoping Robert was there, but he was not. We all came to the conclusion that he had dropped out, and he had.

After rehearsal, I asked Darius if he would play Zakee. We could easily get someone else to play Bryson because it was a smaller part. He didn't like the idea. He said he liked being Bryson. The following week, he too, dropped out. Now the play was two men short - - Zakee and Bryson roles. The play was in six weeks. What were we going to do?

It seemed as if, Ronald had run out of men. He didn't have any replacements. I prayed about it, and the Lord put Marlon, Brandi's boyfriend, on my mind. I called him the next day. He said he would play Bryson for me. Pele had already said he would play Zakee as well as direct. With the addition of Marlon, we were full cast again. But for how long? So many things were happening with the cast members, I was beginning to think my play was jinxed…but I knew it wasn't. Quite contrary. It had God's blessings. Satan was just trying to have his way.

The cast stabilized after Marlon joined. I now had a committed cast. They worked hard. Their hearts were in the play. It made me feel good to know that I could depend on them to see the play through.

On March 14, Ronald asked for more advertisement money - - $1776. I gave it to him. He said everything was set. We were ready to put the play on...then he pulled the plug on the play the next week, a week before it was due to open.

He arranged a mock play and invited outsiders to critique it with a questionnaire. The results were by a majority consensus that the play was not ready. Later he gave the "new" play dates, May 5 & 6. These dates were final. He assured me. Of course, the cast was just as upset as I was. It seemed as though the play would never happen. Fortunately, they continued to come to rehearsal. I was thankful of that. I prayed constantly for the play, and God continued to answer.

By now, it was obvious to everyone that Ronald was shady. He lied constantly. I discovered that he frequently did not remember his lies. He'd say one thing today and another thing tomorrow. His lack of character was getting on my nerves, but I was determined to have the play anyway. I had put too much money into it to back out now. One thing about me, I am not a quitter. Nothing Ronald could do could make me stop the play. He realized it, too.

Ronald called me into his office Friday, March 30. I went not knowing what to expect. He let me in and escorted me to his office.

"Have a seat, Deeva," he said as he opened the door. I sat down, waiting for him to speak.

"I knew the play was not ready, but you would not have believed me. That's why I had the mock play," he said sitting up at his desk twirling a pen in his hand. "I have the results right here," he said reaching for a folder on his desk. "Read the questionnaires for yourself. Deeva, you don't want to go to The 14th Street Playhouse and bomb out. You will ruin your chances of doing anything else with the play. I plan to take it on the road. But I can't take it anywhere if you flop at the first showing. I had an investor at the premiere last week. He's still interested. We're talking about $250,000. That's too much money to blow by being too fast. I have other investors who are interested, too. Either way, you can sell *Uncaged* after the play. I've lost a lot of money in the play already. I'm in the business of making money, not losing it."

"Me, too. I can't take another date change. We will end up losing the cast members we have. So far they have been committed to the play, but you keep changing the dates. That's not right."

"Look, Deeva. I said May 5 & 6 are the final dates of the play. That will give us enough time to make sure it's right. I checked with the box office and they said the play was sold out for April 1."

"What happens to their money?" I asked pleased to know the show was sold out, but disappointed at the same time because we didn't capitalize on it. And how long can he keep jerking my fans around? By the time the play is performed, no one will come.

"Their money will be refunded. We're in this boat together, Deeva. I can't afford to lose anymore money."

"Me, either."

"The play is shaping up. It will be ready in May. Well, that's all I have to discuss. Do you have anything else you want to say?"

"No. I'll just be glad when we have the play. The delay is getting on everyone's nerves. I see it in the cast. I'm feeling it, too."

"Don't worry, Deeva. You will be a rich woman when it's over."

We both smiled. I left the office shortly thereafter. The thought of having an investor really interested me. I hoped he liked the play and was willing to take it to a higher level - - a movie. With the possibility of the play going to different cities, surely it would attract a lot of attention. The possibilities were endless - - movie, merchandise, TV and radio appearances, commercials, as well as a spot in other movies. Deeva Denez and *Uncaged* would be household names. I smiled all the way home as I continued to broaden the list.

Brandi told me Tia had called when I entered the house. I had been so wrapped up in thought, I had forgotten I was supposed to visit her after I left Ronald's office. God blessed her with a son, Marc Anthony, last year on November 25, three days after Mya's second birthday. She probably called to see what happened. I called her back as soon as Brandi ended her conversation.

"Hello," Tia said as she answered the phone.

"Tia, I'm sorry. I forgot about coming over today. When I left Ronald's, my mind was on our conversation."

"What did he say about the play?"

"He changed the dates to May 5 & 6. He said this time it is final."

"Yeah, right! I thought the play was good when I came last week. You could have pulled it off easily. He's jerking you around. If I were you, I would have fixed him long ago."

"He told me about investors that he has. A lot of money is involved. The play has to be right in order to cash in on what they have to offer."

"Wait-a-minute. I have to get Marc. He just woke up and is crying."

I waited for three minutes.

"I'm back. I'm breastfeeding him while I talk to you. He's a greedy little thing."

"So, you're adjusting to motherhood pretty well?"

I guess so. As long as I feed him, he's happy. It's not much to it so far. The hardest part is getting enough sleep, especially since I went back to work last month."

"Do you still want another child?"

"I sure do. I hope I have it within the next five years. I want to have my children before I turn thirty-five."

"You have plenty of time. You can be like me and have a child in your forties."

"No, thank you. I prefer to have mine by thirty-five."

"Well, since you have Marc, I hope you have a little girl the next time."

"Me, too. I've always wanted a boy and a girl. Her name will be Lauren Ashley."

"Who knows, you may have them back-to-back. Sometimes when it's hard to get pregnant, it's not uncommon to get pregnant soon after you have the first one."

"That's okay. As long as I have them, and they are healthy, I don't mind having them close together. How is Mya?"

"She's fine. I just walked in the door. I haven't seen her since I've been home. She must be asleep or looking at TV. How is Derrick handling fatherhood?"

"He's so funny. You should see him sneaking, feeding Marc. I caught him one night sitting in the dark giving Marc a bottle. I couldn't do anything but laugh. He loves Marc, and Marc is crazy about his dad."

"That's good. I hear Mya crying. Let me get off the phone and see what's going on with her. Maybe we can get together next week."

"Okay. Bye."

"Bye," I said as I hung up the phone. I ran up the steps as the receiver touched the phone cradle. Mya's cries led to Brandi's bedroom. When I stepped across the threshold, I saw Francine taking something out of Mya's hand. Brandi was sprawled across the bed watching TV. "What's going on I asked?"

"Mama! Mama!" Mya yelled running to me still crying.

I picked her up. She pointed her finger at Francine, who was sitting on the edge of the bed looking at us.

"Francine took my lip (lip-gloss)," she said crying.

"No! It's mine! You took it from my room!" Francine screeched with the lip-gloss in her hands.

"It's mine, Mama," Mya said crying.

"Let me see it," I commanded Francine. She gave it to me. It was the same lip-gloss Mya had found outside two days ago. "This is her lip-gloss," I said handing it to Mya.

"That's mine," Francine defended as I gave it to Mya.

"No, it's hers. (I felt like since she found it, it was hers to keep. I had seen that same lip-gloss for days, but ignored it. Anyone could have seen it at the base of the front steps. Mya saw it and picked it up. I cleaned it off. To me, since she found it, it was hers.)

"You bought her one like mine?" Francine asked.

I didn't answer the question. "Come on, Mya. Go in Mama's room. I'll read you a book," I said as I turned to leave.

"Mama," Brandi said to my back.

"Yes," I responded, turning toward her.

"Tomorrow, I want to go to church with you," she said facing me, looking from the TV.

"That's fine," I said, going to my room.

"I hate her church," I heard Francine say as I left.

Lately, it seemed as if Francine and I were bumping heads. She kept an attitude – something I detested. Once she was sweet and innocent - - that's how she was when I first met her at the age of six, four and a half years ago. Every since Brandi came, last June, Francine changed. She clung to Brandi and distanced herself from me. She didn't seem like "my" little girl anymore, but my stepdaughter. Since she was next to Mya, I'm sure she felt displaced. No longer was she the baby, but the middle daughter. Francine was eight years older than Mya and seven years younger than Brandi. Since Brandi came back into her life last year, she wanted to identify with her. By doing so, she distanced herself from Mya and me. I was an adult and understood what was happening, Mya didn't. Mya wanted to bond with a sister, who was grasping for her place and identity with the family.

Each day, I found it more difficult to balance my role. Especially since Francine and Raymond Jr. were becoming intolerable by the day. Every since their mom, Stacy, came into the picture, four years ago, it had been a constant battle. Stacy was out of their lives until I came on the scene. She told me that she wanted them to know their real mother. What she failed to realize was that she had an opportunity to be their mother the five years before I came into the picture. But being their mother wasn't important then. Only after she heard her children rant and rave over another woman did she want to be in their lives. Of course, the kids were glad to finally have their mother in their lives. I was glad for them. Somehow, I would have to deal with the constant rejection and distance they had placed between us. My prayer was that one-day the gap between us would be bridged by the loving hand of Jesus Christ, my Lord. He could do it. I prayed that He would.

Mya cuddled up to me when I took her into our room. She bathed her lips with the lip-gloss. How could such a little thing give so much joy? Often times, it's not the big things that give us joy, but the little things in life. Joy is something God wants us all to have along with peace and happiness. Not as the world gives it to us, but as He gives it. (John 14:24) The world can't give it, and the world can't take it away. When we truly know Jesus, His joy comes along. So does His peace and His happiness. These things are not centered on the things of this world but are of Him.

As I watched Mya engrossed in her lip-gloss, I smiled. She knew how to enjoy the simple pleasures of life. "Are you okay now?" I asked as she swiped her lips again.

"Want some, Mama?" she asked putting it to my lips.

"Sure. Give Mama some," I said volunteering my lips.

She smattered the substance on my lips. "I love you, Mama," she said as she finished.

"I love you, too," I said as she continued glossing her own lips again. I sat and watched her, re-living a million memories of her. God truly is an awesome God, I thought as I reminisced.

199

CHAPTER THIRTY-TWO

The next day, I went to church with the kids. Raymond always stayed at home. The only time he went to church was on second Sundays in Dublin. The kids and I went with him, with the exception of Brandi, who stayed behind because of lack of car space and lack of interest. It felt good having Brandi with me. She usually had her own plans on Saturday. I was delighted she wanted to go to church with me today.

We arrived at church fifteen minutes late. It seemed as if we were moving in slow motion to get ready. Pastor Ware was a stickler about being on time. It seemed like no matter how hard I tried to be on time, I was always late. I didn't allow my tardiness to hinder my worship of Jesus. I was sorry I was late, but at least I made it. That was the main thing to me - - being there.

Since the church was not crowded, we found an empty pew, two rows from the front. Sister Dixon and Mother Hindsman were leading testimony and praise service. As we walked in, Sister Copeland was giving her testimony. By the time we got settled, she finished. Sister Janice Wallace stood up as Sister Copeland sat down.

"Giving honor to God, who is the head of my life and Jesus Christ His Son. I give honor to Pastor Ware, First Lady Ware, to all the ministers and everyone else who is present. This week, I was told some disturbing news. I was diagnosed with breast cancer. I start chemotherapy in two weeks. Before my diagnosis, I took salvation and my walk with Jesus for granted. But now I don't. I know that the God that I serve, the living Jesus Christ, who died for my sins and the sins of the whole world, can heal my body of this affliction. He is my hope, my salvation, and my strength. There is no one like Jesus. I have given my life to Him. I look to Him to see me through. I know that He will never fail me or forsake me because His Word tells me so in Hebrews 13:5. Hebrews 13:6 tells me, '...The Lord is my helper, I will not fear. What can man do to me?' At first, I was apprehensive about taking the chemo, but now I have peace. My life is in Jesus' hands. He will take care of me. I ask that all of you who know the words of pray to pray my strength in the Lord," she said as she sat down with tears in her eyes.

Mother Hindsman, sang, *Victory is Mine* after Sister Janice sat down. Sister Dixon followed with, *Can't Nobody Do Me Like Jesus*. We praised Jesus for another forty-five minutes with testimonies, songs, and praises. Pastor Ware called Sister Janice up front to be prayed over and anointed for healing after praise and testimony service. Pastor Ware was obeying the Scriptures in James 5:14-16, *"Is anyone among you sick? Let him call for the elders of the church, and let them pray over him, anointing him with oil in the name of the Lord. And the prayer of faith will save the sick, and the Lord will raise him up. And if he has committed sins, he will be forgiven. Confess your trespasses to one another, and pray for one another, that you may be healed. The effective, fervent prayer of a righteous man avails much."*

Minister Green gave the announcement when Pastor Ware finished. Afterwards, Pastor Ware, a lean dark-skinned man came forward to give the sermon.

"At this time, let me pray," he said as he reached the microphone. *"Father in the name of Jesus, I thank you for this day. I thank you for another opportunity to give Your Word. Please guard my lips that I only say what You would have me to say. Bless the hearing, that Your people will receive Your message through me. In Jesus' name I pray. Amen and Amen,"* he said lifting his head and opening his eyes. "Brethren, I want you to keep Sister Janice in your prayers this week. We believe God for her healing. Amen.

My sermon today comes from Luke 21, starting at the 8th verse. I often say, we're living in the last of the last days. Today, I want to show you in the Scriptures just where we are in Bible prophecy," he said opening his Bible, turning pages. "Verse 8 says, *'And He said*: (referring to Jesus) *'Take heed that you not be deceived.'* "We know that Satan came to deceive the whole world. That's what Revelation 12:9 says. Brethren we know the truth, therefore, we should not be deceived. Let me read on. *'For many will come in My name, saying, 'I am He.'* Jesus correctly predicted that many false prophets and preachers will rise up saying Jesus is the Christ, but lying about His message. I get so sick and tired of all the phony, so called, preachers I hear on the radio and see on TV. They use Jesus to get people to come to them, so they can get their money. Money is their god. Let's continue reading. *'Therefore do not go after them.'* Listen to Jesus' warning. Don't go after them. So the question may arise, how can I tell a true preacher from a false preacher? Turn your Bibles to Revelation 12. Revelation 12 speaks of the birth of Jesus and His true Church. It tells of how Satan wanted to destroy both Jesus and His true Church. Let's pick up the story in verse 13, *'Now the dragon (That's Satan) saw that he had been cast to the earth, he persecuted the woman who gave birth to the male Child (Jesus). But the woman was given two wings of a great eagle, that she might fly into the wilderness to her place, where she is nourished for a time and times and half a time, from the presence of the serpent.'* God's true Church is a small, persecuted church. Jesus said in Matthew 16:18, *'And I also say to you that you are Peter, and on this rock I will build My church, and the gates of Hades shall not prevail against it.'* The Church that Jesus started at His first coming will be here at His second coming. Let's still see how we can identify His true Church from the many false churches. Let's read verse 15, *'So the serpent spewed water out of his mouth like a flood after the woman, that he might cause her to be carried away by the flood.'* Satan wanted to destroy Jesus' Church. To me the flood represents false teaching. *'But the earth helped the woman, and the earth opened its mouth and swallowed up the flood which the dragon had spewed out of his mouth. And the dragon was enraged with the woman, and he went to make war with the rest of her offspring, who keep the commandments of God and Have the testimony of Jesus Christ.'* Brethren, God's true Church will keep His commandments. His commandments are not done away with as these hypocritical preachers proclaim. I'm so sick and tired of their lies that lead God's people astray. Believe the Word of God. God's true Church keeps His commandments.

Quickly go back to Luke 21. I want to wrap this up and tell you where we are in Bible prophecy. Luke 21:9 says, *'But when you hear of wars and commotions, do not be terrified; for these things must come to pass first, but the end will not come immediately.'* Man have fought wars in the past, present and will in the future. We know this to be true. So first, we have false prophets, followed by wars. Let's see what's next in verse 11, *'And there will be great earthquakes in various places, and famines and pestilences...'* Famines and pestilences or diseases are the result of wars. All these things we have experienced, but they will come in the future in a more severe degree. Let's read the last part of verse 11, *'and there will be fearful sights and great signs from heaven.* What are these Scriptures talking about?

Turn your Bibles to Revelation 6. By the way, these same Scriptures are found in Matthew 24 and Mark 13. Revelation 6 explains these Scriptures. Revelation 6 tells about six seals. The first seal is false prophets, who ride on a white horse with a bow and a crown and go out conquering. We find Jesus the True servant of God described in Revelation 19:11-13, *'Now I saw heaven opened and behold a white horse. And He who sat on him was called Faithful and True, and in righteousness He judges and makes war. His eyes were like a flame of fire, and on His head were many crowns. He had a name written that no one knew except Himself. He was clothed with a robe dipped in blood, and His name is called The Word of God.'*

Go back to Revelation 6:3. This explains the second seal, war. *'When He opened the second seal, I heard the second living creature saying, 'Come and see. Another horse, fiery red, went out. And it was granted to the one who sat on it to take peace from the earth, and that people should kill one another; and there was given to him a great sword.'* His horse was red because it represented bloodshed.

Let's read the third seal, famine, in the next verse. *'When He opened the third seal, I heard the third living creature say, 'Come and see.' So I looked, and behold, a black horse, and he who sat on it had a pair of scales in his hand. And I heard a voice in the midst of the four living creatures saying, 'A quart of wheat for a denarius, and three quarts of barley for a denarius; and do not harm the oil and the wine.'* The black horse represents death. It's saying here that food will be expensive because it will be in short supply. A denarius is equal to one day's wages.

Read verse 7 to find out about the fourth seal or pestilence. *'When He opened the forth seal, I heard the voice of the fourth living creature saying, 'Come and see.' 'So I looked, and behold, a pale horse. And the name of him who sat on it was Death, and Hades followed with him. And power was given to them over a forth of the earth, to kill with sword, with hunger, with death, and by the beast of the earth.'* This forth horse is pestilence or disease. It will kill a forth of the people. I want you to understand that once these seals are opened, they will continue to destroy mankind until Jesus returns. They will get worse, not better.

Now, read the fifth seal in verse 9. *'When he opened the fifth seal, I saw under the alter the souls of those who had been slain for the word of God and for the testimony which they held. And they cried with a loud voice, saying, 'How long, O Lord, holy and true, until You judge and advenge our blood on those who dwell on the earth. Then a white robe was given to each of them; and it was said to them that they should rest a little while longer, until both the number of their fellow servants and their brethren, who would be killed as they were, was completed.'* Finally, I have come to where we are in Bible prophecy. We are at the fifth seal. Others have died before us for Jesus' sake. But there are others to follow. This will be the time of the Great Tribulation, yet ahead spoken of in Revelation 7:14. This Tribulation - this martyrdom of saints - must occur and be completed before God pours out the vials of His wrath and His plagues at the second coming of Christ. The Great Tribulation is the wrath of Satan. He knows that his time is short when God intervenes, when God's plagues fall, when Christ returns to rule the earth. The day will come when our faith will be tested. We will give our lives for Jesus. Will you be able to stand in that dreadful day? Paul tells us in Romans 12:1 & 2, *'to present our bodies as living sacrifices, to be holy and acceptable to God. We are not to conform to this world, but be transformed by the renewing of our minds, that we may prove what is that good and acceptable will of God.'* It's time out for shuckin and jivin. We need to get real! This is also why the rapture theory is false doctrine. It proclaims that Christ will return before the Great Tribulation to receive His own. The Scriptures clearly states that Jesus will come after the Great Tribulation and many saints will be killed during this time. Amen.

In conclusion, the sixth seal is the heavenly sign spoken of in Luke 21:11, the last part that we read - - *'the fearful sights and great signs from heaven.'* Look at verse 12, *'But before all these things, they will lay their hands on you and persecute you, delivering you up to the synagogues and prisons. You will be brought before kings and rulers for My name's sake. But it will turn out for you as an occasion for testimony.'*

Remember we read about the true Church earlier, who keep the commandments of God and the testimony of Jesus Christ. You will be given an opportunity to testify for the Lord. If you deny Him, He will deny you. It's something to think about. Before I close, let me read the heavenly signs, so you won't be ignorant of them. They will follow after the Great Tribulation. Revelation 6:12-14 says, *'I looked when He opened the sixth seal, and behold, there was a great earthquake; and the sun became black as sackcloth of hair, and the moon became like blood. And the stars of heaven fell to the earth as a fig tree drops its late figs when it is shaken by a mighty wind. Then the sky receded as a scroll when it is rolled up, and every mountain and island was moved out of its place.'*

Clearly, these heavenly signs have not taken place, which proves again that the sixth seal has not been opened yet. The fact that we still have mountains and islands proves it. The Great Tribulation hasn't occurred either, but the other four seals are in operation. Be not deceived, brethren! Believe the plain teachings of the Scriptures," he said closing his Bible.

One day I'll have to give a sermon on the seventh seal; That Great Day of God's Wraths upon the sinners of this world. This is sometimes known as The Return of Jesus Christ or The Day of The Lord. Most of the remainder of Revelation is concerning it, which ushers in the return of Jesus.

Let me pray. *Father in the name of Jesus, I thank You for the Word that was* given. *I pray that You will give them understanding of the six seals, and especially the fifth seal and the Great Tribulation to come. May we be able to stand in that evil and dreadful day. Help us to really get to know Your Son, Jesus Christ and be willing to give our very lives if that is Your will. In Jesus name I pray, Amen.*

Brother Dix will now come forth to receive the offering," Pastor Ware said as he sat down. Brother Dix came forward, along with Minister Copeland to take up the offering. Cheryl, Brother Dix's wife and Sister Janice's daughter, asked her right side to stand and give their offering. Since I was on her right, I stood up. Next, she asked her left side to stand. They did. After everyone gave, Brother Dix blessed the offering. Pastor Ware came forward again to welcome our visitors and dismiss us. Brandi stood up and said a few words. She even sang a song. We left twenty minutes later after fellowshipping with the other church family.

CHAPTER THIRTY-THREE

Going to church was always the highlight of my week. It gave me the spiritual charge I needed to fight Satan's fiery darts. The Lord that I serve - - Jesus - - is greater than Satan. Therefore, I knew I was victorious every time! Everyday I thanked my heavenly Father for His Son, Jesus Christ. Without Jesus, I would be lost and die in my sins. But because of Jesus, I can have eternal life, and my sins, as well as the sins of this world, are forgiven.

Everything went well with rehearsal for the month of April. Each night the performance got better. They were still funny. It was the best form of entertainment I had had in a long time. Towards the end of the month, Ronald printed flyers for the play. He said the tickets would be available soon. But soon never came because he canceled the play again. He told us a week before the scheduled date of May 5 & 6. The cast and I were furious, to say the least. My main concern was holding on to the cast. I didn't want to lose them; they had been too faithful. When I talked to them, they reassured me they would not leave.

Ronald's explanation was that the play was still not ready to him. The "new" dates were May 26 & 27, Memorial Day weekend. He wanted me to pay him $3200 more dollars to keep from canceling the play. I told him I didn't have $3200 to give him. I had given him too much money already. He was insistent about canceling. He demanded that I give him $1500 to keep the play. I agreed to $1500 over three installments because I had spent too much money, thus far, not to have my play. By now, I knew he was a crook, but I was determined to have my play. He also changed the contract agreement for the play to continue. His share was 25% instead of 23%, and my share was 75% instead of 77%, but I was now responsible for paying the cast for their performance and rehearsal. The next day he handed the cast contracts making me responsible for paying them. I was shocked, to say the least.

The next week, the first week in May, I came up with a payment for the cast. Ronald had told them from the beginning that they would get $50 per rehearsal. I kept that pay scale. My payments started that week. I made a rehearsal sign up sheet to keep track of their pay. It was understood that they wouldn't be paid until after the play. Up until now, Ronald had not paid them anything. They had worked too hard not to get paid. He had told them that he would pay them $250 per hour, per performance. The play lasted two and a half hours. My pay scale varied with each performer. Janil was paid the most because she had more lines and stage time. Marlon was paid the least and everyone else fell in between.

When I presented my pay plan to the cast, they were pleased. In most cases, I was paying them more than what they wanted according to a questionnaire I passed out earlier. I wanted to be fair with them. And going by what I should gross, there shouldn't be any problem with me paying them their due. I could pay them and still have some left for me.

It was at this time I decided to drop Paula as my publisher. So far, she hadn't done anything. My books were not in any bookstores. No book signings had been scheduled. She had not paid me for any of my books nor told me how many books had been sold. Each time I brought the subject up of payment and inventory she became indignant. She treated me as if I was some sort of pest bothering her since she was so busy working on other peoples' work. I had had enough of her and her non-professionalism. God showed me during this time that I could publish my books myself. I had learned a lot while I was doing nothing. The good part was, I could publish my books for others and myself. My desire was to help as many people to get published as possible. I thanked Jesus for the experience with Paula. Her lack of promoting me caused me to learn how to do everything myself. Only God can turn our mishaps into miracles. The Literary Connection, thanks to Paula, would be a renowned business, helping others to get published and fulfill their dreams.

I wrote her a letter, immediately. I wanted to make sure that when I got paid for the play, there would not be any misunderstandings. People love to pop up when money is involved. Also when Ronald's investors offered me a deal, I didn't want to be bound by any contract with Paula. I knew, even though, she hadn't kept her end of our contract, she would be looking to get paid - - it's a fact of life. In addition, I planned to re-publish *Uncaged* for the third time after the play. I planned to publish *The Bearer of the Sign* as well. It had been written before Mya was born, but I was waiting until *Uncaged* took off first. After the play, I would publish both books. My life as an author would start again. I looked forward to the author arena. Thanks to Lisa and Paula, I had been out of circulation since *Uncaged* was first published December of 1997. I was determined to come back with vengeance! I prayed constantly that a demand was being created for my work, and that all this was in God's marvelous plan to accelerate my work, which is really the work of God. I know God has strange ways of doing things. I prayed that this was one of them.

Late Wednesday night, May 9, Ronald called me at home. I was in my bed asleep when the telephone rang. "Hello," I said as I answered the phone.

"Deeva, I have some bad news," Ronald said, hurriedly.

"What is it?" I asked, disturbed.

"I just got a call from Greg. He's gone to California because he has a part in a movie."

"A part in a movie?" I repeated.

"Yes, and he doesn't know when he will be back."

"The play is two and a half weeks away. Do you have someone to replace him?"

"No. But I talked to Pele before I called you, he may have someone. He said he had to make a few phone calls first."

I sat straight up in bed. "He was at rehearsal tonight. I'm surprised he didn't say anything."

"Deeva, I have to be honest with you. Greg got locked up. They just picked him up to take him to Alabama. I don't know how long he will be gone."

"It's going to be hard to replace him. He was really good as Carl," I said.

"He was trying to prove himself," Ronald added.

"What do you mean?" I asked.

"Greg is gay. His roommate called me tonight and told me what happened."

"I didn't know he was gay. He fooled me. But I guess that explains the earrings, tongue ring and nipple rings."

"Well, Deeva, I'll call you after I hear from Pele. I should hear something by tomorrow."

"If he has someone, tell him to bring him to rehearsal."

"Okay. I'll talk to you later.

"Okay, bye," I said as I hung up the phone.

I reclined in my bed unable to fall back to sleep. I kept thinking of Greg being locked up and gay. I liked how he played Carl. Then I thought about how he was the only cast member besides Madame Lee who had not been replaced. I reminded myself that with each replacement, the performance got better. I also thought about the play that was canceled this past weekend and twice before. I told myself that Greg was never meant to be in the play. He must have been part of the reason, along with Ronald, for the cancellations.

The more I tried to fall back to sleep, the more I thought about Greg, Ronald and the play. I kept telling myself, that the play would only get better. Finally, an hour later, I dozed off. As I slept, I dreamed I was at rehearsal at an unknown location. All the cast members were present. Greg was among them. They carried on as usual. When I left rehearsal, it was broad daylight outside. I walked to the nearest corner to go home. A young man came behind me and tried to kill me with a broken bottle, but I fought him back and killed him with it. Then the dream took me to a house. It was night, and I was sitting in a parked car in the driveway. Greg was outside the house, unlocking the door from the driveway to go inside. He saw me sitting in the car then came to me, leaving the door opened. A man from nowhere went inside. As Greg reached the car, a couple came up on the passenger side. The woman opened the door and looked at me. Her body turned into a demon as she spoke.

"We're going to destroy you!" she said with a demonic face that was full of wrath.

"I looked at Greg to warn him of the intruder, but he had turned into a demon as well. He looked at me smiling. I looked at him and the others before the dream ended without them causing me any harm.

I pondered the dream as I slept. All this time, I thought Greg was my friend. But the dream clearly showed me that he was indeed an enemy, out to destroy me. God knew his heart and intentions. I didn't. God didn't want him in the play. He may have done something detrimental during his performance to ruin the play, I thought.

The next evening at rehearsal, Pele brought his friend to play Carl. Ronald also had Jason, Greg's understudy, who dropped out months ago. I had asked Marlon if he was interested in playing Carl. We could always get someone to play Bryson since it was a small role. Ronald told Marlon if he tried out for Carl, then he would lose his role as Bryson. It too would be opened to the best man. Actually, Ronald never liked Marlon playing Bryson. He didn't think he was any good. He had told me so on many occasions. I defended Marlon each time because I knew he was an excellent actor and dependable - - two qualities I needed the most at this time.

Ronald asked the three men who wanted to go first? They could pick any scene in the play. Jason volunteered. Jason said he wanted to do the first scene. Janil and Dana took their positions.

"Here's your hubby now," Dana said, which was Jason's first appearance on stage after entering through the front door.

Jason walked slowly, but confident to Janil, his wife, while giving Dana an admiring glance. He kissed Janil. "Hi, honey," he said turning to Dana. "So this must be Cynthia," he said extending his hand. "Pleased to finally meet you."

They continued the scene until the end. Jason was smooth. He was very good to me. I liked his mannerisms and special touches that he gave to Carl. I couldn't wait to see the other two perform.

Next, Pele's friend and an old cast member of Ronald's performed. His name was Ta'nal. Both Ta'nal and Jason were dark and short. Jason was slender whereas Ta'nal was stocky, but not fat. He was cocky. He said he wanted to do the first scene, too. Once again, Janil and Dana started the scene. Ta'nal came in on que.

It's amazing how each person makes the same scene different. Ta'nal was real. He acted like a real person playing the part. Neither actor could portray the real Carl. I realized that a long time ago. But Ta'nal was very convincing. He seemed like a real husband. His performance was great, but I liked Jason's performance better.

Marlon wanted to play Act One, Scene Four. Carl walks out on Vanessa at the end of Scene One when he finds out that she is pregnant. He returns at the end of Scene Three. Scene Four, she returns from the hospital after losing her baby. Vanessa (Janil) is sitting and sobbing silently when Carl walks in the front door. She doesn't budge.

Carl is standing behind the couch. His voice is cracking. "Vanessa, we nee…" he clears his throat and walks around to the front of the couch. "Vanessa, we need to talk." Vanessa ignores him. Carl kneels down in front of Vanessa, putting his hand on Vanessa's knee, which she quickly moves. "Vanessa, we really need to talk."

Vanessa then said her lines. Marlon was good as Bryson, but he left much to be desired as Carl. Clearly the two best candidates were

Ta'nal and Jason. To get more input on how to objectively decide, I suggested that they do Scene Four and let Marlon do Scene One. They did. After which, Ronald, Pele and I voted. Pele voted for Ta'nal. I voted for Jason. Ronald didn't say whom he voted for but asked the other cast members to vote. The majority voted for Ta'nal. No one voted for Marlon. Both Janil and Dana said that Ta'nal had more "chemistry" with them. Jason turned them off. They couldn't connect with him. Since they were the main characters, and would have to perform with the person selected, their opinion was important. Ta'nal was, therefore, the new Carl.

Ronald immediately asked Jason if he wanted to try for Bryson? He declined and left the office upset. He said he wanted to be Carl and no one else. He told Marlon he could be Bryson. He didn't want it. I felt bad for Jason. He really out performed Ta'nal. But because he wasn't attractive, he missed out. If I had my way, he would have been Carl, but even I can't have my way all the time. And this was one of those times. After rehearsal, I asked Ronald for his opinion. He said Jason was the best. We both agreed on Jason, but the rest of the cast wanted Ta'nal. So Ta'nal had two and a half weeks to learn his lines for the May 26 & 27 play dates. He and Pele felt he would be ready. I prayed he would.

The next day, something came over me to call The 14th Street Playhouse. It was like God prompted me to do it. I had called before when flyers were first printed for the February date and Lynda, a good friend of mine, said that *Uncaged* was not mentioned as one of the plays that were being performed. So, I called to listen to the recording, and she was right. It was like God told me to call again to check again, so I did. This time, however, instead of a recording, I got a real person. A cordial woman answered the phone.

"This is The 14th Street Playhouse. How may I help you?"

"I was calling to see when *Uncaged* is playing."

"Let me check," she said. "I can't seem to find any listing for *Uncaged*. Are you sure you have the right number?"

"Yes. I am the author. My play is with R. B. Productions. The play is scheduled for May 26 & 27."

"No, I'm sorry but your play is not scheduled for those dates. You need to call your producer," she said as she hung up.

I stared at the phone, not believing my ears. My play is not scheduled, and it's two and a half weeks away! God wanted me to

Deeva Denez

know this. I'm going to get dressed and go to Ronald's office before I explode!!

CHAPTER THIRTY-FOUR

I was still angry with Ronald when I got into my car to go to the office. I had had enough of his lying, conniving ways. How many times was he going to lie about the play's date? How low could he go? I couldn't answer my questions, but I would demand that he did.

James Bignon was playing as I turned the ignition. His song was perfect for my situation, *If I Hold My Peace*. The words go like this: "If I hold my peace, let the Lord fight my battle. I know victory shall be mine. If I hold my peace, if I wait on Jesus, I know victory shall be mine. If I go to God in prayer, if I hold my peace and leave my burdens there, I know victory shall be mine. If I hold my peace and let the Lord fight my battle, I know victory shall be mine. If I step out on His Word, I know victory shall be mine. Victory shall be mine! Victory over trials and tribulations shall be mine! Thank you Lord, victory shall be mine. No weapon formed against me shall prosper. The Lord gives you victory over liars and deceivers. If I put on the whole armor of God, victory shall be mine! I will not be denied. I claim it in the name of Jesus! Victory shall be mine!!!" I thanked Jesus for that song. It strengthened me and gave me hope. If I hold my peace and let the Lord fight my battle, victory shall be mine! There is no other way to fight Satan and his cohort of demons. I was definitely in a spiritual warfare. But since I had Jesus on my side, and He is greater than Satan, victory shall be mine. I prayed as I drove.

Dear Heavenly Father,

Please fight this spiritual battle that I am engaged in. You have shown me in a dream that I have enemies that want to destroy me. In the name of Jesus, I declare victory. I know Father that this battle is not mine, but Yours. I give it to You this day. I don't know what Ronald has on his mind, but I have gone too far to quit or turn around. I want my play, and I know with You on my side, I will have it. I don't know what other obstacles are in my path, but I pray that You either remove them, help me around them or help me to go over them. Whatever they are, they won't stop me unless it is Your will. Lord, I'm not a quitter, but a Christian fighter, who does not know defeat. I thank You for the victory, in the name of Your Son, Jesus Christ. Amen.

By the time I reached Ronald's office, the peace of God had engulfed me. It was the kind of peace that the world can't give you and the world can't take it away. I was confident that Jesus was with me. He would direct my path and give me words to say. When I rang the bell, Ronald came to the door wearing a beige leisure suit. He let me inside. His top lip was swollen with several stitches. He smiled as if nothing was wrong. I smiled, too, not wanting to stare at his mouth. After locking the door, he led the way to his office. I had not called him beforehand to tell him I was coming. I just showed up.

He sat down in his chair, and I sat in the first chair. He sat back in his chair and stared at me, waiting for me to speak. "I called The 14th Street Playhouse today," I said calmly.

"I know. Nina called me as soon as you hung up. What are you trying to pull?" he asked agitated. "You had no business calling, checking up on me. I'm ready to call your play off!"

"I called to hear the recording. I wasn't expecting to talk to a person."

"I'm telling you now, I don't like what you did. Nina told me you talked to her supervisor. You almost cost us the play," he said sternly.

I looked at him in total awe. How could he say that to me? Wasn't he the one who lied about the date? "I found out my play is not May 26 & 27. As a matter of fact, they didn't have any dates for *Uncaged*."

"Look, Deeva, I have people at The 14th Street Playhouse, like Nina, that do things under the table for me. She reserves dates, so that I don't have to put a lot of money down. You messed me up today when you called. She makes sure no one else gets my dates. Look, Deeva, stay out of my business!" he said indignant.

"Your business IS my business, regarding MY play," I said emphasizing MY point.

"Deeva, you were wrong for calling and checking up on me. Stick to writing books, and I will handle my end without your help, thank you," he said looking at me with contempt.

"Ronald, you seem to be missing the point here. According to The 14th Street Playhouse, *Uncaged* is not scheduled in May or at any other time. Furthermore, I'm sick of you lying about the play dates. I am going to have my play or you will have to refund every cent of my money back or else."

"Or else what?" he asked.

"Or else I will take you to the God that I serve and let Him have His way with you. He can do a much better job of getting you straight than I can. Let me tell you now, you do not want to fall into the hands of the living God, Jesus Christ. He can deal with you worst than any court."

"Noooo, no, Deeva, you don't have to do that. I will handle things. But promise me you won't call The 14th Street Playhouse anymore. You really messed me up today."

"So, when is the play?"

"I'll let you know tomorrow."

"Listen, Ronald, you can't drag this out much longer. It's time to have the play!"

"You will get your play, Deeva. I'll have you a date by tomorrow," he said standing up.

I stood up, too. "No more games, Ronald. It's time to get serious about this play."

"I will have you a date tomorrow, and the tickets and flyers by next week. You will have your play."

"Okay," I said as I walked from his office. He escorted me to the door, locking it as I left.

I felt good leaving Ronald's office. I felt as if God had indeed fought my battle with Ronald. I smiled at the thought of Ronald, who didn't want to be put into the hands of Jesus. Although he was Muslim, he knew Jesus was with me.

Ronald called the next day to tell me the play dates of June 9 & 10. He reassured me that these were the dates. He would have tickets and flyers by next Friday, May 18, three weeks from the play. The following Friday, Ronald held true to his word, he passed out tickets, something we have never had. Now, with tickets, the play seemed real.

The cast's next biggest obstacle was the music for the play. We had been trying for months, to no avail, for Ronald to get the instrumental version of the three songs of the play. He had said his brother, who owned a recording studio, was going to take care of it. When we asked the brother, whose studio was above Ronald's old office, he said he didn't know anything about it. Greg had also suggested a music store on Glenwood Road before he left. I went to the owner, and she said she could order the music I wanted. It should be in the store within a week. I kept going back, but she never produced any music. Finally, Dad, in the play or Casey Banks said he knew of someone who could help us. This person owned a studio near him. Thankfully, his friend was able to help us. He produced the instrumental versions two weeks before the play. God was with us every step of the way.

The remaining time before the play, the cast perfected their roles. Ta'nal came through like a charm. He had learned his lines by the second week. By now, he was really getting into his character. Everyone seemed happy about the play. I knew they, like me, were waiting on THE day, which was soon approaching. Ronald had talked them into wearing their own clothes, so he wouldn't have to pay for wardrobes. Ronald was shrewd, to say the least.

The day of the play finally arrived. Pele instructed the cast to be at The 14th Street Playhouse by 9 a.m.. They needed time to setup and rehearse before the first show at 4 p.m.. I arrived at the playhouse promptly at nine. I parked across from Dad's car on the side street behind the playhouse. Looking up at the marquee, I smiled as I saw *Uncaged* in bold, black letters. Quickly, I reached for my camera to take pictures. I had been through hell and high water to come to this point. I wanted to remember it forever with pictures. Somehow, all the trials and tribulations seemed to vanish as I took snapshots of *Uncaged*. Today is what I had been waiting for, for a long time. No matter what happened today, I would rejoice.

After my photo session, I entered the playhouse. Jason was in the lobby, sitting at a table near a window. He was Ronald's right hand man. We talked for a few minutes before I asked him where to go. He told me the Main Stage was to my left, but we were performing on Stage Two, downstairs. Curious as to how the Main Stage looked, I peeped inside. It was huge and nice. Another show was playing on the Main Stage at 8 p.m.. I smiled then went downstairs to the Stage Two. Downstairs was also nice. It had a small lobby with restrooms nearby. A white marble counter was to my right. I wondered what it would be used for. A sign was posted on the wall that said Stage 2. I opened the door and went inside. The room was dark. A passageway was straight ahead. Seven black steps were to my left. A long black curtain separated the two. I went up the steps to the stage that was straight ahead. Looking around the small room, a wave of peace enveloped me. Ronald had said there would be 400 seats. That's what I had based paying the cast with. But glancing at the vacant seats, I knew there were not 400 seats in the small room. I began to count. Two hundred seats were all I counted. I knew then I would not be able to pay the cast with the proceeds of the play nor would I make anything. Ronald had screwed me again. Where would he stop?

I then looked at the stage for the $3200 I had spent for stage props. Only a long black curtain was hanging. A large hole was in the center of the curtain. I thought to myself, surely someone was going to fix it before the play. But my instincts told me if it wasn't fixed by now, then it wasn't going to be fixed later. Janil and Dana entered while I was still looking at the curtain. Again the peace of Jesus was all over me. I was glad because getting upset would not accomplish anything positive. I was determined to enjoy the play regardless of what happened.

"Wow, this is small," Dana said as she entered from the top of the steps. I thought we were going to be in a bigger place?"

I kept quiet because if I said something, I would have disturbed my peaceful state. The words of James Bignon ranged through my head: "If I hold my peace, let God fight my battle, then victory shall be mine."

"I wonder what the dressing room looks like," Janil said walking down the steps.

It's nice. I just put my stuff in it. I'll show you where it is if you want me to," Dana volunteered.

Pele walked on the stage as they reached the bottom steps. "This really is nice," he said walking on the stage. This is bigger than when we were here before."

He must have been referring to Stage Three, which held one hundred seats. I watched them walk across the stage. I was content with sitting in my seat, taking everything in.

"The furniture will be here soon," Pele announced.

"I can't wait to see what the stage will look like with the furniture on it. What all will we have?" Dana asked, walking back-and-forth.

"I'm not sure what Ronald ordered. I won't know until it comes. But I have to get the lights and sound ready before the show. That will take at least two hours. When everything is ready, then we can rehearse."

"Dana show me the dressing room. I need to go to the restroom," Janil interjected.

They walked off behind the stage, and I watched Pele walk on and off the stage. A white man came up the steps while I watched Pele. He had a piece of paper in his hand. "Excuse me, is Ronald Brown here?" he asked me coming toward me.

"No, I haven't seen him yet. But, I'm Deeva Denez, the author of the play, and the director is on stage."

"I was just making sure everything was all right."

"I have a question. I was under the impression that we were supposed to be on the Main Stage with 400 seats."

"No. I have your paper work right here," he said, showing me the form. "Mr. Brown signed for this stage for both nights."

"May I see it because that's not what he told me."

"Sure," he said, handing me the paper.

I took it from his hand and read it. Ronald had indeed signed for Stage Two for June 9 & 10. As my eyes scanned the paper, I saw how much he had paid $1445. The document was signed March 13, 2001. "How much would it cost to be on the Main Stage?"

"That's $3000 a day," he answered.

"I know another show is playing tonight on the Main Stage but nothing is playing tomorrow. Will we be able to get the Main Stage tomorrow?" I asked.

"No. Mr. Brown signed for this stage. And besides, once you get the sounds and lights ready for this stage, you won't have time to change tomorrow. You're paying our people $300 today for their services to get you ready. They won't be here tomorrow."

"I see. Thank you for showing me these papers."

"You're welcome," he said as he walked off.

I sat and thought about the papers as I continued to watch Pele. All I could think about was how low could Ronald go?

CHAPTER THIRTY-FIVE

To keep my mind off Ronald's deceptions and thievery, I said a silent prayer. No matter what happened, I was determined to make this day marvelous! I had invested too much time and money to let anything spoil today. The rest of the cast came inside while I mediated on Scriptures. The one Scripture that rang loudly in my head was Ecclesiastes 7:8 & 9, *"The end of a thing is better than its beginning; the patient in spirit is better than the proud in spirit. Do not hasten in your spirit to be angry, for anger rests in the bosom of fools."* The first Scripture reminded me of former prophecies. One prophesy by Madame Lee, who prophesied that the end of my life would be better than the beginning. God had told me *Uncaged* would be a movie. I kept both of those sayings in the back of my mind constantly concerning my life and work. Therefore, no matter what Ronald, Paula, or Lisa did to me, they could not stop my destiny. They could delay it temporarily, but not stop it. No person can close a door that God opens or open a door that He closes. The second Scripture helped me to maintain my peace. Anger does not solve anything; it only worsens situations and eliminates peace.

Janil and Dana came back up the steps to join the rest of the cast. Since everyone was hungry they decided to go eat. I didn't want to leave. I was content with staying put, Brandi, however, took my order for Chick-fil-A. Soon after they left, Pele, who stayed behind, announced that the furniture was here. I enjoyed watching the rental crew place the furniture on stage. They brought in an off white sofa and love seat with earth tone colors of different shades of brown and beige; two wooden end tables with white lamps; a matching coffee table; and a round wooden dining table with a matching china case. Pele instructed them on where to put every piece. I smiled when they left. With the addition of the furniture on stage, it was beginning to feel real.

By the time the cast returned, Pele was still working on the lights and sound. Jason was in the booth helping. Every time I saw Jason, my heart ached for him. I felt how much he wanted to be on stage. If I had my way, he would be performing today. Maybe, he would get a chance in another play, I thought. I ate my food alone while the cast dispersed in all directions.

At one o'clock, Pele finished with all the preparations. He told the cast it was time to rehearse the play on stage. Janil took her position on the sofa, and the play began. Each scene got better and better. Something always came over me whenever Pele performed Zakee. It was if I relived that part of my life over again.

Chills went all over my body when Pele held Janil's hand. The real Zakee never touched me; we only talked. Through his conversations, he changed my life. I never loved a man the way I loved Zakee. My feelings were stronger than I had experienced with anyone. He touched a place in my heart that no other man touched. The feelings I had for Zakee will remain with me forever because of the impact he had on me at a time in my life when he made a difference. Because of Zakee, *Uncaged* was written. At the time God told me to write *Uncaged*, I thought it would be written in sixteen chapters. It wasn't until I completed the thirty-five chapters in *Uncaged* that I realized that the story was still incomplete. That it would take three books to finish the story. Thus, with the writing of this chapter the story, that I started writing on April 21, 1995, is almost finished today, February 27, 2002.

As I write today, I wonder if this book will be completed on my divorce date with Carl on March 13. Time will tell. But, now, let me stop digressing and get on with the story.

The second most touching scene in the play was the scene with Mom and Dad. In that scene, Dad asked me to forgive him for all that he did to me. He even admitted his wrongs. In real life, neither happened. Something went all through me to hear his words. Because of the two scenes I just mentioned, I never tired of watching the play. It was well worth the time and money for those two scenes alone.

After the preliminary play, the cast had forty minutes to rest up for the real thing. Ronald had come by now, and said he would let the people in outside the playhouse. I didn't discuss anything with him. I just took my seat on the front row at the center of the stage, so that I could enjoy the show. I had my camera ready to take pictures of the guests and friends that came. Today was my day, and I was going to delight in every minute of it.

For the first show, my parents joined me. I had guests each show. Ronald made arrangements to video the second show. The playhouse was half-full for the first show. The performance was great! The cast played during rehearsals, but they performed for the show. Everyone acted superbly, and I was proud of them.

The second show we had a full house. My sons sat with me that show. And since the video was taken for that show, they were in the video. After each show, Ronald introduced me. He really pumped the play, the cast, and me up. I was grateful for everything. Ronald had a way of saying the right things at the right time.

The next day, everything went smoothly. The performance was still great! When it was over, however, everyone was tired. Ronald told them it would take two weeks to get paid. We all packed up and called it a night.

Two weeks after the play, Ronald called me at home to tell me the check had arrived. I told him I would be there in twenty minutes. This was the day I had been waiting on. Excitedly, I drove to the office. Payday was here! Several of the cast had called me at home to ask when they would get paid. Today, we can all get paid. They had been so patient and committed; I wanted to give them everything they deserved immediately.

As I pulled up into the parking lot, I saw two cast members' vehicles – Dana's and Ta'nal's. Pele opened the door when I rang the bell.

"Hello, Miss Denez," Pele greeted me as I entered the office.

"Hi, Pele. Is Ronald in his office?" I asked anxious to see him.

"Yes, he's waiting for you. We all are," Pele added.

"Who are we?"

"Dana, Ta'nal, Ronald and me. Ronald told us the check came today. That's why we're here, to get paid," he said walking by my side to Ronald's office.

"I need to see and cash the check first before I can pay anyone," I said approaching Ronald's door. He smiled as he saw me and waved for me to come inside.

"Come on in, Deeva," he instructed from his chair. "Close the door. This won't take long."

"Pele, I'll see you and the cast members when I finish talking with Ronald," I said as I closed the door.

"Okay, Miss Denez. We'll be waiting," he said as he walked off.

Still smiling, I sat down across from Ronald. I placed my purse on the floor and got comfortable in the chair. "Where's the check?" I asked, excitedly.

"Here it is," he said putting the check in front of me.

My eyes widened as I read the amount. I studied it for a second before speaking. I was really at a total loss of words, but somehow these words came out, "What happened to the money? This check is for $225."

"I know. That's all we made."

"There were more people that came to the play than this."

"That's the check, Deeva. You can call The 14th Street Playhouse to verify it," he said picking up the phone.

"No, that won't be necessary. You did something with the money. I just don't know what," I said looking at him in disbelief.

"You're broke," he said sarcastically. "How are you going to pay the cast with that check?"

"I don't know, but I will pay them every cent that belongs to them."

"You paid them too much," he said arrogantly. "I pay according to time spent on stage. They get $250 an hour, but if they are only on the stage for ten minutes, their pay is $40. If I had to pay them, I would have had the play at another playhouse with larger seats. I would have made sure I got paid. You're in the hole, Deeva. They have contracts. They can take you to court."

As Ronald spoke, I saw his demon. His was the second demon I had seen in my life. The first demon was in Bryson. When I saw Ronald's demon, everything fell in place. That explained the lying and money greed - - those were the characteristics of his demon. Bryson had a lying, sex demon. I listened, watching his demon.

"I have an investor, who was at the play. He's interested in buying *Uncaged* for $130,000 with all rights. He can give you $20,000 when you sign. You can have the check within a week. Then you can pay the cast."

"$130,000 is not enough money to sell *Uncaged*, especially to give up all my rights."

"Sell the damn thang, Deeva! You can make your money on the next book. I will have the last say so when you sign. I want 30% of everything."

"I'm not interested in your investor, Ronald. I'm not selling *Uncaged* for $130,000. What happened to your investor for $250,000?"

"I haven't heard from him. The one for $130,000 is the one that is interested."

"No, thank you, Ronald," I said getting up. In my mind, I didn't want to have anything to do with him or his investor(s). I would rely on God to come up with the $16,000 to pay the cast.

"The cast is here to get paid. Remember they have contracts. You can't pay them with this check," he said waving it into the air. "How are you going to pay them?"

"They will get paid. Let me go out to them and explain the situation." He got up and followed me. The trio was waiting outside Ronald's office. I walked up to where they were seated.

"Do we get paid today?" Ta'nal asked before I said anything. Dana and Pele looked at me, waiting for my reply.

"Here's the check, Deeva," Ronald said, placing it into my hand.

"This check is only for $225. There is no way I can pay anyone with this check. I know you have been patient and want to get paid. I will pay you every cent you deserve, but I need time to get the money."

"How much time are you talking about, Miss Deeva?" Ta'nal asked.

"I need my money," Dana added. "I turned down jobs to do this play. I have bills to pay," she said with a furlong look.

"I understand, Miss Denez," Pele said looking disappointed.

"Right now, I don't know how much time it will take me to get all the money up since I wasn't expecting this check to be so small. I know I can have some money by this week."

"When, Miss Deeva," Ta'nal asked. "My wife just had a baby, and she's not working anymore."

"Give me until Thursday. I don't know how much I will have, but I will have something."

"Okay," Pele answered. "What time?"

"Is 3 o'clock all right with everyone?" I asked.

"Yes," they replied.

"Should I contact the other cast members?" Ronald added, smiling as if he was loving every minute of it.

"No, that won't be necessary. I have their numbers. I need to see how much money I can come up with first."

"Okay, I'll see everyone back here Thursday at 3," Ronald announced.

I left them at the office. I had to figure out where to get $16,000 to pay the cast. I prayed all the way home. This surely called for an act of Jesus Christ because I did not have the funds.

Thursday I came up with $2000. I divided it equally between Pele, Dana, and Ta'nal. Miraculously, The Lord made it possible for the cast to be paid. By using three other sources, I was able to pay the cast all the money within two weeks. Jesus performed a miracle that I couldn't believe! If anyone had told me before the play that I could come up with $16,000 in any length of time, I would have told them they were lying. But to come up with it in two weeks, I would have told them, they had lost their mind! But God is good and can do the impossible.

I could tell Ronald was stunned when he saw the money. He thought I was broke, and I was. But I serve the living God, who owns the whole world and the fullness thereof. I may have been broke, but my God owns everything. And for me to have access to what he owns is a prayer away.

Ronald wanted to take the play on the road after everyone was paid. He had chosen July 28 as the next play date. I told him my niece was getting married on that day. He then chose August 4 weekend. That weekend was fine, but I didn't want to do any more business with him - - a snake is always a snake. If they bite you once, they will bite you again when the opportunity arises. I didn't know how he stole the money. I just knew that he did.

Two weeks after I had paid the cast, Ronald appeared on TV on the 5 o'clock news. He had been investigated for fraud and theft with his modeling business, which was under his new business name. The TV program showed scenes of him obviously lying about how he could get his models into commercials. It even told of an incident where one model's brother beat Ronald up for taking her money. I thought back to his swollen lip with stitches. The news featured Ronald all week. The next week, I saw Renae at Kroger and she said Ronald was in jail. I smiled and thought about God's Word, which is always true. Romans 12:17-21 explains my feelings on the matter. *"Repay no one evil for evil... Beloved, do not avenge yourselves, but rather give place to wrath; for it is written, 'Vengeance is Mine, I will repay,' says the Lord...Do not be overcome by evil, but overcome evil with good."*

Don't think for a minute that people get away with evil acts. Put them in God's hands. He will get your sweet revenge. I prayed that God would put him out of business, so that he would not steal from anyone else.

CHAPTER THIRTY-SIX

Many family members and friends saw Ronald on TV. Frequently, they asked if he did me right. No one had heard me complain about him. I told the truth – he was a snake to me, too. He took all of the money. One work associate, who came to the play, called me at home one evening in July.

"Hello," I said answering the phone in the kitchen.

"Vanessa, this is Pat."

"Hi, Pat. How are you doing?"

"Are you busy?"

"I'm working on *Uncaged*. Since the play, I'm re-editing it, so I can re-publish it. I'll do *The Bearer of the Sign* when I finish *Uncaged*."

"I have something to tell you, but I don't know if I should," she said apprehensively.

"Pat, say what you have to say."

"I saw your producer on TV a couple of weeks ago."

"Yes, you and everyone else. The last time I talked to Renae, he was in jail, but he should be out now."

"When I came to the play with my two daughters, he asked us if we had tickets outside the playhouse. I thought that was odd selling tickets outside. He had a very large wad of money in his pocket. I've never seen so much money. I said something to him to let him know what he was doing was not right. He started joking with me then. I also told him I knew you. He talked for a few more minutes, then we went inside. I wanted to tell you earlier, but wasn't sure I should say something."

"I'm glad you called. I knew he stole the money, I just didn't know how he did it. I stayed inside the playhouse the whole time, so I didn't see anything. I never dreamed he would stoop so low until I saw the check for the play."

"Girl, the play was good. Even though he stole the money, you still benefited. He took the money, but you reached a milestone in your life."

"It still hurts me to know he did me that way. I believe in holding up my end, but somehow, I keep running into crooks and thieves who want to take my money, but not do their parts."

"You said yourself, their actions have benefited you to the point where you can now publish your own books as well as other writers. The last publisher because she didn't do anything you started your own business, The Literary Connection. God has a purpose for your producer, too."

"It was prophesied to me before the play, that I would have my own theater company. That must be the hidden blessing behind Ronald's thievery. But Pat, it still hurts me to know what he did. I am human."

"That's why I hesitated to tell you. I knew it would hurt you. Look at it this way, Vanessa, God put people in our paths to do us wrong to advance us to where God wants us to be. If everything always went right, we would be complacent. He made us overcomers, therefore, He must have things for us to overcome. You and I are both living proof."

"You're right. Thanks for the encouragement."

"Look, Vanessa, I have to go. I'll see you at work."

"Okay, bye," I said as she hung up.

So that's how he stole the money. I thought to myself, looking at the phone. A wave of bitterness swept over me. *"Lord, help me to forgive him,"* I cried aloud. *"I can not let bitterness, hatred, malice, or strife have any parts in my life. I must use the lesson of Uncaged and forgive him. Please console me in Your Word, so that I can get rid of these feelings."* I went upstairs to my bedroom and got my Bible. Before I opened it, God gave me Ephesians 6:12, *"For we do not wrestle against flesh and blood, but against principalities, against powers, against the rulers of the darkness of this age, against spiritual hosts of wickedness in the heavenly places."* God was reminding me that my battle was not against Ronald, per se, but his demon(s). Jesus died for Ronald just like He died for me. The difference between us was that I knew Jesus and Ronald didn't, that's why he did the things he did. I prayed that he find Jesus as I searched the Scriptures.

God led me to Ephesians 2:1-13, *"And you He made alive, who were dead in trespasses and sins, in which you once walked according to the course of this world, according to the prince of the power of the air, the spirit who now works in the sons of disobedience, among whom also we all once conducted ourselves in the lusts of our flesh, fulfilling the desires of the flesh and of the mind, and were by nature children of wrath, just as the others. But God, who is rich in mercy, because of His great love with which He loved us, even when we were dead in trespasses, made us alive together with Christ (by grace you have been saved)...For by grace you have been saved through faith, and not of yourselves; it is the gift of God, not of works, lest anyone should boast. For we are His workmanship, created in Christ Jesus for good works, which God prepared beforehand that we should walk in them. Therefore remember that you, once Gentiles in the flesh – who are called Uncircumcision by what is called Circumcision made in the flesh by hands - - that at that time you were without Christ, being aliens from the commonwealth of Israel and strangers from the covenants of promise, having no hope and without God in the world. But now in Christ Jesus you who once were far off have been brought near by the blood of Christ."*

After reading the Scriptures, my bitterness subsided. I said a prayer to forgive Ronald of his wrong doings toward me. I left him in the hands of the Lord and prayed again that he have the honor of knowing Jesus before he dies. Then and only then would his life be changed for the better. Feeling myself again, I went back downstairs and continued to edit *Uncaged.*

Brandi and I worked hard getting *Uncaged* ready to be re-published for the third time. Since Paula did not give me the disk of her version, I had to start from square one. The more I read, the more errors I found. By now, I knew how to edit. I learned a lot in the past four years. Because of all my misfortune with my work, I became a better writer, editor, evaluator, and publisher.

Brandi was my computer person. I corrected everything on paper and she entered the corrections in the computer. To this day, I disdain the computer. I avoid it at all costs. My forte is paper. I write and edit on paper. I learned to do that which I am good at and leave the other things to other people who can do a much better job.

Before July was over, we had *Uncaged* ready to be published. Our next task was *The Bearer of the Sign.* We worked feverously getting it ready. By August 10, we finished. Since both books were sent off, I concentrated on completing my third book, *The Image: A Prophetic Birth.* My goal was to have it completed by February 2002.

August 18, I celebrated my 45th birthday. Raymond and the kids went to church with me that Saturday. My birthdays were the only time he went to my church. It was part of my birthday wish and present. Raymond and Pastor Ware had been friends for nearly twenty years. They talked occasionally over the phone, but they rarely saw each other. I thought Raymond would attend church regularly since his friend was the pastor. Obviously, I was wrong. His presence on my birthdays, however, made them special.

Praise and testimony service was going on when we arrived. First Lady Ware had just finished singing *My God is Real* as we took our seats. Sister Janice Wallace stood up to testify.

"Praise the Lord church, she said standing to her feet. "Giving honor to God, who is the head of my life and Jesus Christ His Son, to all the ministers and saints of God. I was told this week that my cancer had spread to other parts of my body. The doctors have given me six to eight weeks to live. When they told me my prognosis, I said thank you Jesus. They looked at me strange and asked me why I said that. I then told them, I didn't care what they said, my life was in Jesus' hands. Although they had done all that they could do, Jesus can do more. He can heal me of the cancer if it is His will. I trust in Jesus. I know church that my cancer is not my battle. I have given it to the Lord. Last week when I was in the hospital, I was swollen up real bad. I had a liter of fluid around my heart. The doctors said I should have died with all that fluid. But I thank Jesus that I didn't die, but is still standing and is still alive. When I think of the goodness and mercy of Jesus, I praise Him with my whole being. He truly is good to me. For all those who know the words of prayer, pray my strength in the Lord," she said as she sat down.

Several others testified and sang before Pastor Ware came forth. He had on a beige suit with a beige, black and white tie. His tall, slender body hovered over the podium as he prayed.

"Father in the name of Jesus, I thank You for this day You have allowed us to see. Send your Holy Spirit to teach Your people this day. Guard my lips that I say nothing of myself, but only what You would have me to say. Bless the hearing that Your people will hear what You have me to say. In Jesus' name I pray. Amen.

"Praise the Lord, everybody," he said reaching for the microphone, moving from the podium. "This week, I struggled with my spiritual man. I didn't want to read my Bible. Every time I picked it up and read a Scripture, it was like I was just reading words. I came to the alter to pray, and I didn't have nothing to say. I felt so empty inside. Look like the little prayers I did say, just bounced off the wall. It seemed like I was talking to myself instead of God. I went like this for three days. Oh, ya'll know what I'm talking about. I'm sure you've experienced it, too. Well, anyway, the fourth day when I opened my Bible, God led me to the Scripture that set me free," he said walking back to the podium. He opened his Bible.

"Turn your Bibles to 2 Corinthians 4, starting at verse 7. *'But we have this treasure in earthen vessels, that the excellence of the power may be of God and not us.'* Brethren, God gave us this temporary body of clay to show our weakness and show how much we need the power of God in our lives. One day our earthen vessels will be changed to a glorified body like Jesus and God the Father. Look at the next verse. *'We are hard pressed on every side, yet not crushed; we are perplexed, but not in despair; persecuted, but not forsaken; struck down, but not destroyed.'* That's exactly what I felt this week. Those negative feelings had me spiritually paralyzed in the beginning of the week. I was thinking about things at home, things here at the church, my health and up coming surgery, as well as my finances. It was like the weight of the world was on my shoulders. Let me tell you, our clay bodies can't take too much pressure because we are so fragile. That's why we have a living God, who cares about us and tells us to cast all our burdens on Him in 1 Peter 5:7." His voice cracked as he paused to compose himself before continuing. "When I think about how much God loves us; how He gave Jesus up for us, it makes me breakdown. This thing is real people; God loves us more than we can really comprehend. Like Sister Janice testified earlier, even when you hear bad news, you know that you're not alone, and that you have a present help in times of trouble. As believers, we're more than conquerors. We're children of the living God!

Verse 10 says, *'always carrying about in the body the dying of the Lord Jesus, that the life of Jesus also may be manifested in our body.'* Jesus now lives His life in us. We must walk as Jesus walked and talk as Jesus talked. Our lives must reflect His.

Skip down to verse 15, *'For all things are for your sakes, that grace, having spread through many, may cause thanksgiving to abound to the glory of God.'* The things that we do in this life should glorify God. Now the next two verses are what really set me free.

When I read these Scriptures, they were what I needed to deliver me. Verse 16 says, *'Therefore we do not lose heart. Even though our outward man is perishing, yet the inward man is being renewed day by day.'* Brethren, even though these vessels of clay die daily, our inward, spiritual man is growing stronger each day. This physical body may be racked with pain or filled with cancer, but our spiritual person gets stronger in the Lord. We need to change our focus as to what our physical bodies are going through and concentrate on what Jesus is doing through us. It is His life that He is living in us.

Read the last two verses, *'For our light afflictions, which is but for a moment, is working for us a far more exceeding and external weight of glory, while we do not look at the things which are seen, but at the things which are not seen. For the things which are seen are temporary, but the things which are not seen are eternal.'* My present financial situation is temporary. *God is able to supply all of my needs according to His riches in glory in Christ Jesus.* No matter what my situation is, God is able to deliver me from them all. My body ages daily on the outside, but the inner man is renewed and strengthened. My situation at home and the things of the church are temporary. So why should I be concerned with these temporary things? My focus should be on the things that are above and are eternal. I command you today to change your focus from the temporary things of this world to the eternal things of God.

Let me pray. *Father, in the name of Jesus, I thank You for the word that went forth and I pray that it falls on fertile soil. Don't let the enemy come and snatch it away from Your people. In Your Son, Jesus Christ. Amen and Amen.*

Now, Deacon Dix and Minister Copeland come forth to receive the offering," he said as he sat down. They took up the offering as instructed. Pastor Ware came back to the podium to dismiss us after the offertory. We left twenty minutes later.

When I got home, I had a letter in the mail from Dekalb Hospital. The letter had the results of my recent mammogram - - normal. I was very thankful and praised God for it the remainder of the day. It was the perfect birthday gift.

CHAPTER THIRTY-SEVEN

A month later, to the day, I had proof read the galleys for the last time for *Uncaged*. This was the first time I had read the galleys. In the past, that task was left up to my publishers. Lisa and I both opted not to read them, trusting what she had submitted. When her edition of *Uncaged* came back, it was full of errors; something I knew had to be corrected. That's why I sought a second publisher, Paula, to make my book right. Needless to say, her version was better, but it was still not right. I prayed that I had found all the errors before I sent it back this time.

Tosh Fomby, a member of my writer's group, designed my cover. I accidentally discovered she was an artist when I went to her house for a meeting. Her drawings covered her den. I told her I needed a cover person, and she asked for the job. The situation worked perfectly because I knew her, and she knew my work. Everybody in the group had heard every chapter of *Uncaged* as it was being written.

Tosh also designed the cover for *The Bearer of the Sign*. When I first saw it, I was awe struck. The cover was awesome to me. I would have never imagined either cover. I was glad God directed both our paths to accomplish His work. By November, I had completed the last galley of *The Bearer of the Sign*, and *Uncaged* was published. My plans were to promote both books together. Therefore, I waited to schedule any book signings. Thinking back on my two publishers and the birth of Mya, three years ago, I remembered I had not had a book signing in three years. In addition, *Uncaged* had been off the shelves for two and a half years. I felt as it I was starting all over, and I was. I prayed that during my hiatus, a demand was being created for my work. God works in mysterious ways. I hoped this was one of them.

Also in November, Raymond Jr. and Francine went to live with their mother in Augusta. Every since they came back from their summer visit, they had changed for the worst. They kept confusion in the home, especially, concerning Mya and me. It was as if they had rejected both of us. Mya could do no right with them. They always found something to say against her. Their attitude about my daughter worked my nerves. I defended Mya, which made them reject me as well.

Raymond asked Brandi to live with her mother at the same time Raymond Jr. and Francine left. Brandi was due to go to Georgia State University in January. There was so much peace in the house when they left. I was thankful that Raymond came to his conclusion. Mya could finally have her own bed and bedroom and stop sleeping with us. Raymond and I sacrificed a lot for them. Now, we could enjoy ourselves as husband and wife. In fact, after they left, I felt like I was on a honeymoon. The days and weeks that followed strengthened our marriage.

Thanksgiving was Mya's third birthday. I'm not one to celebrate birthdays. They are spiritual in meaning to me. It is a time to give thanks to God, The Creator, for giving my loved ones and me life. This occasion was no exception. Early Thanksgiving morning, I said a prayer for Mya.

Dear Heavenly Father, I come to You this day of Thanksgiving to sincerely thank You and give You praise. I thank You for Your Son, Jesus Christ, who You gave to this world for our sins. I thank You for keeping food on our table, clothes on our backs, a roof over our heads, and all our bills paid. Thank You for Your gifts of grace, eternal life, the Holy Spirit, and salvation. I thank You for Your divine protection upon my family. Please continue to keep Your loving hand around us for as long as we sojourn on this earth.

Father, I pray that you will continue to keep this land called America free. Protect our borders and protect our cities. Cleanse us of all impurities and immoralities. Help us to turn our hearts back to You and Your Son Jesus Christ. May we all reflect on Your goodness, love, mercy and blessings this Thanksgiving Day. Continue to strengthen, encourage and uplift those affected by the attacks of September the 11th. May Your love endure forever!!

Mya is truly a delight to my soul. I thank You for allowing me to share her with You. She is a fighter, and I pray that she press on toward the prize of Jesus all the days of her life. In Jesus' name I pray. Amen.

After I prayed, I felt an urge to write Mya a letter. She was three, and I was forty-five. I didn't know how long we had together. She was too young for me to tell her what I wanted to say. When she is old enough to understand, I may not be around, or my mind may not be as sharp as it is now. Therefore, I will write my letter today because tomorrow is not promised to anyone.

Dear Mya,

Today, as I write this letter, you are upstairs in your room watching TV with your dad. I am downstairs at the kitchen table typing on my word processor. Each morning when you wake up, you first get me up out the bed by saying, "Get up, Mamma. It's time to get up!" you say as you pull the covers off my face. You still like to sleep in my bed although you have your own bedroom now. Each night, you start in your bed, but end up in my bed before morning breaks. I always smile when I hear the pitter, patter of your little feet running into my room in the middle of the night.

Although we have been together for three short years, I often remember the years before your birth - - when you were an image, a promise from God that you were coming some day. Now that you are here, and I can see and hold you everyday, I do. If only you knew how much joy you bring to my life. You are too young to understand. But despite our age difference, the love that we have for each other is understood. You know that I love you, and I know that you love me, too. Your father loves you as well. You healed a place in both our lives.

I told your dad that you are the perfect daughter for me. He swears that we are just alike. I can't say that I fully agree with him although you do have my personality for the most part. Surely, your stubbornness and ill temper sometimes are not my traits. They must be unique to you. Your dad disagrees, however. I see him in you, but he says you are the spitting image of me. I remind him of your nose and hair that are both Miller traits. Sure you have my big almond shaped eyes, light-brown complexion, dimples like my mom and me. Right now, you are a sweet little girl, and I hope you stay that way.

Mya, I love you. I went through a lot to get you here. I knew by ending my first marriage, you would come. I have never regretted my divorce to this day. My only remorse was not getting divorced the first time I filed instead of the third time. By filing earlier, I would have saved myself a lot of mental and emotional scars. But thank God through forgiveness they were healed.

I pray that as I get older, you do not reject me because of the gray hairs on my head. Since I had you, they have multiplied by leaps and bounds. On several occasions, I've been asked if you are my grandchild? Of course, I say no, but I know as the years pass, our age difference will be more noticeable. I don't mind strangers asking questions about our relationship, but if you ever feel like I am too old to be your mother, it would break my heart. I pray that it never happens, but I also know that it is possible, especially, with our youth oriented society.

I'm reminded of your calling in life - - to be a gospel singer for Jesus. You were created for the glory of God to serve Him and draw others to Him. My calling is for the lost and scattered sheep of Israel. Through my first three books, I have completed my mission that was set before me. I pray that you will complete yours, too. Your oldest brother, Carl Jr., will be a preacher for Jesus. He laughs every time I tell him. He, too, will dedicate his life to Jesus and draw people unto Him. You and Carl Jr. will continue what God has started in me. Don't be concerned that there are no preachers or singers in our family, per se. Jesus will anoint both of you to do His will at His appointed time. I just pray that I live to see both of you do what you are called to do.

On a more serious note, I must use some time to talk to you about the facts of life. Life is not fair – that is a fact! Don't go through life thinking you will always get your way. Life doesn't work like that. As long as you live, although you are "free", you will have to live by rules and regulations. You have the laws of man as well as the law of God – The Ten

Commandments. You cannot keep God's Law on your own. He must write them on your heart, and only Jesus can keep them by living in you and giving you the Holy Spirit. You will hear much controversy about The Ten Commandments being done away with. Don't believe it! If you live by them, you will do well. Read your Bible daily, so that you will be grounded in the truth and not be carried away by every wind of doctrine. The Ten Commandments are found in Exodus 20. Pay special attention to the Fourth Commandment – Remember the Sabbath day, to keep it holy. Six days you shall labor and do all your work, but the seventh day is the Sabbath of the Lord your God. In it you shall do no work....For in six days the Lord made the heavens and the earth, the sea, and all that is in them, and rested the seventh day. Therefore the Lord blessed the Sabbath day and hallowed it." The Sabbath is Saturday, which is the seventh day. It pictures a future rest of God (Hebrews 4:1-13). When God made the week, the only day he named was the Sabbath. Even when Jesus walked the earth, the Sabbath day was the only day that had a name. The other days were referred to by the day of the week. The first day of the week is Sunday. Look at the Gospels of Matthew, Mark, Luke and John after Jesus' death; they refer to the first day of the week. For example, John 20;1, says, "Now on the first day of the week, Mary Magdalene went to the tomb early, while it was still dark, and saw that the stone had been taken away from the tomb." Jesus lived during the time of the Roman Empire. After His death, a lot of things were changed by the Roman Emperor, which was prophesied in Daniel 7:25, "He shall speak pompous words against the Most High. He shall persecute the saints of the Most High, and shall intend to change times and law. Then the saints shall be given into his hand for a time and times and half a time." The saints of God will be persecuted for living the truth of God. Still obey God.

Dear Mya, the world we live in, as you know it, has been changed from the days of the Bible because the fourth beast described in Daniel 7:23, "The fourth beast shall be a fourth kingdom on earth, which shall be different from all the other kingdoms, and shall devour the whole earth, trample it and break it in pieces." Because of this fourth beast or the Roman Empire, which also makes up the Babylon Mystery Religion of the Roman Catholic Church (Revelation 17:5), everything has been changed. Truth has been cast down to the ground, so that it could prosper (Daniel 8:12). For instance, our days of the week were named by the Roman Empire in honor of their gods. Remember, God only named the seventh day, which is the Sabbath. According to the Romans, the first day is Sunday because the sun was their main god, thus Sunday worship. The second day, they named Monday in honor of the moon. Wednesday was for Woden. Thursday was for Thor. Friday was connected to their fish god, that's why people like to eat fish on Friday. Saturday was named after Saturn, another god. The same was with our months. January was named after Janus, a god with two heads that looked forward and backwards. Remember God's new years starts in the spring when new life begins. The Passover is the fourteenth day of the first month called Abib (Deuteronomy 16:1, Leviticus 23:5). All the days that God wants us to observe are in Leviticus 23. They are His true days and not the pagan days of the Roman Empire such as Easter, which is named after the pagan goddess Astarte or Ishtar - - the goddess of the rising light of day and spring. She is also a fertility goddess. That's where the "Easter" bunny comes from and her eggs. Eggs and rabbits have nothing to do with Jesus. Christmas also has nothing to do with Jesus. Jesus was not born on December 25. Nowhere in the Bible can you prove it. The Scriptures clearly prove otherwise, that He was born in the fall during the time of the Feast of Tabernacles (Leviticus 23:34-36). The seventh

237

month is the fall either September or October, depending on how God's calendar falls. Remember the Romans changed everything and God honors all of His Holy Days. Jesus died on Passover. The Holy Spirit came on the day of Pentacost (Leviticus 23:15&16).

The next event to take place is the return of Jesus with the blowing of trumpets (Leviticus 23:24). Be not deceived my little one, but believe the truth. God's Word is the truth. The more I write, the more I feel I need to say. There is so much to tell you in such a short amount of space.

Before I close, I must mention how to eat. Health is everything. Again, God gave instructions on what to eat. Read Leviticus 11. God explains about clean and unclean foods. He made the animals, so He should know which ones to eat. If you decide to become a vegetarian, that's okay, too, because in the beginning with Adam and Eve, they did not eat meat, but God gave them every herb that yielded seeds and every tree whose fruit yielded seed to eat (Genesis 1:29).

Make sure you read your Bible daily, so you can know the will of God. Pray and praise Jesus daily also. Give all your problems to Him; He can handle them, you can't.

Lastly, I must talk to you about choosing the right man in your life. Do not go by outward appearance. The heart and mind of a man makes the man - - how he thinks and acts are two very important characteristics to notice. Always pray to God to make sure he is the right one for you because only God knows the heart of every man and woman. Lean not to your own understanding. Avoid men who drink alcohol, curse, and do drugs of any kind, gamble and smoke. You want a clean man, one who fears God and walks in His ways. Not every man or woman who goes to church is a true saint of God. Use wisdom and discernment of the Holy Spirit to choose your friends and mate. Never totally depend on a man. Always have your own money and bank account. Don't let any man lower your self-

esteem. Always think highly of yourself. Also be cautious of your brothers and sisters. Don't let them use you. You are so much younger than they are and may trust them naively. Stay prayerful. Love the Lord, Jesus Christ. Live holy. Be thankful for all things. Manage your money wisely. Be temperate in all things. Remain pure. Keep your virginity for your husband, only he deserves your prize possession. I love you. Happy Birthday!

Love,
Mom

CHAPTER THIRTY-EIGHT

Later that day, we went to my parent's house for Thanksgiving. My whole family was present, including my niece and her new husband. Mom cooked everything. She had a nice variety of foods. It seemed as though she cooked everyone's favorite foods. No one can cook like Mom. After dinner, we sang happy birthday to Mya and ate her birthday cake. For the first time, she blew out all of her candles. That was a sure sign that my baby was growing up. Her birthday was special to her because she had a birthday hat.

My uncle Mark, the one who went to see Madame Lee with Mom and me, came by later with his family. They stayed for a little while. It felt good seeing my brother and sister and their families. With our busy schedules, we rarely saw each other although we lived close to one another. It was good occasions such as Thanksgiving that brought us all together as well as sad occasions such as funerals. I was thankful for the good occasions.

Two weeks after Thanksgiving, Mya had her three-year check-up. I was shocked to find out that she only weighed 24 pounds. I knew she was thin, but I had no idea she was that underweight. Her main problem was being congested. She had really gotten bad two days prior to her visit. Dr. Flowers spent most of the time suctioning the mucus from Mya's nose. Mya had a history of allergies, which caused her congestion. Dr. Flowers prescribed two nose sprays and two medicines. She also had a bacteria infection in her nose. I immediately filled Mya's prescriptions to get her well again.

That same day, I made a deposit for Pastor Ware because I was the treasurer for his radio ministry, Believers Walking in the Way of Righteousness. Coincidentally, his bank was across from Ronald's office. Every week I made my deposits, I looked at his office. This week I noticed his sign was gone and had been replaced by an H & R Block sign. I smiled, knowing his business was gone. The way he cheated people out of their money, justice was rightly done. God is a God of justice. He will fight our battles. He will take care of our enemies without our help. Vengeance truly is His. He will repay.

When I got home from the bank, my mail was waiting for me on the kitchen table. A small brown box was among the envelopes. I opened it first. To my delight, *Uncaged* was inside. I smiled again because victory was mine! The long hard road I had traveled to keep *Uncaged* alive had come to an end. I had given birth to *Uncaged*. This time it will go all the way. My enemies tried to stop me, but they couldn't. It was God's will that *Uncaged* be written and published; nothing and no one could thwart the will of God.

Uncaged was now viable. It too, like Mya, was an image before I wrote one word. It was the book with the pregnant image of me. God said, "Your book will be published first, then you will deliver." He showed me a big book that came in front of the pregnant image of myself. Now, *Uncaged* had been given its prophetic birth.

I understand now, that the book I saw in the image was so big because it contained all three novels – *Uncaged*, *The Bearer of the Sign*, and *The Image: A Prophetic Birth*. I saw one large book, not knowing I was to write a three book series. I knew, however, after I wrote *Uncaged* that the story was not complete. Therefore, I had to write *The Bearer of the Sign*. And since my daughter(s) was not born at the end of that story, *The Image: A Prophetic Birth* had to be written. God showed me the completed story in one book. The three books combined have 120 chapters, which breaks down to approximately 750 single space pages or 1500 double space pages. This has been a seven-year project. Seven is God's number for completion. I started April 21, 1995. Today is April 9, 2002. I am almost done with this book. In my heart, I believe I will finish on or before April 21, 2002, so that I will not go into another year.

Today God has revealed to me the duality of the two images. The first image of a baby girl was indeed that of Mya. He could have stopped there, but He didn't because there was more to come besides the birth of a child. Because her image was first, she was to be born before the second image fully manifested. The second image - - a very pregnant image of me with a big book coming in front of it, coupled with God's prophetic words, "Your book will be published first, then you will deliver." Means: My book, which in one sense meant *Uncaged* will be published first before the baby girl will be delivered. That happened. *Uncaged* was first published December 1997, and Mya was born November 1998. Here is the duality that God has just revealed to me today. My book, which is the completion of the three books, will be published first before my business, The Literary Connection, is born. My business is the second birth to come from me. Mya was first, and my business along with my success is second. This also goes with the prophecy given at the beginning of this book by the minister at the Word of Faith Church. He prophesied about the birth of a baby and a business. The Literary Connection is past the embryo form. It has developed into a real business. All it needs now are clients to give it life. If you desire to be my client, you can reach me at: 2794 Stardust Ct., Decatur, GA 30034. My number is 404-288-4811.

God is doing an incredible work. First, He showed the timely birth of Mya. Second, He showed the birth of my business. Third, but not least, He has shown the work He is doing with mankind - - our birth into His kingdom on earth. We now bear His image in the flesh, but we will also be just like Him - - full of righteousness and truth - - at Jesus' return when our fleshly bodies will become spiritual, immortal bodies. Indeed, *The Image: A Prophetic Birth* is more than a book. It is our destination, our purpose in God's master plan that was laid since the foundation of the world. Are you ready for God's ultimate purpose in your life? Nothing else really matters in this life, not even the last details of this book. May the peace of God be with you until the return of His Son, Jesus Christ when you will be transformed into the image - - a prophetic birth!!

About the Author:

Born and raised in Atlanta, Georgia, Deeva Denez is the second of three children. A graduate of Georgia State University, she has pursued a career in medical technology for the past twenty-five years. Because of her own writing experience and her desire to help other writers, Deeva founded The Literary Connection, which promotes, facilitates, and publishes new authors. She was featured at *The Black Arts Festival* and *Sisters' Only* in Atlanta. Deeva resides in Decatur with her husband and family.

Printed in the USA
CPSIA information can be obtained
at www.ICGtesting.com
LVHW081614311023
762279LV00005B/31